FRENCH PROFILES
Prophets and Pioneers

FRENCH PROFILES

Prophets and Pioneers

G. P. GOOCH
C.H., D.LITT., F.B.A.

1724

LONGMANS

LONGMANS, GREEN AND CO LTD
48 GROSVENOR STREET, LONDON W1
RAILWAY CRESCENT, CROYDON, VICTORIA, AUSTRALIA
443 LOCKHART ROAD, HONG KONG
PRIVATE MAIL BAG 1036, IKEJA (LAGOS)
44 JALAN AMPANG, KUALA LUMPUR
ACCRA, AUCKLAND, IBADAN, KINGSTON (JAMAICA)
NAIROBI, SALISBURY (RHODESIA)

LONGMANS SOUTHERN AFRICA (PTY) LTD
THIBAULT HOUSE, THIBAULT SQUARE, CAPE TOWN

LONGMANS, GREEN AND CO INC
119 WEST 40TH STREET, NEW YORK 18

LONGMANS, GREEN AND CO
137 BOND STREET, TORONTO 2

ORIENT LONGMANS PRIVATE LTD
CALCUTTA, BOMBAY, MADRAS
DELHI, HYDERABAD, DACCA

FIRST PUBLISHED 1961

PRINTED IN GREAT BRITAIN BY
WESTERN PRINTING SERVICES LTD, BRISTOL

CONTENTS

Preface   vii

PART I
BEFORE THE REVOLUTION

1 Bayle and the Cult of Reason   3
2 Fontenelle and the Cult of Science   12
3 Abbé de Saint-Pierre and Perpetual Peace   20
4 Anglo-French Contacts in the Eighteenth Century   29
5 Voltaire in England   44
6 Voltaire as Historian   62
7 The Golden Age of Freemasonry   137
8 Condorcet and Human Perfectibility   145

PART II
AFTER THE REVOLUTION
THE CATHOLIC REVIVAL

9 Chateaubriand and the Charms of Christianity   157
10 Joseph de Maistre and the Vatican   171
11 Lamennais and Christian Democracy   190
12 Montalembert and Church Schools   204
13 Lacordaire in the Pulpit   216
14 Ozanam and the Claims of Charity   226
15 Louis Veuillot and the Press   235
16 Bishop Dupanloup, Friend of Children   244

SECULAR SOCIOLOGISTS

17 Saint-Simon and the Industrial Age 249

18 The Optimism of Michelet 259

19 The Pessimism of Taine 273

20 Georges Sorel and Revolutionary Syndicalism 286

PREFACE

FRANCE has played her full part in the making of the modern world and the modern mind. If she cannot boast of such Copernican figures as Newton and Darwin, she can point to a galaxy of prophets and pioneers who have widened the frontiers of thought ever since Rabelais and Montaigne broke the spell of tradition and encouraged their readers to contemplate the panorama of time and space with open eyes. Some such torch-bearers, each with a message of his own, are portrayed in these pages.

French history divides at the Revolution of 1789, and no other European state but Russia has experienced so sudden and drastic a break in the continuity of its national life. With the exception of Bossuet, who was content with the institutions and ideologies of the reign of Louis XIV, the brightest luminaries of the seventeenth and eighteenth centuries, from Bayle and Fontenelle to Voltaire and Condorcet, preached the need of change and resented the obscurantism in high places which blocked the road to a Brave New World.

The Revolution and its offspring the Empire raised the question what kind of edifice should be erected on the site left vacant by the disappearance of Monarchy and Feudalism, the Nobility and the Church. That the nation should obtain some share in shaping its destiny was generally agreed. But how much? And what principles should inspire the new régime? Political and social institutions are the embodiment of ideas and ideals, and in nineteenth-century France two main schools competed for support. Should the watchword be 'back to religion' or 'forward on secular lines'?

Part II describes the plans for reconstruction of some of the leading spirits of the Restoration, the Second Empire and the Third Republic. The Church knew best, claimed the Catholics.

vii

Let the great industrialists take the lead, argued Saint-Simon. More democracy, pleaded Michelet. Only the educated class was fit to rule, preached Taine, only the *Syndicats*, shouted Georges Sorel.

Some of these studies have appeared in the *Contemporary Review* and my thanks are due for permission to reprint. 'Anglo-French Contacts in the Eighteenth Century' was an address to the Johnson Society. 'Voltaire as Historian' first appeared in *Catherine the Great and Other Studies*.

PART ONE

BEFORE THE REVOLUTION

I

BAYLE AND THE CULT OF REASON

THE governing principle of the intellectual history of Western
Europe since the sixteenth century has been the secularisation
of thought, the transition from a theocentric to an anthropocentric
approach, the decline of traditionalism and ecclesiastical authority,
the growing conviction that the unfettered use of the reasoning
faculty in the search for truth is a duty no less than a right. It was
not reason alone which came into its own. The emancipation
of conscience from authority, declared Acton in a challenging
phrase, was the main content of modern history. Just as reason
is the pathfinder in the detection of error and quest for truth,
conscience, the inner light, the voice of God, told us what was
right and what was wrong.

In this far-ranging transformation of outlook and method
Pierre Bayle played a leading part. Inheriting the critical spirit of
Montaigne and handing on the torch to Voltaire and the Encyclopaedists, he is gratefully saluted as a major emancipator of the
mind from its fetters of superstition by Lecky in his classical study
of rationalism and by Bury in his history of freedom of thought.
A bold thinker if ever there was one, exclaims Brunetière in his
fine tribute to one of the brightest luminaries in the French literary
sky. In this world, declared Goethe, there are few voices and
many echoes, and Bayle was not born to be an echo.

Unable to breathe in the France of Bossuet and Louis XIV, the
pastor's son fled to a safer anchorage in Rotterdam, where he
could write and publish whatever he liked. Even there his views
were far too liberal for Jurieu and other colleagues as intolerant
as the dignitaries of the older Church. Not even his bitterest foes,

3

however, could find fault with his blameless life—he was most respected and admired by those who knew him best. Voltaire pronounced him *une âme divine*. His biography by his friend Desmaizeaux reveals a scholar dedicated to the disinterested search for truth and the combating of intolerance at whatever risk to himself. The combination of wide erudition with a sparkling play of mind entitles his *Dictionnaire Historique et Critique* to rank among the books which have made history. It was described by Frederick the Great as a breviary of good sense, Voltaire described his writings as the library of the nations, Goethe found it in his father's library, and Gibbon paid homage to the author as a calm and lofty spectator of the religious tempest. While the main purpose of encyclopaedias has been to provide information, Bayle regarded the child of his brain as an instrument for the diffusion of ideas which he believed to be of vital significance for the welfare and happiness of mankind. His ambition was realised, for the Dictionary became the bible of the Age of Reason. His admiring American biographer Howard Robinson describes him as the spiritual father of the eighteenth century and founder of modern rationalism. Translations and abridgements carried the Dictionary into many lands with its enfranchising message of intellectual and spiritual independence. *Nullius addictus jurare in verba magistri*.

Born in 1647 in a remote village in Languedoc, Bayle was educated by his father, and anticipated the juvenile experiences of Gibbon when he entered a Jesuit College at Toulouse, the only institution providing higher education in the district. Calvinism had begun to lose its grip and he looked round for an alternative. His father and elder brother, himself a pastor, took his conversion calmly, convinced that the new phase would not last long. Seventeen months later his announcement of his return to Protestantism brought tears of joy to his family, whom he never saw again, for the lapsed Catholic fled to the safer anchorage of Geneva. Continuing his study of philosophy and theology he quickly decided that neither Rome nor Calvin satisfied him. While taking his time to decide what to do with his exceptional gifts he accepted an invitation to become tutor to the son of Count Dohna, owner of the Château at Coppet. Two years later, thirsting for a wider stage, he obtained a similar post in a family at

Rouen, and six months later he settled in Paris, reading omnivorously in the libraries and revelling in the intellectual stimulus
of the capital. At the age of twenty-eight Bayle was appointed
Professor of Philosophy at the little Protestant Academy of
Sedan. On its suppression six years later he accepted a call to the
chair of Philosophy and History at Rotterdam, which was to
remain his home for the rest of his life. Though no longer in
danger, his ship was never to reach calm waters, and henceforth
his battle with Calvinist zealots was as fierce as with the champions
of the older faith.

In 1680 a comet brighter than any witnessed within living
memory flashed across the sky. What did it portend? Was it not
a clear warning to man to repent of his sins? Such was the interpretation of Catholics and Protestants alike, and the former
flocked to the confessional in order to be prepared for the worst.
Disgusted by this lapse into primitive superstition Bayle published his *Réflexions sur le Comète* in 1682. His thesis was far too
bold a challenge to the Churches for him to reveal his name.
Comets, he declared, were purely natural phenomena and had
appeared throughout the ages in many lands, including several
in recent years in France. If men continued to believe that they
were signs from above it was because they refused to employ
their reason. They were part of the ordinary operations of nature,
masses of matter being transported from one portion of the
heavens to another in accordance with the laws of motion. Such
a conception, he explained, was fully consistent with religious
belief. 'The Author of nature pursues His exalted way and
follows the general law which He has established. Nature is
nothing else than God Himself and works of nature are not less
the effect of His power than miracles. We should never attribute
to miracles what we can explain by natural causes.' When he
accepts Christ's miracles as of an order entirely supernatural,
acts done out of love for mankind, he may have been insuring
himself against the thunders of the Protestant Academy in which
he held a post, since his intellectual audacity was unmatched by
a zeal for martyrdom. The conception of an ordered universe
struck at the belief in miraculous interventions almost universal
throughout the ages. There was not a word in the book on comets
to suggest that the miracles described in the Old and the New

Testament could not have taken place. Such an assertion would
have been not only dangerous but contrary to his temperament.
Detesting dogmatism in all its manifestations, he never dog-
matised: he merely cautioned his readers not to be too certain
about many matters in a very mysterious universe. Beliefs possessed no greater authority merely because they had prevailed for
a long time. When his Geneva friend Minutoli warned him not
to stray too far from the beaten track in dealing with the Old
Testament he replied that he venerated the Sacred Books and
disavowed anything in his letters which contradicted them. In
this sphere his letters to friends reveal much more than his writings. 'The theologians argue about words. We are reminded of
Ixion who believed that he was embracing Juno and discovered
that it was a cloud. They dispute about trifles and think that they
are setting forth the most profound mysteries of philosophy and
theology.' Much he really believed, we can only guess. Bury
assumes that he was a complete free-thinker. That his early
writings were anonymous tells its own tale. 'The more I study
philosophy,' he wrote to his brother, 'the more I doubt. The differences between sects only concern probabilities, some more, some
less. There is no finality and I doubt if there ever will be, so profound are the workings of God in the world of nature as in the
world of grace. I am a philosopher without being committed,
regarding Aristotle, Epicurus and Descartes as inventors of con-
jectures which may or may not be true.'

Bayle's second plunge into the troubled waters of controversy
occurred when Father Maimbourg's *History of Calvinism*, published in 1689 and dedicated to Louis XIV, denounced that faith
as the most terrible enemy France had ever known, worse even
than its parent Lutheranism, for it was not merely a heresy but a
source of disorder in the state. In his reply, *General Criticism of the
History of Calvinism*, Bayle complained that the author had approved the Bartholomew massacre and had omitted to issue a
much-needed warning against immorality in France. The infallibility of the Church was a chimera, for there was no infallible
oracle in the world. Conversion was a crime, and there was more
Christianity in Seneca than in the work under review. The Jesuit
author retaliated by having the work burned by the common
hangman in the Place de Grève in Paris, and the death penalty

was threatened for anyone offering it for sale. The hard-hitting book was rapturously acclaimed by the Jansenists, who were regarded in the highest quarters as only less pestiferous than the Calvinists.

When the Edict of Nantes was revoked in 1685 and the persecution of the Huguenots reached its height, Bayle returned to the fray in *La France toute Catholique*. Intolerance, he declared, was a disgrace to the Church. 'You have made your Christianity stink and its name has become justly odious to infidels.' There was a personal as well as an ethical reason for such language, for Bayle's brother, who had succeeded their father in his parish, had been imprisoned and had died of the brutal treatment he received. Stirred to the depths by the *dragonnades* and other horrors, he repeated his protest in a treatise entitled *Philosophic Commentary on the words of Christ wherein it is proved that there is nothing more abominable than to make conversions by force*. The *Preliminary Discourse* contains a fierce denunciation of the persecuting Church, the only good feature of which was the revelation of the unchanging character of Rome.

This broadside was described on the title page as 'translated from the English of John Fox'. England, he explained, had begun to feel that this wolf, this tiger, had forgotten its savage nature! 'Thank God, the French converters have shown us what to expect if we ever fall into their clutches. They would bring to the stake those who do not go to mass if they had the power.' Catholics, it was clear, could not be trusted to leave harmless citizens at peace. While some people were surprised how many free-thinkers and deists there were, he wondered why there were not more in view of all the crimes religion had authorised. *Tantum religio potuit suadere malorum.*

Passing from the burning invective of the *Preliminary Discourse* to the solid argument of the treatise, Bayle reminds his readers that reason is given us by God and is presumably to be used. There might be doubt about speculative thought but not about problems of conduct. The light of nature comes from God: it is the primitive means of distinguishing truth from falsehood, good from evil. 'Compel them to come in' is contrary to the most distinct ideas of reason and to the spirit of the Gospel. Intolerance and torture breed hypocrisy, destroying divine and human morality, providing a pretext for States to exclude or expel preachers, and depriving the Christian religion of its arguments against false religions. They were unknown to the Fathers of the first three centuries, and made any complaints of persecution elsewhere ridiculous. To the common argument that the multiplicity of religions is harmful to the State he replies that such a danger only arises where the one declines to tolerate the other and desires to destroy it by persecution. If mutual toleration prevailed there would be the same harmony in a country with ten religions as in a town where the different classes of artisans give each other mutual support: each would vie with the others in piety, good conduct and skill. Each would pride itself on drawing closest to God by its good works. Their patriotism would increase if the sovereign protected them all and held the balance between them. Co-operation is the source of infinite benefits. Thus toleration is the best method of restoring the golden age and of providing harmony among different voices and instruments. All the trouble arises when one of two religions exerts a cruel tyranny over the other and compels it to sacrifice its conscience; for some kings display an unjust partiality and provide the support of the secular arm for the furious crimes of a mob of monks and priests. In a word, disorder is caused not by toleration but by the lack of it.

Bayle's passionate appeal was addressed to intolerant Protestants not less than to Catholics. So long as he was castigating the older Church for persecuting Protestants he was applauded by Jurieu. When, however, he campaigned for universal religious toleration and branded the execution of Servetus as a hideous blot on the Reformation, the fiery Calvinist excused it, turned against him, and pursued him with virulent invective to the end of his life. *Jurieu injurieux*, as Bayle called him, was the unbending champion of rigid Calvinism and had inherited the stark intransigence of its founder. Bossuet contemptuously described him as the Archbishop of his flock, who claimed not merely the authority of an Archbishop but in the infallibility of the Pope. *Les extrêmes se touchent*, for the Calvinist and the Ultramontane alike believed in a monolithic Church. Jurieu's suspicions were aroused when Bayle demanded toleration not merely for Jews but for Unitarians then known as Socinians. He published an angry reply before he discovered the identity of the anonymous author, who was flagellated as an indifferentist and a *libertin*. A ruler, he declared in a sentence which might have been written by Bossuet and countersigned by Louis XIV, had a right to suppress a false religion. Though the so-called Wars of Religion were supposed to have ended with the treaty of Westphalia in 1648, here was a direct invitation to renew the devastating conflict.

Bayle replied that Jurieu had no right to lecture Louis XIV since their principles, though not their beliefs, were much the same. He expected the victory of Protestantism in France about 1689, after which the Papacy (Anti-Christ) would soon disappear, a kingdom of God on earth would be inaugurated, the refugees would return, Jews and Moslems be converted. God, he asserted, had created William of Orange to execute His will. Jurieu's polemics were not in vain, for the Rotterdam Consistory deprived the iconoclast of his chair.

The incident led Bayle to think of migrating to Berlin where the Great Elector had welcomed Huguenot refugees after the revocation of the Edict of Nantes. He made soundings through his friend Abbadie, happily installed as a pastor to the *émigrés* in the Prussian capital, but the project was dropped when the ruler died in 1688.

Though silenced in the lecture-room he had other means of reaching the outside world. The success of the recently founded *Journal des Savants* encouraged him to launch a monthly review entitled *Nouvelles de la République des Lettres*. Bringing wide learning and manifold interests to his task the editor devoted much of his space to reviews. Though forbidden in France copies were smuggled in and the paper was widely read beyond the frontiers.

The absorbing occupation of the last two decades of Bayle's life was the *Dictionnaire Historique et Critique* which keeps his name alive. How much it was required was indicated by the success of Moreri's *Grand Dictionnaire Historique* published in 1674, the first which was alphabetically arranged, of which seven editions had appeared before it was supplemented and partly superseded. The idea occurred to Bayle as he discovered that Moreri's work swarmed with errors, and his initial intention was to content himself with correcting them. Even when an enterprise of wider scope was undertaken he envisaged no complete work of reference which would have been beyond his powers. Some famous names are absent, and some obscure careers are included as pegs on which to hang his erudition or his ideology. He knew little of science and felt no great attraction to *belles-lettres* and the arts. His chief interest was in history ancient and modern, in religion and superstition in all their forms, and in the world of learning particularly in the sixteenth and seventeenth centuries. He embarked on his formidable task with an erudition almost unique among his contemporaries, fortified by a robust belief in his capacity to pronounce on every aspect of human achievement. Though he has been called a sceptic, his scepticism was usually a mask to conceal very definite convictions, both positive and negative. He was certain that ultimate problems are for ever beyond our grasp. Every philosopher had produced a different system. While the orthodox of various creeds believed that all the answers had been supplied by some divine revelation, he confronted every claim to superior knowledge with the query Is it true? and every kind of conduct with the query Is it right? His biographies are usually presented in impersonal form, but in many cases they are followed by his own comments.

One of the gravest of his offences in the eyes of orthodox zealots was his conviction that morals were not dependent on any particular creed. He had never met an evil-living atheist, he declared, but he had met many professing Christians who were a disgrace to their Church. There had been good people in every age, in every land, in every political and religious community. Had there ever been a better man than Spinoza? What would the Early Fathers say if they returned to earth?

His most delicate problem was how to treat the Jewish and Christian scriptures. Since many Protestants had substituted an infallible Bible for an infallible Church he had to bear in mind the susceptibilities of readers in both camps, but at times his emotions were too strong to suppress. The most celebrated and the most controversial article was on David, described in the Old Testament as a man after God's own heart. Were we to accept such a statement merely because it appeared in the Bible when a secular historian would have pronounced, without hesitation, a much less flattering verdict? The article raised a larger issue than the morality of a Jewish ruler with whom one could not shake hands. If a reader of the sacred books began to criticise or disbelieve this or that recorded incident or to question some moral assessment, where would he stop? When the Rotterdam Consistory protested the offending article was amended in the second edition of the Dictionary; but the original was republished as a brochure and became available to an even wider circle of readers. Jurieu, described by Bayle as 'my enemy', strove in vain to procure the suppression of the whole work in Holland, but its author was always ready with some formula of submission which averted the worst consequences to the brain-child on which he was at work till within a few hours of his death.

He announced his work as a formless collection of passages ill-suited to the delicate taste of the age; he was frankly surprised at its instantaneous success, which encouraged him to prepare a new edition. Had he revisited the world half a century later and witnessed the vogue of Voltaire and the Encyclopaedists the author of the Bible of the eighteenth century would have been entitled to murmur *Quorum pars parva fui*. Yet his satisfaction would not have been unmixed. As Faguet has remarked in a penetrating study, he belonged neither to the seventeenth nor the eighteenth century. Completely out of sympathy with the theological dogmatism of the former, he would have been almost as entirely estranged from the scientific dogmatism of the latter. How, he might have asked, can you be so sure of anything? Knowing what we do of the record of mankind, how can you believe in perfectibility? D'Alembert's aggressive atheism would have disgusted him no less than Rousseau's idealisation of primitive man. He would have found himself most at home with Voltaire, sharing his hatred not merely of intolerance and superstition but of cruelty and violence, war and religious strife. Lonely in his life he strove for a saner and gentler world though he had little hope that it could be attained. Since mankind had never been guided by reason, was there much hope that the future would be better than the past?

2

FONTENELLE AND THE CULT OF SCIENCE

No eminent Frenchman has lived as long as Fontenelle, who missed his century by a month, and no-one has made a better use of his time. *Homo sum*, he might have exclaimed, *nihil humani alienum puto*. The most universal mind of his age, as Voltaire described him, earned a name as writer and thinker when Louis XIV was at the height of his power, and he lived to be saluted as the Grand Old Man of the Age of Reason. His talk fascinated the *habitués* of the salon of Mme de La Fayette, and half a century later he continued to shine with undiminished lustre as the literary lion of the highbrow circle of Mme Geoffrin. Starting his career as the author of second-rate tragedies and comedies, satires and poems, which won him entry into the Académie Française at an early age, he quickly sensed that his real bent was not *belles-lettres* but science; and he became the most accomplished *vulgarisateur* of the marvels revealed by astronomers and physicists that France has ever known. Though untrained as a scientist he acquired a working knowledge in several fields. That he was more than a gifted amateur was recognised by his appointment first as member and soon after as *Secrétaire perpétuel* of the Academy of Sciences. Authority, he proudly declared towards the close of his life, had at last ceased to count for as much as reason, and none of his contemporaries except Bayle contributed so much to the atmospheric change as himself. A good deal was known of the mysterious universe, he declared, but much more was waiting to be discovered and meanwhile one could speculate. Perhaps the moon, the planets and even stars might be inhabited. One day we should surely know.

Born in 1657, son of a Norman lawyer and nephew of Corneille, Fontenelle was educated at the Jesuit College in Rouen. Though destined by his father to the bar, the first taste of the profession was enough, for his heart was elsewhere. His precocity in French and Latin verse had won him prizes at school, and Rouen was too provincial for the unfolding of the talents he felt himself to possess. All doors in Paris were open to the precocious nephew of Corneille, and the success of two operas, to which Lully supplied the music, appeared to indicate that he had found his feet. The illusion was shortlived, for the failure of a tragedy which was *sifflé* by a critical audience taught a lesson he was not too proud to learn. The manuscript was consigned to the flames, and though he continued to dabble in *belles-lettres* he turned his main attention to more rewarding activities. His literary apprenticeship was by no means wasted, for his sense of style was of inestimable value in his task of making difficult subjects seem easy and indeed delightful for the general reader. Two centuries later Faguet saluted him as Secretary-General of the Scientific World.

The *Dialogues des Morts*, which Fontenelle published at the age of twenty-six, revealed that his interests ranged far beyond the domain of *belles-lettres* and may be described as a half-way house in his journey from literature to science and philosophy. Celebrities are summoned from their graves and confronted with others of equal fame sometimes of widely separated periods, for instance Paracelsus with Molière. The chief impression left by the work is the wide learning of a man still under thirty. The dialogue form enables authors to express their convictions through the mouths of others while avoiding direct responsibility for any specific paradox or heresy, but it is not very difficult to detect the writer's authentic voice. Love occupies a prominent place, as the contemporary taste demanded, but it is of an unromantic character. Having known neither real love nor its counterfeit, he regards it from outside with a slightly cynical eye. Throughout life, he felt and displayed little admiration for the human species, reserving his approval for the few who used their reason, the highest quality of mankind. The pleasures of anticipation, in his view, were greater than those of fulfilment. Truth was hard to find, and we could not always be sure we had found it. Man was always aspiring and never enjoying, ever on the march and never arriving, longing for certainty but only finding probability. He had as little use for tradition as for sentiment. Sainte-Beuve indeed describes him as all brain, since nature had forgotten the heart, and Mme Geoffrin, who only knew him in old age, complained that he never laughed, cried or loved. His lack of warmth in human relations has been sometimes attributed to delicate health in his early years and to warnings by his doctor to avoid violent emotions. He never married and no scandal attached to his name.

Fontenelle's most celebrated work, *Entretiens sur la Pluralité des Mondes*, was published in 1686, the year before Newton's *Principia* in which the laws of gravitation superseded Descartes' system of fluxions. Leaving aside the problem of the origin of the universe as beyond our ken, he concentrated on the question whether some or all of the heavenly bodies which he delighted to watch on starlit nights might be inhabited. No-one could be sure but it seemed very likely. The thought obsessed him. Never before and never again did he allow himself such expressions of rapture as in the contemplation of the starry heavens, and he declared with a smile that he could not forgive the sun for blotting out that overwhelming panorama in the course of every twenty-four hours.

Reverting to the dialogue form he had adopted with such success in his earlier work, he presents his thoughts in the form of conversations with an intelligent Marquise whom his biographers have identified as a friend. Fascinated by the pageant of the night sky as they stroll in the garden of a provincial château, she begs him to tell her more about it. This device enables him to break up long dissertations into questions and answers, thus greatly diminishing the strain on the reader's attention. No French writer on scientific subjects has possessed a lighter touch.

I have not wished to suggest anything quite impossible and chimerical [he explained in the Preface], but only what seems reasonably probable about inhabitants of other worlds, for my visions have some real foundation. Some scrupulous people may imagine that there is a certain danger to religion in such a notion, and I respect even an excess of sensitivity. Any such difficulties, however, vanish when we realise that the moon-dwellers, if such there be, are different from the sons of Adam. What are they like? I have not seen them, but their vision of the world and of ourselves must be different from ours. Nature displays infinite variety in her works. That is the idea which pervades my book.

The first *Entretien* opens with the assertion that every star may be a world.

Marquise: What sort of people may live on the moon?
Astronomer: I have no idea. If we lived there, could we imagine such strange creatures as the human species, with such crazy passions and such wise thoughts, with so short a span and such long views, so much knowledge of things almost useless and so much ignorance of more important matters, such ardour for liberty and such inclination to servitude, such yearning for happiness and such incapacity for finding it? The moon-dwellers would be extremely clever if they guessed all that. Perhaps some day there may be contact between earth and moon. We are beginning to fly a little, sometimes at the cost of arm or leg. Navigation began with a hollowed tree-trunk and has developed into big ships. The art of flight is only just born, but it will be perfected and one day we shall go to the moon. Have we reached the end of our discoveries? Perhaps the moon-dwellers may learn to fly before ourselves.

If the moon be inhabited [continues the astronomer], why not the other planets, Venus, Mars, Mercury, Jupiter, Saturn, the last two of which possess satellites? In describing each planet to his companion the astronomer draws on his observations with a telescope and warms to his theme. Every fixed star, he adds, is a sun, illuminating a world of its own.
Marquise: The idea of all these worlds terrifies me.
Astronomer: It puts me at my ease. I seem to breathe more freely and the universe assumes a new grandeur. The stars probably possess planets too small for us to see. In the Milky Way the stars are so close together that there will be no night. I believe that matter sometimes forms new suns, that is new worlds, but of course that is pure conjecture.

A Sixth *Entretien* was added in a subsequent edition. Science was marching on, but the plurality of inhabited worlds remained a hypothesis. Yet there was as much evidence for the belief as for some of the recorded events of history. Writing in old age he once more expresses his wonder at the fecundity and magnificence of nature. The range and boldness in this remarkable book, which was widely read, alarmed the Jesuits, and Le Tellier, the King's Confessor, recommended a *lettre de cachet* for the author. His advice was ignored, since there was not a sentence in the *Entretiens* which challenged Christian doctrine. Whether the author's studies and speculations ever altered his attitude to the teaching of the Church we do not know, but it is easy to understand the alarm in orthodox circles. In the words of Faguet the author sowed dragon's teeth with an elegant hand.

A more subtle challenge to conventional ideology was offered in two brief treatises which have been described as little masterpieces of discreet scepticism. They deal with legends and traditions, rituals and practices, floating on an ocean of superstition and trickery, originating in the exploitation of curiosity and credulity, the cults of communities wallowing in a morass of absurdities such as we can scarcely imagine. Stories of unusual events were embroidered by popular imagination as they were orally handed down, for some people revel in invention. The pagan gods were the creation of man, and history is the record of the aberrations of the human mind. This was scarcely astonishing, for nature presents many faces and many problems to philosophers and is full of surprises.

In certain cases it had been discovered that some phenomena which had appeared supernormal if not indeed supernatural had never occurred. For instance in 1593 a boy of seven was found to possess a gold tooth which was widely interpreted as a divine intervention to console Christian peoples for the progress of infidel Turks in Europe. The bubble burst when it was proved that the tooth had been covered with gold leaf. All religions were full of legends accepted as facts, for when error had effected an entry it was a marvel if it was ever evicted. Yet there should be no difficulty in realising that all oracles were the result of fraud. Have we not ample knowledge of the extent to which men have been impostors and dupes? Do we not know when and why they ceased?

The author of *l'Histoire des Oracles*, well grounded in theology and the classics, proceeded to demonstrate that a belief in oracles claiming superhuman powers had no scriptural warrant. Delphi was notoriously a commercialised hypocrisy. Of course demons

and malignant spirits condemned to eternal torments could exist
and deliver oracles if God permitted them. But had He done so?
The Scriptures contained no such assertion. Yet everyone, including the early Christians, believed there was something supernatural about oracles. Antiquity was full of surprising stories
which people could only attribute to genii. When God chose
the Jews as His people He left the rest of the world in darkness
till the coming of Christ. Even then there were plenty of charla-
tans and dupes. The only marvel in the history of oracles is
human depravity, folly and superstition. The older a fable or a
belief, the less likely it is to be true. While Bayle usually soft-
pedalled on dangerous ground, Fontenelle's little treatises
breathed utter contempt for human credulity worthy of Voltaire.
'Use your critical faculties' was his message to his contemporaries. 'Let us make sure of our facts before we worry our
brains in attempting to explain them.' This advice applies in a
far wider field than fables and oracles, and there is no need to
swallow everything related by historians. Few of them had witnessed the events they relate, and few stand above the battle.
The lives of the Saints, for instance, were full of marvels eagerly
and uncritically accepted as useful ammunition in the running
fight with Jews, heretics and pagans. Many Greeks were aware
that oracles were controlled not by demons but by swindlers
who endeavoured to find out what their clients desired to be told.
Where such information was unobtainable, or when the failure
or success of some future enterprise was unpredictable, deliber-
ately ambiguous answers were provided, since any large-scale
failure was bound to destroy the prestige which constituted the
sole capital of the institution. The oracles of the pagan world
diminished in number and influence with the spread of Christianity and disappeared in the fourth century, but their eclipse was
partly due to their notorious abuses. The book closes with an
angry outburst. The conduct of priests, their indolence, the
exposure of their tricks, the obscurity and falsity of their answers,
would have discredited them and caused their total ruin independently of the downfall of paganism, though the process might
have been slower.

The Book of Oracles might have been written by Bayle, just
as the Essay on Comets might have come from the pen of Fon-

tenelle. The message of both these epoch-making books was that
the more we learn of natural agencies, and we gain fresh knowledge from year to year, the less need there is for supernatural
agencies either diabolical or divine. Some perceptive readers
may well have asked themselves what evidence existed for the
more sensational miracles of the Old and the New Testament, a
theme which Fontenelle studiously avoided. His conviction of
the vast superiority of the achievements of the modern world
was reiterated in his intervention in the celebrated *Querelle des
Anciens et Modernes* inaugurated by Perrault which was con-
vulsing Parisian circles. Had trees grown taller or brains been
larger in the ancient world, he asked in *Discussion sur les Anciens
et Modernes*. How could we fail to be superior since we stood on
the shoulders of our ancestors and added to their legacy the
discoveries and creations of many centuries. 'Say if you will that
we cannot surpass them but not that we cannot equal them.'
The creative arts were a delight, but science, of which the ancients
knew little, held the key to the future. The loftiest of human
ambitions was to widen the frontiers of knowledge by unwearying efforts to learn Nature's marvellous secrets.

The most significant event in the career of Fontenelle was his
appointment in 1701 at the age of forty-four to the post of
Secrétaire Perpétuel de l'Académie des Sciences. For the remaining
fifty-six years of his life science was his primary interest and
occupation. As a man of the world with a taste for literature he
was perfectly at home in the salons of the capital, but his heart
was elsewhere. The author of a treatise on geometry knew most
about mathematics and astronomy, but he possessed a working
acquaintance with achievements in other fields. The proceedings
of the Academy were enlivened by his *Eloges* of seventy-five
members and corresponding members at the time of their death.
Most of them deal with long-forgotten names which required only
brief commemoration, but a few, including Newton and Leibniz,
Vauban, Malebranche and Boerhaave, are models of biographical
and academic presentation, in some cases enriched and warmed
by personal memories and therefore of enduring value to historians of science. A new discovery at home or abroad thrilled
him more than the latest victory of French arms. Human nature,
of which he had never thought very highly, seemed unlikely to

change for better or worse. He lived and died in the conviction that there would always be sufficient scientists to continue the quest for knowledge and understanding of the universe, every generation adding to the heritage of the ages.

ABBÉ DE SAINT-PIERRE AND
PERPETUAL PEACE

THE Abbé Saint-Pierre was as much of a misfit in the France of Louis XIV as Bayle himself. Though he entered the priesthood at the wish of his family he had no belief in the dogmas of the Church and little respect for monarchs. The ruling passion of his life was to increase the happiness of mankind at home and abroad. He brought to his task a singularly imaginative mind and a serene confidence in the value of his suggestions. Long before Condorcet proclaimed the doctrine of perfectibility he promised his contemporaries and succeeding generations a golden age if they would listen to his voice and consult their common interests. The road to the Promised Land was blocked by war, but war could be eliminated by the simple expedient of a federated Europe. All that was needed could be secured by agreement between the rulers of the larger states on the basis of the territorial *status quo* guaranteed by a collective stand against aggression. Though chiefly remembered as the author of the *Projet de la Paix Perpétuelle*, he was almost equally proud of his administrative plan for the creation of Councils in the more important departments of state, assisting an over-worked prince who took his duties seriously, and carrying the burdens of government when the ruler was a minor, or ill, or too lazy to play his part. With peace abroad and an efficient bureaucracy at home every country would attain a state of happiness such as it had never known. Saint-Pierre, like Condorcet, was more than a mere dreamer, for there was a solid core of good sense in all his schemes; yet the two chief French idealists of the eighteenth century were so enamoured of their scheme that they underestimated the imperfections of the human beings who would have to implement them. How could anyone expect the princes and peoples of Europe, large and small, victors or vanquished in the War of the Spanish Succession, to be satisfied with the map as traced in the Treaty of Utrecht? How could one expect rulers in the classic age of absolutism to share their power with elected Councils? And how could one expect the members of such Councils to rise above their individual interests and dedicate themselves exclusively to the common weal?

Half a century after the publication of Saint-Pierre's two principal works Rousseau accepted an invitation to summarise them. He seized the opportunity to pass judgement on their value. While gratefully recognising the Abbé's nobility of aim, the most eloquent voice of the century dismissed his Brave New World as an airy dream; since the rulers who alone could inaugurate the golden age were the men most satisfied with the institutions and prerogatives they had inherited and were consequently ill-disposed towards revolutionary changes. 'This rare man,' wrote Rousseau in his *Confessions*, 'the honour of his century and of the human species, perhaps the only man in history who had no passion but reason, went from error to error in striving to make all men like himself instead of taking them as they are and will remain. He planned for creatures of his imagination in the belief that he was working for his contemporaries.' Voltaire, who hated war no less than Rousseau, pronounced a similar verdict. 'The idea of universal peace is more chimerical than that of a universal language. True, war is a plague, and in conflict with human nature and with almost all religions, but it is as old as human nature and older than any religion. It is as difficult to stop men fighting as to prevent wolves devouring sheep.'

Yet the dreamers and planners dismissed by Louis XIV as *les chimériques* and by Napoleon as *les idéologues* are the salt of the earth, for man does not live by bread alone. The author of the first detailed plan for a unified Europe stretched out a hand across the gulf of two centuries and innumerable conflicts to Woodrow Wilson and the architects of UNO. *In magnis voluisse sat est.*

Saint-Pierre was born into an old Norman family in 1658.

While the eldest son followed the tradition of his ancestors by a
career in the army, the younger, on concluding his studies in a
Jesuit college at Caen, obeyed the wishes of his parents to enter
the priesthood, for which he had not the slightest vocation. At
the age of twenty-eight the death of his father provided him
with sufficient means to migrate to Paris where he enjoyed the
delights of society under the auspices of Fontenelle. He studied
the sciences, frequented the salon of Mme de La Fayette, and was
appointed to the sinecure post of almoner to Madame, sister-in-
law of the King and mother of the future Regent. Elected to the
Academy before he had written a book he belonged to no school
and formed none of his own. 'I learned to hear and examine all
opinions and to change mine when I found one more probable,
till then clinging to my own.'

Shocked, like Vauban, Fénelon, and La Bruyère, by the horrors
of the long War of the Spanish Succession, Saint-Pierre turned
over in his ingenious mind how its repetition could be averted.
After studying Le Grand Dessein attributed in Sully's Memoirs
to Henri IV, he resolved to follow up the trail. His ideas were
submitted to the Duc de Bourgogne shortly before his death in
1712. Many hopes were buried in the grave of Fénelon's pupil,
who, in Saint-Pierre's glowing vision, might perhaps inaugurate
a new era of peace on earth. The Abbé's appointment in 1712
as secretary to Cardinal de Polignac, one of France's two pleni-
potentiaries to the Congress of Utrecht, provided the opportunity for the political planner to study diplomacy at close
quarters, and his year's residence in the old city confirmed his
conviction that nothing but a radical change in international
machinery could rescue mankind from the scourge of recurrent
strife. It was in these busy months that he expounded the scheme
published in 1713, Projet de Henri le Grand pour rendre la Paix
perpétuelle expliqué par l'Abbé Saint-Pierre, launched under the
modest guise of a mere elucidation of the plan attributed to the
most popular of French kings. That was a mere pose, for the gulf
between the two schemes was wide and deep. The Grand Dessein
demanded the dismemberment of the sprawling Hapsburg Empire
and the expulsion of the Turks from Europe as the necessary
preliminary for the creation of a federation of the Princes, a
Christian Republic, the members of which would settle their

differences at a Diet and would guarantee each other against aggression. The Hapsburg Empire, the strongest of the Powers, should be reduced to less threatening dimensions by the restoration of Bohemian and Hungarian independence, Switzerland and the Netherlands enlarged, Milan transferred to the Duke of Savoy, and Naples to the Pope. Europe should be divided into six circles, relations within each being regulated by a Council. The six Councils should be subordinate to a Supreme Council which would deal with major matters of general concern, and would render wars within the Christian Republic impossible.

It was as clear to Saint-Pierre as to the rest of mankind that no solid temple of peace could be erected, nor the map of Europe reconstructed, on the basis of the results of war; but his rival scheme of taking the frontiers as he found them and guaranteeing the owners of territory against violent change was scarcely less utopian. Realising, however, that it was useless to expect a ruler to surrender a portion of his dominions, and rejecting redistribution by force of arms, he had no alternative to suggest. His plan required the acceptance of five articles to procure unbreakable peace.

I. The rulers of every Christian state should form a perpetual alliance for mutual defence against the misfortunes of foreign and civil war, thus guaranteeing the safety of their states and their persons, and the regular dynastic succession. That would reduce expenditure, increase the revenue and well-being of their states, perfect the law, settle their differences by peaceful means, and carry out promptly and fully all future treaties and promises.

II. Each signatory should contribute according to his means to the safety and common expenses of the alliance, the sum to be fixed monthly by a majority vote.

III. The signatories should renounce the use of arms to settle their present and future differences, if necessary by majority vote, and the members must always be ready to accept the mediation of their allies.

IV. Any act contrary to the rules of the alliance should be forcibly resisted by the other members.

V. New articles could only be framed by unanimity, and nothing could alter the original five.

Twenty signatures would inaugurate a golden age and would

serve the interest of all, for it would save expenditure, make every citizen very happy and exchange false for true glory. The Emperor could only guarantee the Pragmatic Sanction by the Five Articles, the King of France would secure enormous reduction of taxation, Spain would recover Gibraltar and Minorca from England who would no longer need Mediterranean fortresses for her trade. Spain would open up South America to world commerce, thus doubling or trebling her revenues, and would no longer fear revolts because her possessions would be securely guaranteed. Little states would lose their fear of being swallowed up (for instance Portugal by Spain and the Republic of Geneva by the Duchy of Savoy). Minor German and Italian states would lose their apprehensions, Poland would be assured the succession in the House of Saxony, the Tsar safe guarded against successful revolts in his vast empire. Charles of Sweden loved big schemes and here was one of the biggest. Even the strongest state would be too weak to challenge the combined forces of the Grand Alliance. Every one would profit except the Turks who could easily be expelled though this would involve war. Such was the only exception to the principle of preserving the *status quo.*

Asked for his opinion on the plan, Leibniz replied that many good intentions were revealed and much solid reasoning. Men desired to free themselves from three great curses—war, pestilence and famine. The Hanoverian philosopher agreed that men had their destiny to a large extent in their own hands, and it was merely lack of determination which prevented them from liberating themselves from an infinity of evils. A ruler could preserve his state from pestilence, as the House of Brunswick had done, and could also guarantee his subjects against famine. Five or six persons could end the Great Schism between East and West and reform the Church. But to stop wars another Henri IV with other great princes would be needed to adopt the scheme, and it would be difficult to make them understand it. None of them would dare to act alone. Perhaps a Minister could take it up when death was at hand if it did not endanger the interests of his family. Yet it was always good to inform the public, and perhaps someone might be impressed when it was least expected. There were usually fatalities which prevented mankind from being happy. 'May you live long enough to enjoy the fruits of your labours.' The great philosopher was not optimistic. 'I remember an inscription in a cemetery,' wrote Leibniz to a friend, '"*Pax Perpetua*". The dead do not fight but the living are of a different humour.'

A third volume of the *Projet de la Paix Perpétuelle* was ready in 1715, shortly after the death of the *Grand Monarque* who confessed on his death-bed that he had been too fond of war. Since the book had now become too large a morsel for the public to buy and digest, the Abbé issued a summary in 1728 with a new title *Abrégé du projet de la paix perpétuelle, inventé par le roi Henri IV, approuvé par la reine Elizabeth, par le roi Jaques son successeur, par les républiques et par divers autres potentats, approprié à l'état général des affaires de l'Europe, démontré infiniment avantageux à tous les hommes nés et à naître en général et en particulier pour tous les souverains et pour les maisons souveraines.*

The *Abrégé* answers some of the objections raised against the scheme, for instance what ruler would accept any infringement of his sovereignty or any limit to his dreams of expansion, or submit disputes to a Diet? Moreover, a guarantee of the *status quo* would perpetuate unjust frontiers and evil régimes. To such criticisms the reply was that civil war, one of the principal and one of the oldest scourges of mankind, had been almost eliminated, so there was no ground for despair. And who could provide a better plan?

In 1716 Saint-Pierre published an essay on the reform of the *taille* in which he spoke with what was felt to be insufficient reverence of the late king. Cardinal de Polignac, his former chief at Utrecht, denounced him to the Academy of which he was the Director, but the offender escaped with a warning and a promise not to repeat the offence. A graver crime was committed in his second important work *Polysynodie*, suggested by the Regent's experiment of associating Councils with the conduct of affairs by departmental ministers, subject only to the Regency Council. The case for Councils rested on the notorious inadequacy of autocratic governments to perform their tasks. Think of what they have done and of what they have omitted to do! 'Kings are men and are more governed by women than others, which is a calamity for the state, and they are too inclined to the pleasures of the table.' The Regent's Councils were unsatisfactory owing to the quarrels of the members, and the experiment was soon abandoned. The only way to prevent Ministers from becoming too powerful, argued the author, was to clip their wings.

Ubi consilia, ibi salus. Man had traversed the age of bronze, was now in the age of silver, and would enter the age of gold if Councils were to be introduced. Princes could not carry the burdens of state; many of them scarcely tried. They were rarely respected, loved or obeyed, since the hereditary system provided ten imbeciles for one authentic king. Councils were required for justice, police, finance, commerce, the army, religion and foreign affairs, each with a president, questions of major interest being reserved for the king. Favourites and courtiers should be excluded. Men of character, ability and experience should be nominated by those who knew them best and rewarded by promotion, the best and ablest among them being transferred from one department to another in order to widen their grasp of affairs. The ideal government was limited monarchy, a good ruler with carefully selected councils at his side. The Councils of the Regency era had no real power. Could men of the highest character be found in sufficient numbers to fill the councils? Rousseau declared it impossible, and believed that places would continue to be bought and sold no less than before, while the king, however unworthy, would remain in effective control.

In 1718 Saint-Pierre was expelled from the Academy for criticising its august patron. The late king, he declared, should be called Louis the Powerful and Louis the Formidable, not Louis the Great, for we must not confound power with true greatness. 'Great power, when not employed to procure great benefit for mankind in general and subjects and neighbours in particular, will not make a very estimable man. In a word, great power alone will never make a great man.' Though the Cardinal reiterated his warning and the Abbé's friends urged him to recant, he replied that he could not in conscience change his attitude. His recalcitrance angered Cardinal Fleury, who had been appointed tutor to the young king by Louis XIV himself, and he described the incident as the most important which had ever occupied the Academy.

It is not a question of the glory of the late king [he declared], for posterity will do him justice and his memory will be honoured by all decent people even if one of its members has dared to attack it in writing. No one would be worthy of membership who put friendship and private ties before its honour. Every new member has to eulogise the late king. If we allow this audacity to go unpunished people will say that our praises were venal and that they only continued during the life of the ruler.

The author's strictures on the *Grand Monarque* were scarcely less a censure of his panegyrists. Unanimity in the demand for his expulsion was required, no debate was allowed, and in the secret ballot his old friend Fontenelle alone challenged the decree. The Regent, who was believed to share the offender's estimate of *Le Roi Soleil*, declined to intervene, but the chair remained vacant and the customary *éloge* on a member's death was withheld. Belated justice was done to him many years later by d'Alembert in the commemoration of Maupertuis.

Undismayed by the frowns of his critics and the approach of old age, Saint-Pierre continued to propound schemes of social betterment in a series of brochures, among them the creation of an Academy of Medicine to collect information on discoveries and treatment and to summarise it in an annual report. Keenly interested in public health, he urged village *curés* to learn the rudiments of medical knowledge in districts where doctors were beyond reach. Other projects dealt with the problem of mendicancy, the reform of the *taille*, the suppression of duels, the improvement of education, and the diminution of the number of disputes which came into the courts and clogged the channels of justice. A Political Academy should be created to foster the study of the science of government.

Saint-Pierre ranks with Condorcet among the constructive idealists of France, and he needed no theological or philosophical system to spur him on his way. When death approached in 1743, at the age of eighty-five, he summoned a priest to satisfy his relatives. 'That is the only thing for which I reproach myself,' he muttered when the visitor withdrew, 'the only time I have betrayed truth, for I don't believe a word of it.' It was enough for him to know that he had not lived in vain. Carrying the enthusiasm of youth into old age, describing

himself as the Secretary of Europe, he died in the conviction
that the seed he had planted would ripen to harvest in due
course.

4

ANGLO-FRENCH CONTACTS IN THE
EIGHTEENTH CENTURY

THOUGH Englishmen and Frenchmen had been fighting on and off ever since the Norman Conquest they knew little of each other's way of life till the eighteenth century when the process of cultural cross-fertilisation began in earnest. The story falls into two parts—French visitors to England and British visitors to France.

When Voltaire crossed the Channel in 1726 at the age of thirty-two he was already a successful dramatist and a welcome guest at the smart dinner tables of the capital. Throughout his long career his tongue, like his pen, was as sharp as a razor, and a witty but wounding utterance landed him in the Bastille. Possessing influential friends he was soon out again on condition that he would leave Paris for a time. Here was an opportunity to visit England with which he had a few personal ties, above all with Lord Bolingbroke who had found his country too hot for him after championing the Pretender, had settled in France, married a French lady, and after a decade of exile was allowed to return. The amnesty arrived just in time for him to welcome Voltaire who also brought an introduction to the French Ambassador. He hoped to finance the publication of his *Henriade* by subscriptions in advance. Friends and admirers played up and the poem duly appeared with a dedication to Queen Caroline, who loved the things of the mind as heartily as her husband despised them. Living at Wandsworth with a kindly merchant he had met in Paris, he worked hard at the language.

In an astonishingly short time he wrote it with scarcely a mistake and spoke with sufficient fluency to confront the literary pundits. He saw most of Pope and Swift, and made acquaintance with Congreve and Gay, Thomson of *The Seasons* and Young of *Night Thoughts*. He was presented at Court, received a small subsidy, attended the funeral of Newton in Westminster Abbey, met Walpole and Sir Hans Sloane, father of the British Museum, frequented meetings of the Royal Society, which made him a Fellow, sampled Quaker services, and dined with a leading Quaker, Andrew Pitt, in Hampstead. From the formidable widow of Marlborough and from Lord Peterborough, a veteran from the Marlborough wars, he received materials for a biography of Charles XII of Sweden.

What did he think of us? His answer is to be found in the *Lettres sur les Anglais*, first published in English shortly after his return to France, which inaugurated the era of *anglomanie*. It was a great deal more than the sparkling record of a visitor, for it was also designed as an appeal to his countrymen to follow British models. Unlike Montesquieu, Rousseau and Mirabeau, he felt little interest in political theory. All he wanted was good government, and if it were provided by a Philosophic Despot such as Frederick the Great he was quite content. His simple ideology was expressed in Pope's couplet:

> For forms of government let fools contest.
> That which is best administered is best.

It was above all the tolerant atmosphere which won his admiration. Though neither Roman Catholic nor Noncomformists enjoyed the full privileges of citizenship, they were better treated than religious minorities in most other countries. As a Deist, firmly believing in an *Etre Suprême* who created the universe but rejecting Christian theology, he stood outside the bickerings of the sects. Though no-one possessed less of the placid Quaker temperament, he carried back to France a lifelong admiration for the little community which dispensed with priests and creeds. Neither the Seven Years War nor any other political complication diminished his admiration for the hospitable country where he had spent nearly three years, and he was always ready to receive English visitors such as Boswell in the closing years at Ferney.

Voltaire left us in the spring of 1729 and Montesquieu arrived three months later, at the age of forty. A member of the nobility, a magistrate and a landowner, he was busily collecting material for his majestic *L'Esprit des Lois*. He had already visited Italy and central Europe where he found little to admire in the laws and institutions, and he kept the best to the last. In the brilliant satire on his native country enshrined in the *Lettres Persanes* which had won him fame, he had contrasted the ordered liberty of England with the cramping autocracy of France. Desiring to witness the system in operation he devoted nearly two years to the task. As Lord Bolingbroke had sponsored Voltaire, so Lord Chesterfield, whom he had met abroad, sponsored Montesquieu. He could read and understand English well enough to attend debates in both Houses and in the Royal Society, which made him a Fellow, and to be presented at Court; but he could speak too little to frequent society. While Voltaire, with his keen interest in every aspect of life and thought, went everywhere and saw everyone, Montesquieu came with a strictly limited purpose —the study of our institutions. That he found people cold was largely due to his inability to converse, but his indifference to our citizens was outweighed by his warm approval of the system under which they lived. Like Voltaire he demanded good government; unlike him, he believed that it could only be secured by the division of power. What was needed—and what England possessed—was a limited monarchy, a freely elected legislature, an independent judiciary. His tribute was paid in the celebrated chapters of the *Esprit des Lois* which were to be intensively studied by the authors of the American Constitution who may be described as the spiritual heirs of Locke and Montesquieu. His advocacy of mixed government produced no effect on the *ancien régime*, which stumbled along, regardless of warnings, to the abyss; but his teaching inspired Mirabeau and other Anglophils in the Constituent Assembly in 1789.

Rousseau's visit in 1767 was a shorter and much less successful affair, and it left unpleasant memories on both sides. He had never felt much interest in us, was ignorant of our language, and had never manifested the slightest desire for closer acquaintance; but on being evicted from his native Switzerland and feeling unsafe in France he accepted an offer from Hume to take him to

England and look after him. They had recently met in Paris when Hume was Secretary in the British Embassy, and he had told Rousseau that he admired his writings and would be glad to help him if the need arose. His friend Adam Smith declared that he was as near perfection as human nature allowed, and his disinterested kindness to the neurotic genius confirms the verdict. Little did he know what he was in for when he so generously volunteered his aid. The two men crossed the Channel together, and on landing at Dover the emotional visitor hugged and kissed his benefactor with tears in his eyes. His two novels, *La Nouvelle Héloise* and *Emile*, the former the French equivalent of Richardson's *Clarissa*, the latter a fictional treatise on education, had been widely read in England. Chaperoned by Hume he was received in London with open arms, and Garrick gave a supper party in his honour at his house in the Adelphi. The visitor, who detested cities and crowds, quickly tired of the festivities, and accepted an invitation to the spacious home in Derbyshire of an admirer of his writings named Davenport. At this stage he was joined by his illiterate mistress, Thérèse Levasseur, whom Boswell had piloted from Paris, and who quickly quarrelled with the staff.

Voltaire was vain and touchy, but he had a much better heart than the author of *Le Contrat Social*, who suffered from persecution mania. The English visit had opened under sunny skies, but dark clouds rolled up when news of a *jeu d'esprit* of Horace Walpole reached his ears. On one of his visits to Paris the latter had concocted an imaginary letter from Frederick the Great inviting Rousseau to Berlin. Though not intended for publication it was shown to his friends and found its way into print. The letter was harmless enough, but that he should have been the victim of a hoax threw him into a paroxysm of fury. In fairness to him we must remember that this man of genius with the golden pen was near the borderline which separates eccentricity from insanity. Assuming without the slightest evidence that Hume had a hand in the affair he denounced him as a traitor. This unprovoked onslaught from the man who had received nothing but kindness was too much even for Hume, who broke off personal relations and declared Rousseau 'the blackest and most atrocious villain in the world'. His verdict was echoed by Dr.

Johnson, who only knew him by his writings and the reports of friends.

Boswell: Do you think he is a bad man?
Johnson: One of the worst of men, a rascal. I would sooner sign a sentence of transportation for him than for any fellow in the Old Bailey.

After this volcanic eruption Rousseau shook the dust of England off his feet and recorded his verdict in his *Confessions*: 'I have never loved England or the English.' Let us think of him as the Karl Marx of the eighteenth century, as potent an intellectual ferment and an even more disagreeable character.

Mirabeau liked England and Englishmen as much as Voltaire, and his visit on the eve of the Revolution was a happy interlude. Though he only became a world figure when the States General met in 1789, he had already made his name by his writings, his family quarrels, and his notorious immorality. After spending months in the fortress of Vincennes he crossed the Channel in 1774. The role of sponsor was played by his old school acquaintance Gilbert Elliot, soon to become Lord Minto and Governor-General of India. Under the auspices of this Whig magnate the visitor was a welcome guest in Whig circles. He found Lord Shelburne, afterwards the first Lord Lansdowne, sympathetic, and delighted in the society at Lansdowne House and at Bowood, the stately Wiltshire home of the Petty family. The host was not only a statesman but an intellectual, and the two brightest ornaments of his entourage were Bentham and Romilly, the leading law reformers of the age. Mirabeau also visited Burke in Beaconsfield, for the great orator and publicist was the champion of the system of limited monarchy as established in 1688. The Whig ideology accepted by the Hanoverian monarchs corresponded exactly to the views of the visitor who had suffered from *lettres de cachet* and who fretted at the spectacle of France muddling along under inefficient rulers and bearing with ever-increasing impatience the manifold abuses of the *ancien régime*. What he saw of our way of life during eight crowded months strengthened his conviction that constitutional monarchy was working well and would equally benefit the land of his birth. When the tocsin sounded in 1789 he became the voice of his countrymen who,

D

like himself, desired to retain the Monarchy but to allow the
Tiers Etat a share in government. The most arresting figure on
the French political stage till he died of his excesses two years
later at the age of forty-two was a rare combination of unbridled
physical passions and a cool brain, the oracle of the moderates
who pleaded for the survival of monarchy in the diluted form
suited to the modern world.

Far more Englishmen visited France in the eighteenth century
than Frenchmen England. The English Milord, travelling in his
own carriage as he made the Grand Tour, was welcomed in
French inns not merely because his purse was well filled but
because he represented a country famed for its liberty and prosperity. In the era of *anglomanie* English celebrities who had
made their name found all doors open to them in *la ville lumière*,
the intellectual capital of the Continent.

No Englishman knew French society so intimately as Horace
Walpole. While visitors were occasionally seen in the salons he
alone could claim to be a *habitué*. That he was the wealthy son of
a Prime Minister and nephew of the British Ambassador gave
him a good start, but it would not have carried him very far in a
world where ability counted for more than birth and where an
illegitimate like d'Alembert could rise to the highest posts in the
academic world. No-one could have been more different from the
full-blooded Sir Robert, lover of good cheer, country sports and
the knockabout of parliamentary warfare, than his younger son,
delicate in looks and health, lover of things of the mind, a born
student, a letter-writer worthy to rank with Cicero and Erasmus,
Mme de Sévigné and Voltaire. Macaulay did him less than
justice when he charged him with thinking everything great to
be little, everything little to be great, and trifles serious business.
Interested and well-informed about everything, he admired
French culture and the cosmopolitan society which Paris offered
in the Age of Enlightenment.

His first glimpse of France was at the beginning of the Grand
Tour of 1739–41 when the young man of twenty-four and his
friend Thomas Gray visited Paris and Rheims *en route* for Italy.
Macaulay's description of Lord Chesterfield as a man of the world
among men of letters and a man of letters among men of the world
is equally applicable to the dilettante politician who sat in Parlia-

ment without a break for twenty-seven years. Not till 1765 did he
revisit the country which was to mean so much to him for the rest
of his long life. Carrying introductions to Mme Geoffrin and
Mme du Deffand, he found smiles on every face. Now a man of
forty-eight, his sociable temperament, range of information and
manifold interests made him run after—in his own words—as if
he were an African prince. Though Mme Geoffrin won his
respect by her solid good sense, he found her *Philosophes* rather a
trial, preferring the salon of Mme du Deffand of which he became
the brightest ornament. 'I am in your debt', he wrote to George
Selwyn who had given him an introduction, 'for making over
Mme du Deffand to me. She is delicious—that is as often as I can
get her 50 years back. But she is as eager about what happens every
day as I am about the last century. I sup there twice a week and
bear all her company for the sake of the Regent.' The reference
to the Regent was due to the fact that in her youth she had been
one of his innumerable mistresses for a brief period.

Horace Walpole entered her life at a moment when her quarrel
with Mlle de Lespinasse had led to the departure of d'Alembert
and other *habitués* and left an aching void in her heart. President
Hénault, her partner of many years in a *liaison de convenance*, was
growing deaf and somnolent and could no longer dispel the
boredom felt by the old lady nearing seventy who had lost her
sight. Her salon was her life, and within a year of the stormy
parting scene she found a deeper happiness than she had ever
known in a quasi-maternal friendship with an Englishman whose
face she never saw. It was her Indian Summer, and though her
new friend felt genuine affection for his hostess the association
meant infinitely more to her than to him.

> She is very old and stone blind [he reported to Gray] but retains all
> her vivacity, wit, judgment, memory, passion and agreeableness. She
> goes to operas, plays, suppers and Versailles, gives suppers twice a
> week, has everything new read to her, makes new songs and epi-
> grams admirably, and remembers every one that has been made
> these last four-score years. She corresponds with Voltaire, dictates
> charming letters to him, contradicts him, is no bigot to him or
> anybody, and laughs both at the clergy and the Philosophes. In a
> dispute into which she easily falls she is very warm and yet con-
> vincing, even when she is wrong. Her judgment on every subject

is as just as possible, on every point of conduct as wrong as possible, for she is all love and hatred; passionate to her friends to enthusiasm; still anxious to be loved—I don't mean by lovers—and a vehement enemy, but openly.

Visiting the wittiest woman in France every day he prolonged his sojourn to seven months.

On parting early in 1766 the friends began a correspondence which continued till her death in 1780. Copious selections from her letters were published in 1810 by Agnes Berry, Walpole's literary executor, and extracts from his letters were quoted in the notes. A far more complete collection was edited by Mrs. Paget Toynbee in three stout volumes a century later, and the definitive text fills five volumes in the sumptuous Yale edition. Even now the collection is incomplete, for only about 1,000 of the estimated 1,700 of her letters survive, while of Walpole's letters, estimated at about 700, only about 100, mostly in brief fragments, are available. Some are taken from Mrs. Berry's footnotes, and fourteen from copies made by the French Secret Police and discovered in the Police Archives in Paris. Some may have been destroyed by Mme du Deffand at his request, for he dreaded unfriendly comments in the salons on his friendship and his French. Most of them were doubtless burned by Mrs. Berry at his request.

Mme du Deffand called him her dear tutor and once he addressed her, to her great joy, *ma chère petite*. While she allowed her heart to speak he never allowed her to know how fond of her he was. He constantly urged her to bridle her emotions and she chided him for his reserve. 'You have one failing,' she wrote, 'the fear of ridicule.' He confessed she was right, explaining that since he ceased to be young he had a horrible fear of being a ridiculous old man. She tried to meet his complaints, assuring him: *Je serais votre mère*. In truth she regarded him as her devoted son, and he described her as 'this best and sincerest of friends who loves me as my mother did'. When she lost her pension he begged her permission to make it up, an offer gratefully declined. 'She loves me better than all France', he confided to a friend. Her closing years were sweetened by two more visits and by his weekly letters. She left him her books, papers and a gold box with a portrait of Tonton, her adored little dog, who found a new home at Strawberry Hill. 'I loved her most affectionately and sincerely,' he wrote to a friend, 'I admired her infinitely and my gratitude is without words.' She comes best out of the correspondence, and Lytton Strachey goes so far as to say that it leaves a very damaging impression of Horace Walpole. The censure is too severe, but I wish he had been less inclined to rebuke her occasional exuberance and to stint the tender phrases which would have brought solace to her hungry soul. There was not the slightest danger in opening their hearts to each other, for the blind old lady had long outlived the passions of youth and he had never known them.

Of the distinguished British visitors none spent so much time in France as David Hume, the greatest of British thinkers and for almost a century the most popular of our historians. His first visit, 1734–7, took place when, at the age of twenty-three, he felt in need of a quiet period for study, shielded from the distractions of the homeland. The time was well spent, for it was then that he composed his chief philosophical work, *A Treatise on Human Nature*. He arrived in the capital shortly after the excitement aroused by the curious phenomena at the tomb of Abbé Paris. Though Jansenism was frowned on by the Court, the Hierarchy and the Jesuits, the Jansenist priest had gathered round him devoted disciples who flocked to his grave to pray for his soul. In an atmosphere of mass emotion anticipating the scenes at Lourdes, the sick were cured and the blind recovered their sight. Fearing a revival of the Jansenist heresy the Government closed the cemetery and the miracles ceased, but they were still the talk of the town when Hume arrived. He proceeded to study the evidence for the strange happenings, concluded that they were impostures, and embodied his reflections in his *Essay on Miracles*, the best known of his philosophical writings. Miracles, he concluded, did not occur; they were supernormal, not supernatural. The challenge to authority inaugurated on the Continent by Bayle had grown into the so-called Enlightenment in which Hume took his place at the side of Lessing, Voltaire and the Encyclopaedists. After a spell in the stimulating air of the capital he withdrew to the peace of Rheims, thence to La Flèche in Anjou, renowned for its Jesuit College where Descartes had studied. One of the staff informed him that 'some nonsensical miracles'

had recently occurred there. After three stimulating years abroad
he returned home with an abiding interest in the life and thought
of France.

The first visit was followed by the War of the Austrian Succession, which lasted eight years, and the Seven Years War which
ended in 1763. On the return of peace he was invited by the new
British Ambassador, Lord Hertford, to become his secretary.
The offer was accepted and he was soon promoted to an official
position as Secretary of Embassy and *Chargé d'Affaires* when his
chief was away. By this time his name was familiar as the author
of the first History of England to be widely read abroad, nowhere more than in France where a translation of the volumes
on the Tudors and the Stuarts became a best-seller. He was
lionised in the salons of Mme Geoffrin and Mlle de Lespinasse,
and was received by the Dauphin at Versailles. What a large heart
he possessed was proved when Rousseau sought his protection.
No two men could be more different in social background,
ideology or temperament than the British Tory and the Genevese
democrat, the British sceptic and the theist author of *Emile*, the
polished man of the world and the moody Bohemian. It was
enough for Hume that the author of *Le Contrat Social* was in
distress, and without hesitation he promised him shelter in
England. First impressions were extremely favourable. 'The
celebrated Rousseau', he reported, 'has rejected invitations from
half the kings and princes of Europe to put himself under my
protection. I find him popular in Paris, especially among the
ladies. He is mild, gentle, modest, good-humoured, much like
Socrates.' They crossed together in January, 1766, when Hume's
term of office in Paris expired. The tragicomedy which followed
has been described in a previous study.

Gibbon's first sight of France was in 1753 when the lad of
sixteen was *en route* to Lausanne. During the following five years
under the roof of Pastor Pavillard he quickly abandoned the
Catholic faith which had attracted him at Oxford, fell in love
with Suzanne Curchod, 'sighed as a lover and obeyed as a son'
when his father threatened to stop his allowance, and, in his own
words, learned to think in French. Ten years after his first crossing
of the Channel he paid his first visit to Paris where he could hold
his own with the best talkers at the dinner tables and in the salons.

12 February, 1763 [to his stepmother]. Paris in most respects has fully answered my expectations. I have a number of very good acquaintances which increase every day, for nothing is so easy as making them here. Instead of complaining of the want of them I begin already to think of making a choice. Next Sunday, for instance, I have only three invitations to dinner. We may say what we please of the frivolity of the French, but in a fortnight in Paris I have heard more conversation worth remembering and seen more men of letters among the people of fashion than in two or three winters in London. Among my acquaintances I cannot help mentioning M. Helvétius, author of the famous book *De l'Esprit*. I met him at dinner at Mme Geoffrin's, where he took great notice of me, made me a visit next day, and has since treated me not in a polite but a friendly manner. Besides being a sensible man he has a very pretty wife, 100,000 livres a year, and one of the best tables in Paris. To the great civility of this foreigner who was not obliged to take the least notice of me I must contrast the behaviour of the Duke of Bedford (the British Ambassador). I presented my letter from the Duke of Richmond. He received me civilly. I would apply to him whenever I wanted assistance, and thus dismissed me. I have not heard of him since. Indeed I have often blushed for him, for I find his stateliness and avarice make him the joke of Paris. Instead of keeping open table, he hardly asks anybody.

24 February, 1763 [to his father]. I have now passed a month in this place, and it has answered my most sanguine expectations. I have found several houses where it is both very easy and very agreeable to be acquainted. Lady Harvey's recommendation to Mme Geoffrin was a most excellent one. Her house is a very good one; regular dinners there every Wednesday and the best company of Paris in men of letters and men of fashion. It was at her house that I connected myself with M. Helvétius. At his home I was introduced to Baron D'Olbach, a man of parts and fortune and has two dinners every week. Next Sunday we go to Versailles.

25 March, 1763 [to his stepmother]. I find my conquests multiply every day. I am sorry for the honour of my country, and see how contemptible a figure he (the British Ambassador) makes among our late enemies and constant rivals. My only comfort is that the national character is as much revered as his is despised. What Cromwell wished is now literally the case. The name of Englishman inspires as great an idea at Paris as that of Roman could at Carthage after the defeat of Hannibal. Indeed the French are almost excessive. From being very unjustly esteemed as a set of pirates and barbarians we

are now by a more agreeable injustice looked upon as a nation of
philosophers and patriots.

Suzanne Curchod, the Swiss pastor's penniless daughter whom
Gibbon hoped to marry, found a more eligible partner in Necker,
a German banker who migrated from Switzerland to Paris, and
rose to be Finance Minister under Louis XVI. Her correspondence
reveals that she had cared for the young Englishman more than
he for her. They met again in 1776, a year memorable for both
parties: for the historian owing to the publication of the first
portion of *The Decline and Fall of the Roman Empire*, for her as
the date of her husband's appointment to succeed Turgot. When
the Neckers crossed the Channel in the spring accompanied by
their precocious daughter of fourteen, the future Mme de Stael,
Gibbon strove to make their visit a success.

26 April, 1776 [to his stepmother]. I am a good deal taken up with
the Neckers. We are really glad to see one another, but she is no
longer a beauty.
20 May, 1776 [to Holroyd]. I am very busy with the Neckers. I live
just as I used to do twenty years ago and oblige her to become a
simple reasonable Swiss lady. The man, who might read English
husbands lessons of proper and dutiful behaviour, is a sensible
good-natured creature.
24 May, 1776 [to his stepmother]. My afternoons have been a
good deal devoted to Mme Necker. She and her husband leave
this country next Tuesday, entertained with the island and owning
that the barbarous people have been very kind to them. Do you
know that they have almost extorted from me a promise to make
them a short visit to Paris in the autumn?

If Gibbon's first visit to Paris in 1763 had been a success, the
second, in 1777, was a triumph, for his book had won him a
European reputation. To his stepmother, who expressed apprehension about his plans, he explained that he would not live with
the Neckers, adding that she was 'very far from being an object
of desire or scandal'. Far from being a temptress, she was regarded in certain circles as a Puritan and a prude and the Necker
ménage as a rare example of domestic fidelity.

My second excursion to Paris [he records in his Memoirs] was
determined by the pressing invitation of M. and Mme Necker who

had visited England in the previous summer. On my arrival I found M. Necker, Director-General of the Finances, in the first glow of power and popularity. His private fortune enabled him to support a liberal establishment, and his wife, whose talents and virtues I had long admired, was admirably qualified to preside in the conversation of her table and drawing-room. As their friend I was introduced to the best company of both sexes, to the Foreign Ministers of all nations, and to the first names and characters in France who distinguished me by such marks of civility and kindness as gratitude will not allow me to forget nor modesty to enumerate.

The visit, which lasted from May to October, is much more fully described in his letters. He wrote to the Neckers from his hotel on the evening of his arrival, and a month later reported his impressions to his closest friend Holroyd, later Lord Sheffield, his literary executor. 'My reception by the Neckers very far surpasses my most sanguine expectations. I dine and sup with them almost every day.' Horace Walpole had given him an introduction to Mme du Deffand, 'an agreeable young lady of 82', and he was presented at Court. 'They pretend to like me, and whatever you may think of French professions I am convinced some at least are sincere. I feel myself easy and happy in their company.'

24 July. My connection with the Neckers who every day acquire more power and deserve more respects opened the doors to me, and I seldom dine or sup at my hotel.

13 August. The more I see Paris, the more I like it.

1 September [to his stepmother]. M. Necker has not yet discovered any signs of jealousy. I love him on his own account.

'She was very fond of me,' he reported to Holroyd after the visit, 'and the husband particularly civil. She asked me every evening to supper. Afterwards he goes to bed and leaves me alone with his wife. It is making an old lover of mighty little consequence. She is as handsome as ever and much genteeler; seems pleased with her fortune rather than proud of it.' Her report to a friend reveals that she had not wholly forgiven the friend who had jilted her in the days of her obscurity. 'I have seen Gibbon,' she confided to a friend, 'and it has given me immense pleasure. Not that I still retain any feeling for a man who I believe does not deserve it. Never has my feminine vanity had a more complete or honourable triumph. He has become gentle, humble, bashful.'

One of the greatest of our political thinkers was no traveller or linguist and Burke only paid one visit to France; but that brief experience proved a milestone in the evolution of the father of the counter-revolution. The date was 1773, the last year of Louis XV, no longer *le bien-aimé* but the shameless slave of Mme du Barry. What little he saw of the country he liked. 'The clergy, in all their forms,' he wrote in his *Reflections on the French Revolution* published in 1790, engaged a considerable part of my curiosity. I received a perfectly good account of their morals and their attention to their duties. With some of the higher clergy I had a personal acquaintance, almost all of noble birth. They seemed to me liberal and open, with hearts of gentlemen and men of honour.'

The most abiding memory of his visit was of Marie Antoinette at the age of eighteen, whom he saluted in the most celebrated passage of his book.

> It is now 16 or 17 years since I saw the Queen of France, then the Dauphine, at Versailles; and surely never lighted on this orb, which she hardly seemed to touch, a more delightful vision. I saw her just above the horizon, decorating and cheering the elevated sphere she just began to move in, glittering like the morning star, full of life and splendour and joy. Oh! what a revolution! And what a heart I must have to contemplate without emotion that elevation and that fall! Little did I dream that, when she added the titles of veneration to those of enthusiastic and respectful love, she should ever be obliged to carry the sharp antidote against disgrace concealed in that bosom. Little did I dream that I should live to see such disasters fallen upon her in a nation of gallant men, a nation of men of honour and cavaliers. I thought ten thousand swords would have leapt from their scabbards to avenge even a look which threatened her with insult. But the age of chivalry is gone. That of sophisters, economists and calculators has succeeded, and the glory of Europe is extinguished for ever.

When Sir Philip Francis scoffed at the 'foppery' of this tribute on a woman whom he dismissed as a 'Messaline and a jade' Burke replied: 'I tell you again that the recollection of the Queen of France in 1773, and the contrast between that brilliance, splendour and beauty with the prostrate homage of a nation to her, and the abominable scene of 1789 which I was describing did draw tears from me and wetted my paper. These tears came again when I looked at the description, and they may again.'

The meditations of the eloquent Irishman were received with praise from the Right and an explosion from the Left. 'Burke's book is the most admirable medicine against the French disease,' wrote Gibbon; 'I admire his eloquence and his politics, I adore his chivalry, and I can even forgive his superstition.' George III said that every gentleman ought to read it, and Catherine the Great switched her allegiance from Montesquieu to Burke. Such eulogies were countered by Tom Paine's best-seller *The Rights of Man*, in which, with obvious reference to the panegyric on the unhappy Queen, he charged the author with 'pitying the plumage and forgetting the dying bird'. Soon after the publication of Burke's *Reflections* Anglo-French contacts were transferred from the drawing-rooms and dinner tables to the battlefields and the high seas.

5

VOLTAIRE IN ENGLAND

VOLTAIRE was not only the High Priest of the *Philosophes* and Commander-in-Chief of the army of the Enlightenment but the most arresting figure except Goethe in modern continental literature. His long-range influence on the intellectual climate of France far surpasses that of any other French writer, for Rousseau, who alone might challenge the claim, was a Genevese. Gibbon, his near neighbour at Lausanne, pronounced him the most extraordinary man of the century. For Goethe he was the greatest name in the literature of all ages, the most astonishing creation of nature, the most representative of Frenchmen. 'Le plus bel esprit de ce siècle' echoed President Hénault, who knew all the pundits of the *Ville Lumière*. Centuries would be needed to produce his equal, exclaimed Diderot. 'Ce n'est pas un homme, c'est un siècle,' was the verdict of Victor Hugo. Taine compared him to a fountain whose waters never ceased to play, and Sainte-Beuve declared that he had made France and Paris in his own image. No other writer before Karl Marx has exercised such enduring influence on the thoughts of mankind. French authors could count on readers all over Europe, for French was the *lingua franca* of the Intelligentsia. Leaping into fame with his early plays and poems he lived long enough to be recognised as the uncrowned King of the Republic of Letters. Unstinted homage continues to be paid in the twentieth century in an unceasing flow of biographies and monographs, above all in the superb Geneva edition of his correspondence edited by Theodore Besterman, an enterprise worthy to rank with de Boislisle's edition of the Memoirs of Saint-Simon.

44

None of the serried array of volumes deserves more attention than that which covers Voltaire's residence in England 1726–1729, by far the most significant episode of his early life. What little he knew of France's historic enemy he liked, and closer acquaintance made him a good European. His debt was partly paid in his *Lettres Philosophiques sur les Anglais* which inaugurated the era of *anglomanie* and coloured French thinking till the Revolution. Here was a land combining prosperity with political liberty and religious toleration. His paean to England may be contrasted with the contemporary *Lettres Persanes* of Montesquieu, the former finding little to blame in England, the latter little to admire in France. Both these sparkling publications were Tracts for the Times.

Why, he inquired, should not his fellow-citizens enjoy similar privileges and opportunities? In the words of Condorcet, his disciple and biographer, Voltaire henceforth obeyed the call to combat the prejudices which enslaved his country, a crusader with a mission to break the fetters of the mind. The same question was answered in much the same way by Montesquieu, who crossed the Channel immediately after Voltaire's return. But for one reader of the chapters on the British Constitution in the massive *Esprit des Lois*, Voltaire's scintillating manifesto attracted a hundred. His affection for England, far from being a straw fire, burned with a steady glow till his death fifty years later. A friend in all weathers, he admired what was best in our life and thought.

Voltaire might never have crossed the Channel, and certainly would not have stayed so long, but for the incident in February 1726 outside the home of the Duc de Sully where he was a guest at dinner. When informed that his presence was requested by a visitor he was beaten up in the streets by the lackeys of the Duc de Rohan, a profligate aristocrat of whom he had spoken too freely. Though he had never fought a duel no course seemed open to him but to challenge the contriver of his spectacular humiliation. To avert this revenge he was packed off to the Bastille where under the system of *lettres de cachet* victims of private vendettas were more numerous than offenders against the state. Though allowed books and visitors he fretted behind the bars. 'I have been right down,' he reported to a friend; 'I am only awaiting my convalescence to leave this country for ever.' He

appealed to Maurepas, Minister of the Interior, for permission
to visit England. His release was granted on condition that he
should depart not less than fifty leagues from the capital and not
return without permission. His next surviving letter is dispatched
from Calais. 'I shall only go to London when my health has
recovered from my afflictions. I am not banished. I am permitted,
not ordered, to go.'

During his month at Calais he appealed to the good offices of
Sir Horatio Walpole, British Ambassador at the Court of Louis
XV and brother of Sir Robert, and not in vain. 'Mr. Voltaire',
wrote the latter to his friend Bubb Dodington, a wealthy
figure in English society and patron of men of letters, 'is a
French poet who has wrote several pieces with great success
here, being gone to England in order to print by subscription an
excellent poem called Henry IV, which on account of some bold
strokes in it against persecution and the priests cannot be printed
here. M. de Morville (Foreign Minister) has earnestly recommended it to me to use my credit and interest for promoting this
subscription among my friends.' A few days later he wrote in
similar terms to the Duke of Newcastle. 'I hope you will excuse
my recommending to you at the earnest instance of M. de Morville Mr. Voltaire, a poet and a very ingenious one who has
lately gone to England to print by subscription an excellent
poem called Henry ye 4th. He has been indeed in ye Bastille, but
not upon ye account of any state affair but for a particular quarrel
with a private gentleman, and therefore I hope Yr Grace will
readily give him your favour and protection in promoting the
subscription.' These introductions secured the traveller a recommendation from the Foreign Minister to the French Ambassador
in London, the Comte de Broglie.

More important than any official sponsoring was a personal
acquaintance whom Voltaire felt sure would help him to find his
feet. Lord Bolingbroke, the most dazzling figure at Westminster
at the close of the reign of Anne, had put his money on the wrong
horse by championing the Pretender and had crossed the Channel
when the Elector of Hanover succeeded to the throne. Though
dismissed by Macaulay as a brilliant knave, he was much more
than an ambitious politician. Genuinely interested in history,
philosophy and literature, he found occupation in study and

writing during the years of exile spent at the château of his French wife near Orleans. He had made money in Law's Mississippi ramp by selling out before the crash. He admired the dramas of the clever young author of whom France was talking, and shared his Deism in an age when Bayle had challenged the authority of Bossuet and the Jesuits. Voltaire was welcomed at La Source in 1721, two years before his host was allowed to return to England in 1723, and he continued to speak of him with gratitude to the end of his days. 'I have found in this illustrious Englishman', he reported to his closest friend Thièriot, 'all the erudition of his country and all the politeness of ours. This man, who has passed his whole life in his pleasures and public affairs, has however contrived to learn everything and remember everything. He knows the history of the ancient Egyptians as well as of England, Virgil as well as Milton. He loves English, French and Italian poetry, and says parts of the *Henriade* surpass anything in French verse.' Since the feud between the Pretender and the Hanoverians was not Voltaire's business, there was no political barrier to mar the harmony of a friendship which gave equal pleasure to both.

A second string to his bow was Everard Falkener, a wealthy merchant whose business took him abroad. They had met in Paris, but when we do not know. What a benefactor Voltaire had found was proved in England when his health and prospects were dim. *Zaïre* was dedicated to Falkener, and when the author wished to eulogise Stanislas, former King of Poland, he saluted him as 'a kind of Falkener'. In later years Falkener was appointed Ambassador to Turkey and Postmaster-General, and he received a knighthood. While Bolingbroke unlocked the doors of the literary world, Falkener provided a roof over the visitor's head.

Voltaire disembarked at Greenwich on 10 June, 1726, when the annual Fair was in full swing and the King's birthday was being celebrated. The river was full of shipping and he enjoyed a ramble in Greenwich Park. First impressions were delightful. He moved on to London in the evening, probably spending his first night in Bolingbroke's residence in Pall Mall. The task of learning to write and speak English was accomplished with astonishing rapidity. Among the letters in the new Geneva edition are some in almost faultless English, though they may well have been revised by some English friend. He was soon able to meet the literary stars on equal terms, and he even tried his hand at verse. His studies ranged far beyond the frontiers of *belles-lettres*, for he was soon deep in the writings of Locke and Newton, whose funeral service he attended in Westminster Abbey. No other Frenchman of his time possessed such a range of interests, and this versatility enabled him to establish fruitful contacts with the *élite*.

He continued to cherish his vendetta against the Duc de Rohan, and he had scarcely settled in England than he recrossed the Channel in search of his prey. The quest proved too dangerous, for his visit to the capital violated the condition of his release. The first surviving letter from England, dated 12 August, 1726, confided his disappointments to Thièriot, his most favoured correspondent. 'I have recently paid a little visit to Paris. As I did not see you, you will guess I saw no one. I sought only one man whose instinctive cowardice kept him hidden from me as though he guessed I was on his track. But the fear of being discovered made me leave quicker than I came. I am still very uncertain if I shall retire to London. I know this is a country where the arts are honoured and rewarding; there is difference of condition but no other difference except of merit. It is a country where one thinks freely without being fettered by any servile fears. If I followed my inclination it is there that I should settle with the sole idea of learning to think. But I do not know if my slender means, greatly reduced by all my wanderings, my bad health, now worse than ever, and my taste for the most profound retreat, will allow me to fling myself into the hubbub of Whitehall and London. I have very good recommendations in this country, and they are waiting for me with much friendliness, but I cannot tell you that I get about. I have only two things to do in my life. One is to risk it with honour as soon as I can; the other to finish it in the obscurity of a retirement which suits my way of thinking, my misfortunes, and my knowledge of men.'

The next letter, dated 15 October, was also in a minor key.

I heard from you and from my brother of the death of my sister. What you wrote pierced my heart. What am I to say on the death of my sister except that it would have been better for my family and myself if I had been taken instead. It is not for me to speak to you of the little importance one should attach to this brief and difficult passage which is called Life; you have more luminous ideas on it and drawn from purer sources. I only know the misfortunes of life, but you know the remedies: it is the difference between the patient and the doctor. I have made many mistakes in my life. The bitterness and sufferings which have marked almost every day have been often my fault. I feel how little I am worth. My failings make me pity myself and my faults horrify me. But God is witness that I love virtue.

The next letter, in the same month, is the first surviving effort in English.

I intend to send you two or three poems of Mr. Pope, the best poet of England and at present of all the world. I came again into England in the latter end of July, very much dissatisfied with my secret *volage* into France, both unsuccessful and expensive. I had only some bills of exchange upon a Jew called Medina for about 8 or 9 thousand livres. At my coming to London I found my damned Jew was broken. I was without a penny, sick to death of a violent ague, a stranger alone, helpless in a city where I was known to nobody. My lord and my lady Bolingbroke were in the country. I could not make bold to see our Ambassador in so wretched a condition. I had never undergone such distress, but I am born to run through all the misfortunes of life. In these circumstances my star, that among all its direful influences pours always on me some kind refreshment, sent to me an English gentleman unknown to me who forced me to receive some money that I wanted. Another London citizen (Falkener) that I had seen but once in Paris carried me to his own country house wherein I lead an obscure and charming life since that time without going to London, and quite given over to the pleasures of indolence and friendship. The true and generous affection of this man who soothes the bitterness of my life brings me to love you more and more. I have seen often my lord and my lady Bolingbroke. I have found their affection still the same, even increased in proportion to my unhappiness. They offered me all their money, their house, but I refused all, because they are lords, and I have accepted all from Mr. Falkener, because he is a single gentleman. I had a mind at first to print poor Henry at my own expense, but the loss of my money is a sad stop to my design. I question if I shall try the way of subscriptions by the favour of the Court. I am weary of courts. All that is King or belongs to a King frights my republican philosophy. I won't drink the least draught of slavery in the land of liberty. I fear, I hope, nothing from your country. All

D

that I wish for is to see you one day in London. You will see a nation
fond of their liberty, learned, witty, despising life and death, a nation
of philosophers. Not but there are some fools in England. Every
country has its madmen. It may be French folly is pleasanter than
English madness, but by God English wisdom and English honesty
is above yours. One day I will acquaint you with the character of
this strange people. I have wept for my sister's death and I would be
with her. Life is but a dream, full of starts of folly and of fancied
and true miseries. Death awakes us from this painful dream, and
gives us either a better existence or no existence at all.

Pope's fame was at its zenith, and his praise of the unpublished
Henriade which Bolingbroke had brought to England was music
to the author's ears. He thirsted to meet the masters of his craft,
none so much as the recognised monarch of English letters.
Returning one day to Twickenham in Bolingbroke's coach the
poet was thrown into the water by the collapse of a bridge, and
two fingers of his right hand were injured. Writing on 28 October
as a guest of Bolingbroke Voltaire seized the opportunity to pay
his homage.

Sir, I hear this moment of your adventure. I am concerned beyond
expression for the danger you have been in, and more for your
wounds. Is it possible that those fingers which have written *The
Rape of the Lock*, which have dressed Homer so becomingly in an
English coat, should have been so barbarously treated? Let the hand
of Dennis or one of your poetasters be cut off—yours is sacred. I
hope, Sir, you are now perfectly recovered. Really your accident
concerns me as much as all the disasters of a master ought to affect
his scholar. I am sincerely, Sir, with the admiration you deserve,
your most humble servant, Voltaire.

Pope's only rival in celebrity in the world of letters was Swift,
whom Voltaire met when they were guests at the home of Lord
Peterborough, the veteran of the War of the Spanish Succession.
Gulliver's Travels had recently appeared, and Voltaire sent Thièriot
a copy urging him to translate it. It would be immensely successful, he added, for he had never read anything more clever and
amusing. 'It is the English Rabelais without his trash, very amusing by its singular imagination and its light style in addition to
being a satire on human nature.' Thièriot, though a lover of
literature, was a notorious idler, and a translation soon appeared

by another hand. In a letter of introduction to the Foreign Minister, Comte de Morville, Voltaire described Swift as 'an ornament of the nation you esteem and one of the most extraordinary men England has produced'. That Voltaire's novel *Micromégas* was indebted to *Gulliver's Travels* is obvious in its title. Though he forwarded the second volume of *Gulliver* he did not urge its translation. 'Stick to the first; the other is overstrained. The reader's imagination is pleased and charmingly entertained by the new prospects of the lands which Gulliver discovers for him. But that continued series of new-fangled follies, fairy tales and wild inventions, palls at last upon our taste. Nothing unnatural may please long. For this reason the second parts of most romances are so insipid.'

Voltaire's only contact with the master of English comedy was less encouraging. When the visitor expressed his sincere admiration for the dramatist, Congreve snobbishly begged to be regarded not as an author but as a gentleman. 'If you had been merely a gentleman,' was the well-merited retort, 'I should not have troubled to visit you.' Gay, on the other hand, allowed him to read *The Beggar's Opera* before its triumphant reception on the stage. He also met Colley Cibber and was frequently seen at the theatre. He might have admired Shakespeare more if he had seen Garrick's impersonations. With the author of *Night Thoughts*, whom he met at Bubb Dodington's home in Dorset, his relations were closer and continued longer. Though Young was soon to take orders and the visitor to become the *bête noire* of believers their common interest in literature bridged the gulf. He revised the English version of the essay on Epic Poetry, and in later years dedicated his *Sea Piece* to his French friend in flattering terms. Voltaire also admired Thomson, not only for *The Seasons*, the most popular of his poems, but for his plays.

I was acquainted with Mr. Thomson when I stayed in England [he wrote (in English) long after in 1750]. I discovered in him a great genius and a great simplicity. I liked in him the poet and the true philosopher—I mean the lover of mankind. I think that without such a good stock of philosophy a poet is just above a fiddler and cannot go to our soul! His tragedies, he argued, had not received the honour they deserved. They might perhaps lack fire, but, taking him all in all, methinks he has the highest charms to the greatest esteem.

Among Voltaire's purposes in coming to England was the publication of the *Henriade*; and now after the loss of a substantial sum owing to the bankruptcy of the Jewish financier on whom he had counted, he needed help in high places, for how could any London publisher be expected to risk a loss on a French epic? The royal hero, author of the Edict of Nantes and on friendly terms with Queen Elizabeth, was *persona grata* in the land of religious toleration, where writers of merit were esteemed and the nobility were believed to be as generous as they were rich. The obvious method of approach to the ranks of patrons was through the French Ambassador in London.

> M. de Voltaire [wrote Comte de Broglie in March 1727] is ready to print by subscription in London his League, and asks me to procure subscriptions. M. de Walpole (Sir Horatio, the British Ambassador) also tries to get them and will gladly help. But as I have not seen the book, and I do not know if the additions and omissions which he says he has made to the Paris edition and the illustrations are approved by the Court, I can't act without your approval. I always fear that French authors may abuse the liberty allowed in this country to write whatever they like on religion, the Pope, the Government or its members. Poets are particularly inclined to use this licence, to profane what is most sacred. If there was anything of that in the poem I should not like to be reproached for subscribing and inducing others to subscribe. Please tell me what to do.

At the close of 1727 the author moved to Maiden Lane, Covent Garden, a more convenient base for pushing the publication of his epic.

Voltaire was now so generally known that he could approach the highest in the land without personal acquaintance or introductions.

> Though I am a traveller unknown to Your Lordship [he wrote in English to Harley, Second Earl of Oxford] the name of Harlay [*sic*] has been for many centuries so glorious for us Frenchmen and the branch of your house settled in France is so proud of the honour of being nearly related to you that you must forgive the liberty of this letter. I have written and printed a heroic book called the *Henriade* in which one Harlay of your house acts the most noble part, and such a one you should be acquainted with. Having been in some measure educated in the house of the late Achille de Harlay,

the oracle and a First President of our Parliament, I should be wanting in my duty if I durst not trouble your lordship about it and beg the favour of waiting on you before the book comes out.

After this fanfare it is disappointing to miss the name of Harley in the list of subscribers.

Swift was approached in a flattering letter of 18 December accompanying Voltaire's only book published in English during his residence, the essays on the Civil Wars in France and Epic Poetry. 'You will be surprised in receiving an English essay from a French traveller. Pray forgive an admirer who owes to your writings the love he bears to your language which has betrayed him into the rash attempt of writing in English. Can I make bold to entreat you to make some use of your interest in Ireland about some subscriptions for the *Henriade* which is almost ready and does not come out yet for want of a little help? Subscriptions will be but one guinea.' Whether the flattering appeal succeeded in procuring subscribers we do not know. When the *Henriade* appeared a copy was presented through a third party.

> I sent the other day a cargo of French dullness for my Lord Lieutenant [he wrote to Swift]. My Lady Bolingbroke has taken upon herself to send you one copy of the *Henriade*. She is desirous to do that honour to my book, and I hope the merit of being presented to you by her hands will be a recommendation. If she has not done it already, I desire you to take one out of the cargo which is now at my Lord Lieutenant. I have not seen Mr. Pope this winter, but I have seen the third volume of the Miscellaniea, and the more I read the works the more I am ashamed of mines [*sic*].

When the handsome quarto edition, dedicated to Queen Caroline, appeared in 1726 it proved as successful as he expected. Though substantially completed before he crossed the Channel it had profited by his residence in England. The list of subscribers included the King and Queen, most of the nobility, and many familiar figures in public life. Every copy was sold before publication, after which three other less expensive editions were needed in three weeks. 'Though the poem is written in a language not much admired here in regard to poetry,' reported Voltaire to a French friend, 'three editions have been made in less than three weeks, which I assure you I attribute entirely to the subject and not at all to the performance.' That, however, was a *façon de parler*, for the cleverest writer in Europe knew his own worth.

Voltaire's most substantial works designed and completed in England were his studies of the religious wars in France and of epic poetry published in a single volume in the winter of 1727. The former, a by-product of the *Henriade*, saluted Henry of Navarre as the champion of religious liberty and the restorer of peace to a land disgraced by the Bartholomew massacre. Though his sympathies were always with the persecuted, he complains that the Protestants, though free from superstition, tended to anarchy as much as the Church of Rome towards tyranny. To English readers the most interesting portion of the essay on epic poetry was the study of Milton, whom he greatly but never unreservedly admired. In *Paradise Lost* he had scaled the heights, but the subject did not interest his reader. The essay, rewritten in French, reappeared as an Introduction to the *Henriade*. Though a diligent student of Shakespeare, he preferred the Restoration dramatists and declared of *Hudibras* that he had never found so much wit in a book. In the last months of his sojourn he brought over a French company to inaugurate a French theatre in London, but there was too little support and the actors returned to Paris.

When the two essays and his own epic were off his hands, Voltaire turned his attention to the romantic figure of Charles XII of Sweden and sought information from survivors of a heroic age, among them Sarah, Duchess of Marlborough. After telling him what she knew, she is believed to have invited him to help her with her own memoirs. On discovering, however, that he was expected to humour her prejudices a break occurred between the most dictatorial of women and the most thin-skinned of men. With Lord Peterborough his contacts were more profitable, for the veteran commander was the Duke's most efficient collaborator after Prince Eugene himself.

The second half of the English visit as mirrored in the intimate letters to Thièriot is as buoyant as the early phase was depressed by ill-health and financial anxieties. Most were written in English, because, as he explained, they might not be understood by suspicious eyes. He begged his friend to obtain permission for the *Henriade* to appear in France, adding that he would never send anything across the Channel without consent of the French Government. To Voltaire liberty of expression was the breath of life.

> I heartily wish to see you and my friends but rather in England than in France. You, who are a perfect Briton, should cross the Channel and come to us. I assure you again that a man of your temper could not dislike a country where one only obeys the laws and one's whims. Reason is free here and goes her own way. Hypocondriaks especially are welcome. No manner of living appears strange. We have men who walk six miles a day for their health, feed upon roots, never taste flesh, wear a coat in winter thinner than your ladies in the hottest days.

He had found the system of ordered liberty for which he craved.

That the friendship with Falkener continued is shown in a charming letter from the latter. It was easier for the calm and steady Englishman to be at peace with himself than for the mercurial French genius. 'I am as you left me,' he wrote in December 1728, 'neither more gay nor more sad, neither richer nor poorer, enjoying perfect health, having everything which can render life agreeable, without love, without avarice, without ambition or envy. While that lasts I shall boldly call myself a very happy man.'

Voltaire's range of acquaintances was extremely wide. He met Berkeley, but when Andrew Pitt, his Quaker friend, sent him *Alciphron*, an appeal to freethinkers, after his return to France he replied that he was pleased but unconvinced, an admirer not a disciple. 'I believe in God, not in priests.' More to his taste was Samuel Clarke, disciple of Newton, who wrote on philosophy and theology. When they met the visitor was fascinated. 'Clarke jumped into the abyss, and I dared to follow him.' His favourite philosopher was Locke, 'the Hercules of metaphysics, who has fixed the boundaries of the human mind'. Equally interested in science, he met Sir Hans Sloane, President of the Royal Society, and became a member in 1743. He closely followed the Deist controversy inaugurated by Toland and carried on by Collins and Woolston. Among the ladies only Lady Bolingbroke and the adorable Molly Lepel, Lady Hervey, received his homage. No feature of English life attracted him more than the multitude of religious bodies, not enjoying equal privileges, but all permitted

to believe and to worship as they pleased. None of them appealed
to his sympathies except the Quakers who required neither priests
nor creeds, abjured war and violence in every form, and were
model citizens. The Quaker meeting, on the other hand, was not
to his taste.

With the launching of the *Henriade* there was no compelling
reason to remain in England, and in March 1729 he begged
Maurepas to permit his return to Paris, for which the poor state
of his health and fortune, he explained, were the sole reasons.
'I promise to forget the past, to forget everyone, and only to
remember your kindness.' Maurepas sanctioned a visit of three
months for business purposes, adding that his conduct must give
no ground of offence. His appearance at Court, he added, must
be postponed. Voltaire left England for ever after almost three
years of residence. He had made good use of his eyes and ears,
increased his literary reputation, enriched his mind, and become
a citizen of the world. Henceforth British visitors were always
welcome, and in later life he used to say that if he were not
settled in Geneva he would prefer England to any other land.
English literature, science and philosophy were never far from
his thoughts. He saluted Pope's *Essay on Man* as 'the most didactic poem, the most useful, the most sublime, in any language.'
During the busy partnership with Mme de Chatelet he completed
an account of Newton's discoveries. That the two countries
were in opposite camps during the Seven Years War made no
difference to his sentiments. Never has our country possessed a
greater foreign admirer or a more faithful friend.

It is characteristic of Voltaire's interest not only in religious
liberty but in religion itself that the first seven of the twenty-four
Lettres Philosophiques sur les Anglais, the most influential book on
England ever written by a foreigner, are devoted to the sects.
His preference is for the Quakers, proclaimed not only by giving
them pride of place but by allotting them an amount of space
disproportionate to their limited numbers. Though temperamentally there was a gulf between the sharp-tongued satirist
who delighted in a fight and the quiet citizens who abhorred
every form of strife, there was a sufficient area of ideological
agreement to win for them an abiding place in his heart. Reared
among the intrigues and frivolities of Parisian society, he was

deeply impressed by their simplicity and integrity, the shining example they set of good citizenship, and their steadfast fidelity to the Sermon on the Mount. Though a militant foe of the Roman Church he was at all times an unreserved admirer of the moral teaching of Christ. Knowing a good man when he found one, he respected people better than himself. The Quakers appealed to his mind and heart because they appeared to be the most Christian, perhaps the only truly Christian, community in the world.

The book opens with a visit to Andrew Pitt, retired merchant in Hampstead, whom he describes as one of the best known English Quakers.

He was a hale and hearty old man who had never been ill because he had never known the passions of intemperance. Never have I seen anyone with a nobler or more engaging air. 'Friend,' he began, 'I see you are a foreigner. If I can be of use you have only to speak.' [His object, explained Voltaire, was to seek instruction in his host's religion, though the answers to most of the questions were known to him in advance.]
Voltaire: Have you been baptised?
Pitt: No.
Voltaire: So you are not Christians?
Pitt: We are, but we don't believe Christianity consists in sprinkling water over the head. We condemn no one for performing the ceremony, but we believe that those who profess a religion of the spirit should abstain from Jewish ceremonies.
Voltaire: What about Communion?
Pitt: All we have is the communion of hearts. Sacraments are of human invention. You should read Robert Barclay's exposition of our faith.

The conversation then turned to certain customs which differentiated Quakers from other sects, such as their special attire, their refusal to remove their hat in any company or to take an oath, and their use of the second person singular in addressing their fellows. Above all, they never went to war. 'Not because we fear death; but because we are neither wolves, tigers or dogs but men and Christians. God who has commanded us to love our enemies cannot wish us to cross the sea and cut the throats of our brothers.'

On the following Sunday Pitt accompanied his visitor to a

meeting near the Monument, where they found about 400 men
and 300 women assembled in profound silence. The silence lasted
a quarter of an hour after which a member rose and poured forth
a medley of nonsense, supposed to derive from the gospel, of
which, in Voltaire's belief, neither the speaker nor his hearers
understood a word. 'How could sensible people tolerate such
follies?' he inquired as they left.

> *Pitt:* It is the only way of discovering if the speaker is inspired. In
> case of doubt we listen patiently. We also permit our women to
> speak and often two or three are inspired at the same time.
> *Voltaire:* So you don't have priests?
> *Pitt:* No, and we get along quite well. We don't pay men in black
> garments to succour the poor, bury the dead, and preach to the
> faithful. These occupations are too sacred to be discharged by other
> people.

In his third and fourth letters Voltaire describes the origin and
spread of the movement as mirrored in the career of George Fox
and William Penn.

In contrast to the Quakers, whose ideology and way of life—
with the exception of the boredom of the meeting house—
appealed to some of his deepest feelings, the author's treatment
of the Church of England, or, as he calls it, the Anglican religion,
is perfunctory and contemptuous. 'England is the land of sects.
An Englishman, being a free man, chooses his own road to
heaven. Yet their real religion, that in which one gets on, is the
sect of Episcopalians.' The monopoly of official posts by its
members had led to the conversion of so many nonconformists
that only about five per cent of the nation was outside the fold.
From the Catholics it had retained the scrupulous observance of
the collection of tithes and the pious ambition to be the master,
for every country vicar desired to be a pope. They also encouraged
their flocks in holy zeal against nonconformists; yet religious
passions had ended with the civil wars, and even under Tory rule
at the close of the reign of Anne there had been nothing worse
than the breaking of a few chapel windows. The morals of the
clergy were better than in France because they were educated
at Oxford and Cambridge, far from the corruption of the capital,
and most of them were married. The notice of the other leading
sects is equally brief. The Presbyterians, supreme in Scotland,

were rigid Sabbatarians. Though the ministers of different denominations detested each other as much as a Jansenist detested a Jesuit, they all lived in peace. 'At the London Bourse you will see Jews, Moslems and Christians doing business together as if they were all of the same faith. If there were only one religion there would be a danger of despotism; if there were two they would cut each other's throats; since there are thirty they live in peace and happiness.' The author concludes his survey of religion by welcoming the recent revival of Unitarianism.

Passing from religion to politics, Voltaire remarks that whereas civil war in Rome led to despotism in England it created liberty.

The English nation alone has succeeded in limiting the power of kings by resisting them. By a series of efforts it has established this wise government in which the prince, with unlimited power to do good, is prevented from doing harm, where Lords are grandees without insolence and without vassals, and where the people take part in the government without confusion. The two Houses are the arbiters of the nation, the King the super-arbiter.

The establishment of liberty had cost a sea of blood, but it was worth the price. Other countries had shed more but merely increased their chains. In the English civil war the King had unleashed the tempest by continuing to be the master of the nation of which he is only the first pilot. With Magna Carta as a good start the system of mixed government had been gradually evolved, the power of the House of Commons was increasing from day to day, the Law Courts dealt out equal justice to all classes, and everyone paid the taxes sanctioned by Parliament. In this eulogy of limited monarchy the author was addressing himself to French at least as much as to British readers, his advice anticipating the recommendations of Montesquieu by only a few years.

Voltaire admired no less the sensible attitude to the business world. Alone among the nations the English had begun as warriors and ended as merchants. Younger sons of a peer went into business; a younger brother of the Minister Lord Townsend was in the City, and when Harley was Queen Anne's chief adviser his brother held a post in Aleppo. This attitude was unintelligible in Germany where every member of an old family bore the princely title and lived apart from the common herd, or in France where any member of an old family could be a Marquis if he had money to spare, and where the merchant had become so used to contempt that he was stupid enough to blush for his social inferiority. Who is the most useful to the state, the well-powdered *seigneur* who knows the precise hour when the King gets up and goes to bed, and gives himself airs while playing the part of a slave in the ante-chamber of a Minister, or a merchant who enriches his country, issues orders from his office to Surat and Cairo, and contributes to the happiness of the world? A further example of the sense of the islanders was the practice of inoculation against smallpox.

Voltaire found even more to praise in the sphere of philosophy and science, and a series of letters pays eloquent homage to Bacon, Locke and Newton. Recently the old question had come up in conversation who was the greatest of men—Alexander, Caesar, Tamerlane or Cromwell? Someone said Newton, and he was right. 'It is to him who dominates our minds by the force of truth, not to him who makes slaves by violent means; to him who knows the universe, not to him who disfigures it that we owe respect.' Bacon, the father of experimental philosophy, had banished the absurdities of the Schoolmen. Locke, the wisest of men, who had approached the study of the mind without presuppositions, observing the stages of its development, concluded that all our ideas came through our senses and never pretended to know all the answers. To Newton and his disciples he devotes far more space than to any other individual.

However much a *Philosophe* he had become, Voltaire remained primarily a man of letters, and in his survey of England he keeps literature, on which he could speak with the greatest authority, for the closing chapters. Beginning with tragedy he delivers an unenthusiastic verdict on Shakespeare:

> The English take him for a Sophocles, and he made the theatre. He possessed a powerful and creative genius, true to nature and rising to the sublime, but without the slightest spark of good taste or acquaintance with the rules. Indeed his merits revived the theatre. There are fine scenes, portions so great and so terrible in these monstrous farces called tragedies that his plays continue to be acted with great success. Time, the only arbiter of reputations, finally

renders his faults respectable. Most of his odd and gigantic ideas now after two centuries pass for sublime. Nearly all modern authors try to imitate him, but their failure proves him inimitable.

Dryden was almost as reckless in his disregard of rules and probability, and indeed it almost seemed as if human nature was made in England in a different mould. Addison was the first to write a reasonable tragedy, though his *Cato* possessed other qualities besides reason—a masculine elegance and energy in the tradition of Corneille, though disfigured by a good deal of the irrelevance and confusion apparently inseparable from the English stage. Since Addison plays had become more correct. In some ways comedy as practised by the Restoration dramatists, above all Rochester and Congreve, seemed to Voltaire a more natural vehicle of English wit and genius, though none of them had reached the stature of Molière. In poetry he admired the rude vigour of *Hudibras* and above all the polished perfection of Pope, whose *Essay on Man* is described as the most didactic, the most useful and the most sublime poem in any language, though there was nothing original in its philosophy. No other country of the time could have given Voltaire so much to see and to hear, to admire and to wish for France. If the whole picture strikes readers as a little too *couleur de rose* we must remember that its main purpose was to sell England to his countrymen.

6

VOLTAIRE AS HISTORIAN

I. *Charles XII and Peter the Great*

VOLTAIRE, declared Gibbon, his neighbour at Lausanne, was the most extraordinary man of the century. The greatest figure in the literature of all ages, the most astonishing creation of the author of nature, the most representative of Frenchmen, echoed Goethe. Centuries would be needed to produce his equal, exclaimed Diderot. 'Ce n'est pas un homme, c'est un siècle,' exclaimed Victor Hugo. 'Le plus bel esprit de ce siècle,' was the verdict of President Hénault. Taine compared him to a fountain whose waters never ceased to play. No writer before or since has occupied such a commanding position in Europe or exercised such immediate and enduring influence. He possessed a larger *clientèle* during his lifetime than any man of letters before Bernard Shaw. French publications could count on readers all over Europe, since French was the *lingua franca* of the Intelligentsia in every land. Few foreigners could enjoy *Hamlet* or *Faust* in the original, and even in the best translation the magic disappeared. The attention of the world had been focused on French culture and the *Ville Lumière* by the galaxy of genius during the seventeenth century and by the immeasurable prestige of *Le Roi Soleil*. Of this accumulated capital Voltaire was a grateful beneficiary, and in the sixty years of his literary activity he contributed even more than he had received. Leaping into fame with his early plays and poems, he grew in stature and authority till he became the uncrowned king of the Republic of Letters. In addition to the Académie Française he was a member of the Royal Society and of the Academies of La

Crusca, St. Petersburg and Berlin. His acquaintance was craved by princes no less than by literary aspirants, and his letters passed like current coin from hand to hand. Everyone coveted his praise and dreaded the lash of his tongue.

Voltaire's interests extended far beyond the frontiers of *belles-lettres*, and his patronage was solicited for many causes. During the ferment of the *Aufklärung*, when tradition and authority were challenged with even greater vigour and over a wider field than in the hectic century of the Reformation, the Goddess of Reason was enthroned and the sage of Ferney was recognised by friend and foe as the High Priest of the cult. His legacy was the principle of free inquiry. While Chateaubriand complained that he had rendered incredulity fashionable, Quinet hailed him as the angel of extermination sent by God against His sinful Church. As a satirist he ranks with Aristophanes and Juvenal, Aretino and Swift. As a factor in the intellectual climate of modern Europe his place is with Machiavelli and Rousseau, Burke and Adam Smith, Darwin and Marx. That he made Paris and France in his image is the verdict of Sainte-Beuve. A soldier in the army of humanity, he was a builder as well as a destroyer, and many of the things he attacked deserved to die. 'The spirit of intolerance sank blasted beneath his genius,' declares Lecky. 'Wherever his influence passed the arm of the Inquisition was palsied, the chain of the captive riven, the door flung open. He died leaving a reputation that is indeed far from spotless, but having done more to destroy the greatest of human curses than any other of the sons of men.' Whatever the changes in literary fashion, political ideals, academic methods and religious beliefs, Voltaire can never be ignored. *Candide* is as immortal as the *Essais* of Montaigne, the *Pensées* of Pascal, the *Maximes* of La Rochefoucauld and the *Fables* of La Fontaine. The undying interest in the most eminent Frenchman of the eighteenth century is illustrated by the international enterprise of a complete and critical edition of his letters, more extensive in bulk and more widely ranging in the list of his correspondents than his three most serious competitors, Erasmus, Mme de Sévigné and Horace Walpole.

In the evolution of modern historiography the sixteenth century was the age of doctrinal controversy, the seventeenth of massive erudition, the eighteenth of flowing narratives. With the single exception of Gibbon, Voltaire was the leading historian of his age, and it is only the masterpieces of these two supermen which are still widely read. Hume and Robertson retained their popularity till the middle of the nineteenth century, and Montesquieu's *Considérations sur les causes de la Grandeur et de la Décadence des Romains* inaugurated the sociological approach to history; but the twentieth century leaves all three in dignified retirement on the topmost shelf. *The Decline and Fall of the Roman Empire*, the most impressive achievement in the whole range of British historical scholarship, was too voluminous and in the later portions too dull to make a wide popular appeal. The *Siècle de Louis XIV*, on the other hand, a work of manageable dimensions, retains its vogue as an unrivalled panorama of the golden age of the French Monarchy. Equally popular is *The Life of Charles XII*, the earliest biography of a ruler in any language which still fascinates readers more than two centuries after its birth.

During the middle decades of his tempestuous career Voltaire's principal occupation was the study of history. Most of his plays had historical themes, and the *Henriade*, which took Europe by storm, was based on considerable study of the life and times of his favourite hero. In these early works, however, history was merely the raw material of literature, and it was not till he was gripped by the epic of Sweden's warrior king that he embarked on a course of reading which ultimately furnished him with a wider knowledge of world history than any Frenchman, perhaps any European, of his time. Of his major historical writings all but one are of interest and value. *The Life of Charles XII* contained material derived from a number of eye-witnesses. *The Life of Peter the Great* utilised documents supplied by his daughter the Tsarina Elizabeth. *The Age of Louis XIV* was enriched by the confidences of many survivors of the *Grand Siècle*. *The Age of Louis XV*, though necessarily more reticent as the work of the Historiographer of France, possessed the authority of a keen contemporary with many contacts in the highest circles. *The History of the Parliament of Paris*, for which documents were placed at his disposal, was a substantial contribution to constitutional history. The *Essai sur les Moeurs*, at once the most comprehensive and the most individual of his historical writings, provided the first readable survey of the evolution of mankind on the basis of the evidence available in the middle of the eighteenth century. *The Annals of the Empire*, from Charlemagne to the Thirty Years War, on the other hand, is nothing more than its title implies—a work of reference commissioned by a German princess which might have been written by any literary hack. 'Gardez-vous de lire ce fatras', wrote the author to a friend; 'il est d'un ennui mortel.'

The corpus of Voltaire's historical writings makes an impressive show, amateur though he was. 'A great historian,' declares Émile Faguet, 'one of the fathers of history.' *Homo sum*, he might have echoed, *nihil humani a me alienum puto*. Every phase in the slow ascent of man, however primitive or uninviting, seemed to him worthy of attention. While Gibbon's interest began with the classical world, Voltaire commanded a far wider perspective by including the civilisations and ideologies of the East. While Bossuet, with his closed mind, had presented a geographically and chronologically limited section of the human record as the implementation of a divine plan, Voltaire envisaged the whole drama as a progressive liberation of energies, an instinctive urge towards a fuller and more satisfying life. There is no trace of determinism in his approach. He never suggested that progress towards enlightenment, which he prized above all things, was automatic. His vision of *homo sapiens* groping his way towards civilisation, organisation, humanisation, was the forerunner of the doctrine of collective creation formulated by Herder and the Grimms, Savigny and Eichhorn. The story of mankind, he was well aware, was infinitely more than a string of events.

Next to his courageous attempt to interpret the fortunes of man as the unfolding of a mighty drama of effort and experiment, Voltaire's most significant contribution to historical study was his challenge to the dead hand of tradition. In politics he was a liberal conservative, in scholarship an iconoclast. Probability, declared Bishop Butler in a famous phrase, is the guide of life, and Voltaire unflinchingly, indeed gleefully, applied the maxim to the testimony of the past. Though *Quellenkritik*—the expert analysis of sources—was the child of the nineteenth century, a few pioneers, from Lorenzo Valla, Bayle and Père Simon to Vico, Beaufort and Astruc, had pointed the way. The 'Donation of Constantine' had been exposed as a colossal fake, the legends of Livy had been challenged, and some of the elements which went to the making

F

of the Old Testament had been sorted out. Without claiming to be an expert, Voltaire brought his razor-edged intelligence to bear on a multitude of marvels which embellished the narratives of the past, particularly those connected with the Jews and the Christian Church. Though the conception of the uniformity of nature only became an axiom of science and historical reconstruction in the nineteenth century, he adopted it as a working hypothesis. Is it likely to be true? Could this really have occurred? Such was his instinctive reaction to stories which contradicted the general experience of mankind. Like the other leaders of the *Aufklärung*, he was unaware that there were more things in heaven and earth than were dreamed of in their philosophy, and that the exceptional was not necessarily the impossible. Nevertheless it was a useful service to let a stream of cool air into the stuffy chambers where unreflecting chroniclers mechanically repeated from generation to generation the legends invented or accepted by their predecessors. Neither the longevity of a tradition nor the range of its acceptance, he argued, provided the slightest guarantee of its factual truth. Erudition had proved insufficient to reconstruct an intelligible picture of the past, for scholars were frequently as credulous as illiterates. The free play of reason, arbitrary though it might sometimes be, was required to sift the grain from the chaff. The first duty of the historian was to apply the criteria of his own time to the jumbled testimony of bygone days. At the shrill blast of his trumpet many legends collapsed like a house of cards. Complacent credulity aroused his mockery and scorn, and no eighteenth-century historian brushed away so many cobwebs from the temple of Clio.

The Life of Charles XII, written during his residence in England and published at Rouen in 1731, was not only the earliest of Voltaire's historical writings but his favourite child. He had grown to manhood during the years in which the dare-devil exploits of the King of Sweden reverberated through Europe. The swaying fortunes of the struggle between 'the Lion of the North' and Peter the Great were watched with hardly less interest than the campaigns of Louis XIV against the ring of enemies which his ambition had provoked in the West. Voltaire was never too absorbed in his literary triumphs to spare attention for the passing scene, and he was always eager to acquire information from performers on the public stage. He was particularly indebted to the gentle Stanislas, ex-King of Poland, to whose duodecimo Court of Lunéville he paid frequent visits. Other well-informed contemporaries who furnished material included Bolingbroke, the Duchess of Marlborough and Marshal Saxe. All available printed authorities were used, among them *The Wars of Sweden* by Defoe, masquerading as 'a Scots gentleman in the Swedish service'; and Count Poniatowski, a Polish friend of the King, allowed him to read his unpublished memoirs.

The book won immediate success. The theme was a godsend to any writer who knew how to handle it—swift action, a European stage, a colourful hero, unpredictable developments, a tragic conclusion. Voltaire could tell a story as skilfully as he composed an epitaph. Written for the general public, there is no overloading with detail and there is not a dull page. Though the author seldom comments on events it is easy to detect undertones. That he so frequently and so exclusively salutes Charles' courage and austerity suggests that he finds little else to admire. The whole work might serve as a tract against war under cover of a biography. Throughout life he detested violence in every form and pitied the innocent victims of the men of wrath. No celebrated biography is less disfigured by hero-worship, and from time to time his indignation flares up. 'King Stanislas told me that a Russian officer, a friend of his, surrendered to and was shot by a Swedish General. Worst of all was that the King wrote the order in his own hand to break Patkul, the Russian Ambassador to Augustus of Saxony, on the wheel. Every lawyer—and every slave—feels all the horror of this barbaric injustice.'

Beginning with a brief sketch of Sweden and Finland, the climate and the people, Voltaire passes to the dynasty which made Sweden a Great Power. Gustavus Vasa, the father of his country, Gustavus Adolphus, Charles X and Charles XI, four doughty warriors, prepared the way for Charles XII, 'perhaps the most extraordinary man who ever lived'. When the precocious lad was asked what he thought of Alexander the Great, he expressed a wish to resemble him. Ascending the throne at fifteen he crowned himself, like Napoleon, only to find Denmark, Poland and Russia blocking his path. Throughout life the Slav colossus of the North was never far from the thoughts of Voltaire, who briefly outlines

the realm of the Romanoffs. The existence of that immense country, he exclaims, was not realised by the West before Peter the
Great, and it was not an agreeable discovery. The Russians, less
civilised than the Mexicans in the time of Cortez, were the slaves
of masters as barbarous as themselves. All the more memorable
was the achievement of the superman who built a capital, trained
an army, created a navy and broke the power of the Church.
When Charles scattered his troops at Narva, Peter prophetically
remarked: 'I know the Swedes will long continue to be victorious,
but in time they will teach us to beat them.' Since Poland was a
mere pawn on the chessboard, the author analyses the elements of
weakness and laments the plight of that unhappy state whose
constitution was the laughing-stock of the world. 'The nobility
have scarcely elected a king before they fear his ambition and plot
against him.' The implicit invitation to her neighbours to fish in
troubled waters was joyfully accepted, and the elective throne
became the challenge cup of Europe. The War of the Polish Succession, in which Russia championed the claims of Augustus,
Elector of Saxony, while Sweden supported Stanislas Lecszynski,
was merely an aspect of the wider struggle between Stockholm
and St. Petersburg for the hegemony of Northern Europe.

The young King left his capital in 1700 at the age of eighteen
and never entered it again. He dedicated himself to the art of war,
renouncing wine and women, schooling himself to hunger, sickness and cold, and sharing every hardship with his troops. His
hairbreadth escapes confirmed his belief in predestination: fate,
it seemed clear, was reserving him for higher things. At the age of
twenty-two he selected Stanislas for the Polish throne, and this
part of the narrative is enriched by reminiscences of the fallen
ruler who loved to recall his early days. For instance, his baby
daughter, afterwards the wife of Louis XV, was missed in the tur-
moil of war and was found in a village. 'This is the story I have
often heard him tell.' The fumes of victory went to the head of the
first teetotal King. 'Success became too familiar to him; he said it
was more like hunting than fighting, and complained of never
having to contest a victory.' After the laurels of Narva nothing
seemed impossible to his seasoned troops. 'He even dispatched
officers to Asia and Egypt to make plans of the cities and to
report on the strength of these countries. If anyone could over-

throw the Persian and Turkish Empires and then go to Italy it was he. He was as young as Alexander but he was more indefatigable and more temperate. Perhaps the Swedes were better soldiers than the Macedonians. But such plans, which are called divine when they succeed, are regarded as chimeras when they fail. His sole pleasure was in making Europe tremble.'

The tide turned at Pultowa, where the King, drunk with glory and crazed with ambition, met the punishment he deserved. Peter's proposals for peace provoked the haughty reply: 'I will treat with the Tsar in Moscow.' Counting on the aid of Mazeppa, the rebel chief of the Ukraine, he scorned advice. 'Their victories had filled the Swedes with such confidence that they never inquired about the enemy's numbers, but only about their location.' The description of the battle, as fiercely contested as Blenheim and Ramillies, is a spirited performance. 'All who have served with the Swedes', comments the biographer, relying on first-hand testimony, 'know that it is almost impossible to resist their initial onset.' The Russian ranks were speedily broken, quickly rallied, and finally scored a resounding victory. Charles escaped to Turkey, a General without an army, since his troops had surrendered in droves. In a few hours the warrior King lost the fruit of nine years' campaigning and a score of battles. The captured Cossacks were broken on the wheel, a hideous practice prevalent in many parts of the Continent.

Voltaire grasped the epoch-making significance of Pultowa as clearly as his twentieth-century readers. 'The battle was fought on 8 July, 1709, between the two most famous monarchs in the world: Charles distinguished by nine years of victory, Peter by nine years of training his troops to an equality with the Swedes. The former was celebrated for having given away the dominions of others, the latter for having civilised his own; Charles loving danger and fighting merely for the sake of glory, Peter shirking no difficulties and making war only from calculation; the Swedish King liberal from a generous temperament, the Russian never generous except with some object in view; the former sober and temperate in an extraordinary degree, naturally brave and only on one occasion displaying cruelty, the latter retaining the roughness of his education or his race, as terrible to his subjects as he was fascinating to strangers, and addicted to excesses which shortened his days. While Charles bore the title "Invincible" which he might lose at any moment, Peter had already received the title "the Great", which no defeat could forfeit since he did not owe it to his victories.' The biographer leaves his readers in no doubt as to the real hero of the book.

The few remaining years were an anti-climax. Treated as an honoured guest by the Turks, Charles had ample leisure to dream and to scheme. He longed to enlist the might of the Ottoman Empire in another round of his boxing match with Peter, for he still believed in his star. His protégé Stanislas had lost his throne after Pultowa, but might he not be restored when the tide of victory turned? The picture of the *ménage* at Bender is enriched by the testimony of acquaintances, among them a Portuguese doctor Fabricius living in Constantinople, an envoy of Holstein, and Count Poniatowski. The Turks chivalrously provided food and cash, money was sent from France, and the captive King borrowed from merchants at Constantinople. 'Many people journeyed from the capital to see him. The Turks and the neighbouring Tartars came in crowds. All honoured and admired him. His rigid abstinence from wine and his regularity in attending public prayers twice daily spread the rumour that he was a true Mussulman.' For the first time he had leisure to read, and he found solace in the heroes of Corneille and Racine. All proposals for peace with Russia and his return to Sweden were rejected out of hand, and when the Turks at last requested him to leave their country, the ungrateful guest staged a sanguinary resistance. Marching north he was soon in the thick of the fight once more, defending Stralsund to the last and perishing by a shot from an unknown hand—perhaps by a member of his own forces—at the siege of Frederikshall at the age of thirty-six.

The biographer's verdict, severe though not unjust, needs comparatively little revision after two centuries of research, but his English biographer Nisbet Bain suggests that Charles was more of an intellectual than Voltaire admits. Despite certain heroic qualities to which unstinted homage is paid, he is presented as a pocket Attila, storming over northern and eastern Europe without any constructive aims. Living in the moment, he was incapable of creation and indeed had no desire to create. Hegemony passed to the Tsar who made a better use of it, for he employed his successes for his country's good. If he conquered a town the best artisans were transferred to St. Petersburg. The customs, arts and sciences of any place he took were imported to enrich and elevate his own country. Thus of all conquerors he had the best excuse for his conquests. Sweden, on the other hand, lost all her foreign possessions, and had neither trade, money nor credit; her veteran warriors were killed or died of want. More than 100,000 remained in the vast Russian Empire, and as many more had been sold to the Turks and the Tartars. The male population was visibly diminishing, yet their hopes revived when they heard that their King had arrived at Stralsund. The country youth crowded to enlist, leaving the land without cultivators. He thought his subjects were born to follow him to war, and he had schooled them to think so too. He enlisted many fifteen-year-olds. In numerous districts there were only old men, women and children; sometimes the women ploughed unaided. A people thus loaded with taxation would have revolted under any other king, but even the most miserable peasant knew that his master was faring as badly. So great was their veneration that they could not hate him; one could not help blaming him, admiring him, pitying him, or aiding him. All his actions were almost incredible. He carried the heroic virtues to a point at which they became faults. His eminent qualities were a nightmare to his country; he was an extraordinary rather than a great man. His life should be a lesson to kings, teaching them that a peaceful and happy reign is better than so much glory. Like other adventurers, crowned and un-crowned, he dug his own grave, forgetful of the maxim that politics—of which war is a function—are the art of the possible. No contemporary observer realised more fully than Voltaire that the final collapse of Swedish imperialism was an event of minor significance compared with the emergence of Russia as a Great Power.

Voltaire was fascinated by the towering figure of Peter the Great, and he returned at intervals to the epic struggle for the mastery of the North. A half-length portrait, entitled *Anecdotes sur Pierre le Grand*, written in 1748, is notable for the tribute to the Genevese Le Fort who met the young ruler in 1695 and en-couraged him to break with the prejudices of the past. Without the Genevese, he declares, Russia might still be in a state of

barbarism. The reformer of such a backward country could only
build in brick, but elsewhere he would have built in marble.
Merciless he was, but cruelty was traditional at the Russian Court.

When a full-length biography was suggested by the Russian
Court during the later years of the Tsarina Elizabeth and official
materials were offered for his use, Voltaire accepted the invitation
with pleasure. That it was commissioned by the daughter of the
hero to some extent clipped his wings, and the portrait of the
superman could hardly be expected to reproduce every wart on
his swarthy countenance. The story of Charles XII had been one
of private virtues and public vices; with Peter it was the reverse.
Rulers of good character, however, like Charles I, Charles XII
and Louis XVI are judged by their public performances, not by
their observance of the Ten Commandments. Yet the book is
no mere official panegyric, and the final verdict differs little from
that of the earlier portrait. While Charles envisaged life as a military campaign, Peter dedicated himself to the more rewarding
tasks of the political architect. Published in 1759, the *Histoire de
Russie sous Pierre le Grand* breathes a warmer tone than the life of
Charles XII. With the warrior King the whole plan was wrong,
with the Tsar merely some of the methods. There was naturally
a good deal of repetition in the narrative of the wars, but there
was also new material on internal developments. For the first
time the West was enabled to visualise the greatest of the Romanoffs not only as the creator of modern Russia but as a living
personality, part genius, part savage. There had been travellers
and travellers' tales, but little was known of the reforms which
had revolutionised the life of the country and wrought a permanent shift in the balance of power on the European chessboard.

Compared to the Chinese and Indians, the oldest civilisations
with a span of over 4,000 years, the Russian people, as Voltaire
reminds his readers, had arrived late and had made more progress
in fifty years than any other nation by its own efforts in five hundred. Though still underpopulated, it possessed as many inhabitants as any Christian state. Of the twenty-four millions—
the latest figure supplied from official sources—most were
serfs in Poland, many parts of Germany, and, until recent
times, in nearly all Europe. Wealth was reckoned not in

money but in slaves. Since the chief need was population, Peter wisely attempted to limit the number of monks. From the standpoint of national survival those 13,000 drones were lost to the State, and the 720,000 serfs whom they possessed were out of all proportion to their needs. This abuse, added Voltaire in a later edition, was only corrected by the Empress Catherine, who deprived the clergy and monasteries of these odious privileges and strove to turn them into useful citizens. The religions of the Empire, as numerous as the races, included Muslims and primitive pagans. Christian dissidents from the Orthodox Church, such as the Raskolniks, were left in peace, but Peter expelled the Jesuits as a political danger.

At the close of his introductory chapters Voltaire pays preliminary homage to the mighty Muscovite whose achievements had fascinated him since his youth. Writing in the middle of the Seven Years War when Russian armies were in the field, he declares that Russia owed her influence in Europe to Peter alone. Of all the celebrated legislators he alone was fully known, for fables had clustered about all his predecessors. 'We enjoy the advantage of writing truths which would be regarded as fables were they not well attested. In the largest of states everything had to be made. At last Peter was born and Russia was transformed.' Voltaire always admired pioneers.

Though he never visited Russia Voltaire approached his task with a lively sense of its extent and resources. It was larger than all the rest of Europe, he began, larger than the Roman Empire, larger than the dominions of Alexander the Great. So vast a territory required a population to match, but to make it as populous and productive as the countries of western and southern Europe would need centuries of labour and a succession of supermen on the throne. He records with satisfaction that of the thirty-five churches in the new capital five were allotted to Catholics, Calvinists and Lutherans—five temples erected to the spirit of tolerance, an example to other nations including his own. The admixture of race is stressed, and the showman salutes Siberia and the Far East. His interest in religious beliefs and practices finds full scope as he summarises the reports of visitors to those distant lands. The Kamchatkans, for instance, possessed a mythology but no religion, demons and sorceresses taking the place of gods. Yet backward communities were not unteachable. Culture and the arts had been established with such difficulty in Asia, and the edifice had so often been overthrown, that it was surprising that the majority were living above the Tartar level.

The biographical sketch begins with the death of Alexis in 1677 at the age of forty-six, and the provisional partnership of Sophie, his daughter by his first wife, and her brother Ivan, an epileptic imbecile. Peter, the precocious child of a second marriage, grew up among horrors. Like his half-brother Ivan he suffered from convulsions, but he possessed a cool and powerful brain. He taught himself German and Dutch. Ships and shipbuilding, a boyish passion, remained the chief delight of his adult life. At the outset of the reign he inaugurated commercial relations with China. Whenever China crosses the stage Voltaire smiles at his favourite nation.

Peter's visit to Western Europe at the age of twenty-five is described with admiration. His half-brother dead and his odious half-sister a prisoner of state, he felt that he could safely leave his kingdom and seek lessons abroad. He worked and lived like an artisan in the shipbuilding yard at Sardam, learned to perform operations, to make clocks and cast cannons, corrected Dutch maps of Russia, studied astronomy, finished his training in shipbuilding at Deptford, and invited foreign technicians to settle in Russia. He returned by Vienna and Warsaw. Not till Joseph II half a century later did a ruler undertake journeys for such utilitarian aims.

The first searching test was the revolt of the Streltsi, or palace guards, who were believed to aim at the elevation of Sophie during the absence of the ruler. Though in itself a small affair, it indicated a core of opposition to the foreign models and foreign instructors whom Peter felt to be essential for his plans. Yet throughout his reign he took care to keep the higher controls in Russian hands. Like the Japanese of the Restoration era he employed foreign experts to train his subjects. The savage punishments of the Streltsi cast a shadow over the fame of the young ruler, but they notified potential malcontents that they would receive short shrift if they raised their hand against the State. Like Sultan Mahmoud, who slaughtered his Janissaries in the nineteenth century with equal unconcern, he believed that the interests of his backward country demanded totalitarian rule. A further step towards autocracy was the abolition of the Patriarchate, the creation of the Holy Synod under a Procurator responsible to the Crown, and the diversion of large ecclesiastical revenues to the payment of troops. Every blow at the power and pretensions of the Churches—whatever the Church and whatever the creed—is greeted by the biographer with a cheer.

The long war with Sweden fills a smaller space in the annals of the Tsar than that of the King, for in Russian history it was merely an incident. Though the panic at Narva left Charles the first man in Europe, Peter never doubted that Russia's turn would come. His labours for national recovery resemble the efforts of Frederick the Great after the Seven Years War. He imported livestock, created a textile industry, and developed the Siberian mines. In addition to building a new capital, he constructed fortresses from Kronstadt and Archangel in the north to Kiev and Taganrog in the south. How much was at stake at Pultowa was fully grasped by the biographer. 'I have read the letters of several Ministers who shared the general view that Charles would win, but his death would mean only one hero less in the world. That of Peter would involve the ruin of all his achievements, useful as they were to the whole human race, and the relapse of the largest empire into the chaos from which he had begun to extricate it.' Both rulers were under fire. Pultowa, concludes the biographer with something like a shout of triumph, meant the happiness of the vastest empire in the world. The note is a little too shrill, but it is true enough that a Swedish victory would have stimulated the Swedish bull's pathological urge to gore his neighbours.

While the knight-errant blandly ignored the lessons of experience the practical idealist was eager to learn. His visit to Paris in 1717 aroused even more interest than his earlier sojourn in the West, for he was now at the summit of his fame. No living ruler approached him in ability and achievement. He desired to see everything with his own eyes and to test objects with his own hands. He was a mechanic, an artist, a geometrician. 'The Academy displayed its choicest treasures, but none so rare as himself.' He corrected mistakes in maps of his territories. He accepted membership of the Academy, and began a correspondence on experiments and discoveries with those members of whom he wished to be a colleague. 'We must go back to Pythagoras to find such travellers, and they had not quitted an empire in order to learn.' Embracing the statue of Richelieu he exclaimed: 'Great man! I would have given half my territories to have learned from you how to govern the other half.' Once again he invited experts to Russia to instruct his subjects.

The later chapters are dominated by the fate of Alexis, the first of the dynastic tragedies which darken the story of eighteenth-century Russia. The heir to the throne, the son of Peter's first wife Eudoxia Lapouka, never knew happiness, for his mother was immured in a convent when he was six and his father had no time for the nursery. His marriage in his seventeenth year to a Bruns-wick princess who died in childbirth brought no ray of sunshine into his life. Inheriting his mother's dislike of foreign advisers he fell under the influence of ecclesiastical and civilian reactionaries. Voltaire had collected a good deal of information about the frustrated lad in addition to the official material provided for his use. The clergy emerge as the villains of the piece. The books provided for his education seemed to him to condemn his father's revolutionary work. 'Priests were leaders of the malcontents, and he submitted to their will. They convinced him that the whole country was outraged, that his father, who was often ill, would not live long, and that the nation would welcome expres-sions of his disapproval.'

Voltaire sympathises with both parties in the dynastic feud. He has equal understanding for the ruler's consuming anxiety as to the permanence of his work and for the heir's sour dis-approval of the new pattern. The tension increased when in 1711 the Tsar divorced his wife and married Catherine, his Lithuanian mistress, who presented him with two daughters, potential competitors for the throne. It was in vain that Alexis was entrusted with various administrative tasks and was sent to complete his education at Dresden, for by this time the feud was too bitter to be healed and too notorious to be hushed up. Warned by his father that he must change his course or forfeit the throne the unhappy heir renounced his claim. To a second warning, 'Im-prove or enter a monastery,' he replied that he would become a monk.

The drama entered its final stage when Peter visited the West in

1717. Alexis fled to Vienna with his mistress and thence to Naples. He was coaxed back by the solemn oath of his father that he would not be punished, but he was removed from the line of succession, which passed to his infant son, and his associates were tortured to death. The biographer, like the Greek chorus, looks on and cries, 'The pity of it all!' 'The Tsar had to decide between the interests of nearly eighteen millions and a single individual incapable of governing them.' Some charges were denied by Alexis but he admitted others, excusing himself on the ground of anger and drink. In confession he had expressed a wish for his father's death. His confessor had replied: 'God will pardon you; we wish it too,' and admitted under torture that the statement was correct. 'We must not judge the laws and customs of one nation by those of others,' comments Voltaire. The Tsar had the undoubted right to punish his son with death for his flight; that he acted with deliberation and full publicity indicated his conviction of the justice of his cause. He allowed the Bishops to decide after a trial of five months, during which Alexis was interrogated several times. Though he had never thought of parricide, a unanimous sentence of death was pronounced for having left Russia without permission—a curious anticipation of the attempted flight and punishment of Prussia's Crown Prince Frederick in 1730. So confident was the Tsar that he was discharging his duty that he ordered the publication and translation of the proceedings. A commissioned biography was hardly the place to record that Alexis was flogged to death, and Voltaire dutifully reproduces the fairy tale of apoplexy which was served out to Russian embassies abroad.

The closing years of the reign were not the least memorable. Peter was the first modern ruler to seize the possibilities of applied science, and he founded the Academy of Science as an instrument of national policy. 'The arts flourished,' writes Voltaire, 'manufactures were encouraged, the navy was enlarged, the armies were well supplied, the laws were observed.' He enjoyed his glory in full, and resolved to share it with his low-born second wife, the only woman—perhaps the only human being—he ever loved. In 1724 he placed the crown on her head at Moscow and married his daughter Anne to the Duke of Holstein. But there was always some skeleton in the Imperial cupboard. In 1722 Catherine was

proclaimed successor to the throne and in 1724 was crowned
Empress Consort. After the coronation, however, her husband
suspected her—probably without reason—of a *liaison* with a
young chamberlain, and the latter's sister, one of her ladies, was
charged with financial misdemeanours. The chamberlain was
executed and his head, preserved in spirits, was deposited in the
apartments of the Empress. His sister was punished with the
knout. 'These severities which outrage our customs', comments
Voltaire, 'were perhaps necessary in a country where observance
of the law seemed to demand a terrifying rigour.' The Empress
asked mercy for her lady-in-waiting which was refused. When in
his anger he smashed a Venetian vase, she remarked: 'You have
broken an ornament of your palace. Do you think that will make
it more beautiful?' Partially appeased, the Tsar reduced the blows
of the knout from eleven to five. This and similar incidents gave
rise to the suggestion that his agonising death was due to poison-
ing. 'Mere malicious rumours,' exclaims the biographer: the
Persian campaigns had overtaxed his strength. In the winter of
1724–5 he suffered from an abscess and other ailments, and was
often delirious. Claims for the succession could be made for his
grandson Peter, the child of Alexis, and for his eldest daughter
Anne, Duchess of Holstein; but the influence of Menschikoff, the
all-powerful Minister, placed his widow Catherine on the throne
without a hitch.

The book concludes with an impressive catalogue of the reforms of the master-builder. He introduced textile industries,
constructed canals, organised the police, repressed begging,
decreed uniform weights and measures, imported foreign artisans,
worked the iron, gold and silver mines, built forts, improved the
maps. Sometimes he took the spade himself and carried heavy
burdens on his back. Commercial relations were established with
Persia and China, and an Orthodox Church was built in Pekin.
In the sphere of legislation he studied foreign practice; the code
he began to compile was completed by his daughter and reflected
the mildness of her reign. His governing principle was that
service counted for more than birth. The biographer dwells with
special satisfaction on the religious reforms. He abolished the
Patriarchate because he wished the executive to be supreme in
every sphere; the Holy Synod, chosen by the ruler, could only

pass laws which he approved. The idea of competing authorities in a state seemed to him absurd. Though the Patriarch had not sworn obedience, the fourteen members of the Synod, who held senatorial rank, recognised their master who occasionally presided at their sessions.

Like Augustus, Peter found a Russia of brick and left it of marble. Inheriting a sprawling, semi-oriental monarchy dominated by the great nobles and the Church, he left it a centralised autocracy, the prototype of the Enlightened Despotisms of eighteenth-century Europe. After the conclusion of the long war with Sweden the Senate of the Holy Synod conferred the titles of The Great and Emperor on the most influential personage of Eastern Europe since Constantine. 'Half hero, half tiger!' exclaims Voltaire in the life of Charles XII. Soft-pedalling is to be expected in official biography, but the final tribute is more than mere flattery. That his work endured tells its own tale. 'Europe had recognised that he loved glory, but that he used it to do good; that his faults never weakened his great qualities; that he coerced nature, his subjects, and himself, on land and water, but coerced in order to adorn.' A graceful compliment is added to the daughter who had commissioned the work. 'Extreme rigour was necessary at that time towards the lower class; but when manners changed the Empress Elizabeth buttressed by clemency the work which her father had begun by his laws. This indulgence has been carried to a point without precedent, that during her reign no one should be put to death; and she kept her word. She is the first sovereign to respect human life. Malefactors have been condemned to the mines and public works. Thus their punishments are rendered useful to the state—an arrangement as wise as it is humane. Everywhere else the criminal is executed without stopping crime.' Life had always been cheap in Russia, and Peter's volcanic rages left it cheaper still. For Voltaire, as for ourselves, the best measuring rod for civilisation was the degree of respect for the body and soul of the individual citizen, in other words, for the rule of law. Confronted with this exacting test neither the Swedish gladiator nor the Romanoff master-builder deserves high marks. The century of the common man was still far away.

II. *The Ancien Régime*

So long as mankind retains interest in the *Grand Siècle*, the *Roi Soleil* and his degenerate successor, in the poets, the preachers and the captains of the *ancien régime*, Voltaire's surveys of two long and eventful reigns will continue to be read. As a youthful eye-witness of the closing years of Louis XIV and a keen observer of the whole span of Louis XV, he records his own impressions and utilises oral as well as written testimony of men and women who had stood close to the heart of events. The second work is of less interest, partly because the recorder had to be more reticent and partly because there was infinitely less glamour and glory. Yet *The Age of Louis XV* deserves more attention than it usually receives. In these two books the history of France from the death of Richelieu to the eve of the French Revolution is interpreted by the brightest intellect of the age. A third work, on the Parlement of Paris, traces constitutional developments from the Middle Ages to the writer's own time.

No Frenchman before the age of Sismondi and Thierry, Guizot and Michelet, Thiers and Tocqueville, made such notable con-tributions to the history of his country as Voltaire. The first attempt was Mézeray's survey, carried down to the reign of Henri IV, which was published during the Fronde. The three folio volumes, and still more an abridged version issued in 1668, supplied the needs of readers for almost a century. While his use of the sources for the early centuries was uncritical, the value of the book increases as it approaches his own time. Economic and social conditions were sketched, and his independent judgement cost him his pension as Historiographer Royal. His sympathies were with the bourgeoisie to which he belonged and with the cool-headed *Politiques* who frowned both on the Huguenots and the *Ligue*. The next attempt was made by the Jesuit Père Daniel, who rejected some of the Merovingian fables accepted by Mézeray and whose tributes to the role of the Monarchy earned him the coveted title of Historiographer Royal. A less ambitious enter-prise was the *Abrégé Chronologique de l'histoire de France* by Presi-dent Hénault, the distinguished lawyer and discreet lover of Mme du Deffand, who was strongest in the field of institutions and was extremely careful not to risk his skin. None of the three possessed the slightest literary talent and none attempted to paint the life of the nation. France had to wait for Voltaire to produce a readable narrative, as England had waited for Hume.

'I consider Louis XIV as a benefactor of mankind,' wrote Voltaire to d'Argenson in 1740. 'I write as a man, not as a subject. I desire to portray the last century, not merely a prince.' Though the author was a cosmopolitan who felt equally at home in every civilised land, his book is a glowing tribute to the genius of France. Published in Berlin in 1751, it was revised in 1756 and assumed its final form in 1768. To please all his readers was impossible. 'Voltaire has sent me his book,' wrote President Hénault. 'The weakness of the first volume is that the King is unfairly treated. But the second volume makes up for it.' Émile Faguet, on the other hand, long afterwards complained of the glorification of Louis XIV. As a matter of fact Voltaire is a fairer judge than Saint-Simon into whose unpublished Memoirs he dipped during his last visit to Paris. He read everything available, published and in manuscript—Dangeau's voluminous journal, the Memoirs of Torcy and Villars, the papers of Louvois and Colbert. After the first edition he obtained from the Duc de Noailles the Memoirs or rather Memoranda of the King himself. Among the oral witnesses were Villars, Fleury, the Duc and Duchesse du Maine, and Caumartin, the helpful friend of his youth. He was also privileged to examine the archives in the Louvre. The finished portrait is not very different from that which has been painted by Lavisse.

The *Siècle de Louis XIV* opens with an expression of the author's aim: to depict not merely the career of a celebrated ruler but the mind of man during the most enlightened age the world had ever seen. There had only been four happy periods when the arts ripened to perfection—classical Greece, the age of Caesar and Augustus, the Renaissance, and seventeenth-century France. The latest was the best, not indeed in artistic achievement but in the advance of reason. It was the more remarkable since it followed a period of barbarism and civil war. Yet the historian confines his eulogy to the lofty realm of the spirit, for the actions of rulers had not kept pace with the advance of mind. All ages were alike in criminal folly. The book is written in complete independence by a man who brings his own scale of values to the task.

G

Though justly proud of the cultural achievements of France, Voltaire, like Gibbon, Lessing, and Goethe, was more of a European than a patriot. The vision of Europe as a cultural unit was continually before his eyes. Christian Europe, excluding Russia, he declared, was like a great republic divided into states, with a common substratum of religion and public law; for instance, the person of ambassadors was respected and prisoners of war were not enslaved. In a community connected by so many ties religious wars were a form of madness peculiar to Christians. Though attempts had been made to maintain a rough equilibrium, since Charles V the balance had inclined to the House of Austria. Detesting war as heartily as any of the Quakers whom he had met in England, he was too much of a realist to dream of a warless world. His sombre picture of France after the assassination of Henri IV anticipates Vandal's celebrated denunciation of the Directory before the emergence of *le petit Caporal*. Though not quite so cruel and frenzied as the wars of the *Ligue*, when religious fanaticism was mated with political faction, the era of the Fronde is denounced as a welter of ambition and intrigue. France's greatest soldiers, Condé and Turenne, fought successively on both sides, and the climax of degradation was reached when the former enlisted the aid of the Spaniards against his fatherland. The disunion of the rebels was the salvation of the Court, but the dictatorship of the cunning Mazarin, who cared for nothing except money and power, was a shady episode. His principal achievement was to secure Alsace for France. Was he a great Minister? That, replies the historian cautiously, was for posterity to judge. When the young monarch came of age his day was over, and his death relieved a tension which was becoming unendurable.

Voltaire was a convinced royalist, for he thought little of the political capacity of the common man. But there was no unction in his attitude to kings. His florid compliments to Frederick the Great and Catherine the Great were merely the current coin of the age, as they fully understood; awe was as foreign to his nature in the courts of Europe as in the courts of heaven. Yet he was unstinted in his homage to born rulers of men, and the *début* of Louis XIV stirs him to enthusiasm. For the first time since Henri IV there was a firm hand at the helm and tortured France was grateful for the boon. The prestige of the throne was quickly restored,

Dunkirk was purchased from England, a fleet came into being. By 1665, at the age of twenty-seven, he had reached the summit of ambition. 'He was young and rich, well served and blindly obeyed, fearing no foreign ruler and eager to distinguish himself by foreign conquests.' The campaigns are described with spirit but without emotion. In the war with Holland the author's sympathies are with the Dutch, who fought heroically under William of Orange against desperate odds and kept up the struggle till the Emperor, the Great Elector and other princes came to their aid. Though he salutes the genius of Condé, Turenne and Vauban, he describes Louvois as more valuable to the King than any of his generals.

The second interval of peace which followed the Treaty of Nimwegen in 1678 is painted with more satisfaction than the victories in the field. Louis XIV ruled a nation happy in itself and a model to other states. He had added Franche Comté, Dunkirk and part of Flanders to France, naval bases were established at Brest and Toulon, and Strasbourg was acquired without drawing the sword. He would never have approved the devastation of the Palatinate which Louvois had ordered if he had witnessed the horrors it involved. With the turn of the century and the War of the Spanish Succession, however, the tone becomes more severe and the arrogance of the monarch is roundly denounced. 'It was against him rather than against France that the Allies were leagued. The King deteriorated, not only in the shaping of policy but in the choice of his agents. Chamillart, virtually Prime Minister, was unfit for his post. The King held the reins too tightly; commanders in the field had often to ask leave before launching an operation, whereby favourable opportunities were sometimes unused.' In a word Le Roi Soleil possessed too much power. Voltaire had as little use for monarchical absolutism as for Divine Right: Limited Monarchy was far the best system. 'Elsewhere the people have blindly to acquiesce in the designs of their kings, but in England the king must acquiesce in those of his people.' Thanks above all to Villars' belated victory at Denain the War of the Spanish Succession achieved its purpose by planting a grandson of the French monarch on the Spanish throne, though at the cost of prolonged and terrible suffering. At the close of his stirring narrative the historian reiterates his admiration for the

supreme practitioner of a difficult art. 'He possessed an elevation
of soul which urged him to the accomplishment of great things
in every sphere. The splendour of his rule was reflected in his
most trivial actions.' Voltaire, who lived into the reign of Louis
XVI, realised how far and how fast the French Monarchy had
fallen, though he had no notion that it was so near collapse.

The latter portion of the book is the most interesting because
it is the most personal. The chapters entitled 'Anecdotes of the
Reign', containing material collected from eye-witnesses, round
off the portrait of the King. The earliest sign that he was born
with a great soul was the victory over his passion for Marie Man-
cini. It was the fault of his mother and Mazarin that he had received no systematic education and had read little beyond the
plays of Corneille. He should have been taught some history,
especially of recent times, but the available manuals were almost
unreadable. Yet he learned his *métier* quickly, and France was
grateful for the dignity and brilliance of the Court after the horrors of civil war and the secluded life of his colourless father. A
new era opened with his marriage fête in 1660 and that of his
brother to his English cousin Henrietta in 1661. It is not the
monarch alone who receives high marks. 'Nature herself seemed
to take a delight at this moment in producing men of the first rank
in every art,' but the ruler could hold his own with the best. 'He
towered above everybody by the grace of his figure, the majestic
nobility of his countenance, and the sound of his voice, at once
dignified and charming. An old officer faltered when asking a
favour, saying, 'Sire, I never trembled like this before your
enemies.' Fêtes never interfered with his incessant labours. His
generosity was unprecedented, not only to French writers, among
them Racine, but to foreign scholars, though he knew too much
of human nature to expect much gratitude. 'Every time I fill a
post I make a hundred people discontented and one ungrateful,'
he remarked. His worse fault was sensuality. Few women could
resist him, and even his genuine affection for the La Vallière
synchronised with frequent infidelities. Her successor, the
Montespan, was detested for her arrogance and pomp. The whole
Court was a hotbed of amorous intrigue, and Louvois indulged
in several mistresses. Superstition was as rife as immorality. The
Marquise de Brinvilliers was justly executed for poisoning her

family, but there was much foolish talk about love potions and pacts with the devil. Medical science was in its infancy, and natural deaths, such as that of Henrietta, were attributed to crime.

Next to the monarch the most interesting portrait in the gallery is that of Mme de Maintenon, who was described to him, among others, by Cardinal Fleury. In a well-known study Döllinger saluted her as the most influential woman in French history, but that was not the view of her contemporaries. She rarely interfered, declares Voltaire, either to render a service or to make mischief. 'She had scarcely any feelings of her own, and her only care was to conform with those of the King.' There was no outward show of greatness. She was an agreeable and docile companion of the ruler who was more deeply attached to her than she to him. Though he admits that no marriage contract was drawn up, he asserts that the ceremony took place in January 1686 on the advice of the King's Confessor, Père La Chaise, 'in a small chapel at the end of the apartments later occupied by the Duke of Burgundy'. The Archbishop of Paris pronounced the Benediction. Only the Confessor and two valets were witnesses.

The anecdotal chapters are followed by surveys of the administration, commerce and finance, arts and sciences, and ecclesiastical affairs. Though he never used the words *L'état c'est moi*, Louis was more entitled to do so than any of his predecessors or successors on the French throne. He read every document that he signed. His most enduring achievement was the creation of a navy. 'He had defects and made grave mistakes, but if those who condemned him had been in his place would they have equalled his achievements? No one has surpassed him as a monarch. He was aware of his faults though unable to correct them. "I have been too fond of war," he confessed in a memorandum for his son; "do not imitate me in that, nor in my extravagance." Though his life and death were alike glorious he was not mourned as he deserved. His eminent qualities and his noble deeds eclipsed all his faults. He was never ruled by his Ministers, and he did more good to his country than twenty of his predecessors together.'

France, we are reminded, was weak in historians and composers but pre-eminent in literature and painting, architecture and sculpture. To these creative activities Louis XIV gave more

encouragement than all his predecessors added together. A brief
digression on the Arts and Sciences in Europe enables the author
to pay tribute to England. Since the Restoration, he declares with
his ignorant contempt for the Middle Ages, the English had made
greater progress in all the arts than in all previous times. Milton
was the glory and wonder of the age. Dryden and Pope were
admirable, Swift a better Rabelais, Addison's *Cato* a masterpiece,
Newton and Locke the leaders of science and philosophy. Leibniz is saluted as perhaps the most universal genius in Europe,
Galileo as a giant. Looking round the Continent Voltaire proudly
concludes: 'We have shown that during the last century mankind,
from one end of Europe to the other, has been more enlightened
than ever before.' There spoke the High Priest of the *Aufklärung*:
not territory, nor power, nor riches were the test of progress, but
enlightenment and the arts of peace. None of his contemporaries
could have produced so widely ranging a survey of intellectual
life. Though the humanities were his special province, he was
deeply interested in science. He knew enough physics to understand Newton, and he had carried out experiments in chemistry.

The concluding chapters on the Protestant churches and the
Catholic heresies are among the most characteristic. The Church
in France, contrary to general belief, was not wealthy; there were
no Prince Bishops as in Germany and Austria, and a good deal
of money flowed away to Rome. The Gallican Articles of 1682,
strictly limiting the authority of the Vatican, are naturally
approved by the old foe of Ultramontanism. The revocation of
the Edict of Nantes, on the other hand, was one of the greatest
calamities, not only for the victims but for France. The Protestants, who formed about a twelfth of the population, were loyal
and useful citizens who had taken no part in the Fronde. Fifty
thousand families left the country in three years, and the total loss
amounted to half a million. Voltaire had met Huguenot exiles in
England and Holland, among them Cavalier, their best-known
chief. Though his sympathies were always with the oppressed, he
admits that there were fanatics among them, and fanatics of every
colour he abhorred.

The feud between Jansenists and Jesuits is treated with scant
sympathy for either side. While the disputes of the classical
philosophers were peaceful, those of the theologians were always

violent and often led to bloodshed. Voltaire hated the Jesuits as much as Arnauld himself, not merely for what they taught but for what they had done. They were indeed completely discredited by the murder of Henri IV, the Gunpowder Plot and the *Lettres Provinciales*, which contained as much Attic salt as *Tartuffe*. Pascal, however, was unfair in saddling the whole Order with the extravagances of a few Spaniards and Flemings; he might have detected similar monstrosities among Dominican and Franciscan casuists. The Jansenists receive gentler treatment, though their doctrine of grace, derived like that of Calvin from Augustine, was part of 'the wretched controversies of the Schoolmen'. The piety of Port Royal is acknowledged, but the Jansenist movement fizzled out with the convulsions and miraculous cures at the tomb of the Abbé Paris. The Bull *Unigenitus*, issued on the eve of the death of Louis XIV, registered the triumph of the Jesuits and of Father Le Tellier, his Confessor, who had persuaded him that the best means of atoning for his sins was to hammer the heretics.

From Jansenism to Quietism was but a step. Mme Guyon, declares Voltaire, wished to be the Saint Theresa of France. 'The ambition to have disciples, perhaps the strongest of all ambitions, obsessed her mind. Though herself a lightweight, she secured the patronage of Mme de Maintenon and of Fénelon, tutor to the King's grandsons, 'the most brilliant figure at the Court'. Like a man in love, he condoned all her faults and she hailed him as her son. It is a tribute to the Archbishop of Cambrai that the arch-enemy of the clergy felt his fascination, and he regrets that the big battalions were on the other side. Mme de Maintenon, hating discord, withdrew her protection, and Bossuet was called in to dissect the writings of Mme Guyon. When he denounced them she was sent to Vincennes, and now he demanded that Fénelon himself should condemn his friend. When the Archbishop pub-lished a milder version of Quietism in his *Maxims of the Saints* Bossuet pronounced it heretical, and the King requested con-demnation by the Pope. Fénelon recanted, a humiliating proce-dure which Voltaire himself, forced to more than one face-saving surrender, cannot condemn. No ecclesiastic in the portrait gallery is painted in such glowing colours. 'His personality and *Télé-maque* won him the veneration of Europe. He was universally beloved.' Despite the charm of this radiant figure the historian dismissed the mystics as 'the alchemists of true religion'. The whole controversy is exhibited as a storm in a tea-cup. 'These disputes, which long claimed the attention of all France, are over. One marvels at the rancour and bitterness they caused.' At the end of his journey through the longest reign in French history, Voltaire draws a lesson from the other side of the world. Jesuit missions had been permitted entry at the close of the sixteenth century, but they were soon forbidden as the effect of innovation was feared. The Eastern peoples had never dispatched missionaries to Europe, and the mania for proselytising was a disorder of recent times. The beginning of wisdom was to live and let live. Different peoples—and different persons—had differing traditions and varying needs. The simpler a religion the less there was to quarrel about. All theologies and philosophies were guesswork. What mattered most was conduct, and in the field of morals the West had little to teach the East. There is very little propaganda in the book, but the articles of the author's creed stand out as clearly as the Ten Commandments: intellectual enlightenment, the encouragement of the arts and sciences, religious toleration, mild laws, sound finance, the avoidance of war, and above all a spirit of humanity. Neither idealising nor despising the average man, Voltaire believed that on such lines the sum of happiness both for individuals and nations could be vastly increased.

The *Précis du Siècle Louis XV* is planned on a less comprehensive scale. Appointed Historiographer of France in 1746, Voltaire commenced his official duties with a narrative of the War of the Austrian Succession which was submitted for approval to d'Argenson, Minister of War. Other portions of the reign were described at intervals in later years, and revision continued till the close of his life. The book is enlivened by material from such prominent actors in the drama as Marshal Villars, the Duc de Richelieu and the Duchesse de Maine. The curtain rises on the Regency, when gaiety returned in a flood after the gloom of the declining years of Louis XIV. The Regent died of his debaucheries in the prime of his life. 'We laughed at his death as we had laughed at his government, for the French are accustomed to laugh at everything.' Yet he was not wholly contemptible. 'His only faults were his passion for pleasure and his liking for innovations. Of all the descendants of

Henri IV Philip of Orleans most resembled him in his valour, his kindliness and his lack of pose, but he possessed a richer culture.' The chief sensation of the Regency was the crazy scheme of the Scottish adventurer John Law, who founded a bank and a Mississippi Company, assumed control of the national resources with the title of Controller General, and issued paper money in a flood. In the pursuit of his vaulting ambitions he was naturalised and became a Catholic; for a brief space Paris was at his feet. 'I have seen him entering the Palais Royal followed by Dukes and Peers, Marshals and Bishops.' When the bubble burst the magician fled from France. 'I have seen his widow at Brussels, as reduced as she had once been proud and triumphant at Paris.'

The portrait of Cardinal Fleury, the King's tutor, who held the reins for twenty years after the death of the Regent, is painted from personal acquaintance. 'If any mortal was ever happy it was Fleury,' who retained health and power till his death at the age of ninety. He was moderate, mild, conciliatory, economical, a lover of peace, and in consequence less criticised and less envied than the flamboyant Richelieu and the greedy Mazarin. Like his contemporary Walpole he disliked adventures and wisely allowed war-weary France to lick her wounds. 'It was a happy time for all the nations which vied in commerce and the arts and forgot its past calamities.' Though no superman and lacking elevation, he gave his countrymen what they needed and craved. The long peace was interrupted by the War of the Polish Succession in which France vainly backed Stanislas for the throne, while the Emperor and Russia championed Augustus III, Elector of Saxony. A far graver enterprise was the War of the Austrian Succession, in which Fleury joined as regretfully as Walpole embarked on the Spanish war of 1739. The account of the campaigns provides the fullest treatment of any aspect of the reign. A long digression describes the romantic escapade of the young Pretender in 1745, details of which the author derived from an eye-witness of the expedition. Having seen England flourishing and contented under the Hanoverians, he extends his sympathy to the prince but not to his cause. London, he could testify, was full of traders and sailors who were far more interested in maritime successes than in events beyond the Rhine. A full account of Anson's voyage round the world was rewarded by the gift

of a gold medallion with the hero's head from his grateful
family.

Voltaire turns with relief to the eight years of peace between the
devastating struggles of the Austrian Succession and the still
fiercer flames of the Seven Years War. 'Commerce flourished
from St. Petersburg to Cadiz. The arts were held in honour. All
the nations were in touch. Europe was like a large family reunited
after disagreements.' Fresh misfortunes, however, seemed to be
heralded by earthquakes in Portugal, Spain and Morocco. In
Lisbon, where one-third of the city was destroyed and 30,000 lives
were lost, the Portuguese thought to secure God's mercy by
burning Jews and other innocents. The catastrophe left an
abiding impression on the historian who embodied his reflections in the most moving of his poems and the most popular of
his tales.

Though he had quarrelled with Frederick before the outbreak
of the Seven Years War, Voltaire pays unstinted homage to his
military abilities. 'Louis XIV was admired for resisting Germany,
England, Italy and Holland in union. We have witnessed a more
extraordinary event: an Elector of Brandenburg, standing alone
against the House of Austria, France, Russia, Sweden and half the
Empire; a prodigy attributable to the discipline of the troops and
the superiority of the captain. Luck can win a battle; but when the
weak resists the strong for seven years in open country and repairs
the gravest misfortunes, that is more than mere luck.' In this respect the war was without precedent. The second King of Prussia
was the only ruler who possessed a treasure and the only one who,
having introduced real discipline into his armies, had created a
new power in Germany. The father's preparations enabled the
son to seize Silesia. France's military record, by contrast, was
lamentable; Rossbach was a panic, not a battle. She was equally
unsuccessful in India where the conflict of British and French
brought misery on the gentle inhabitants. 'The Indians would
have been the happiest people on earth if they had not been
known to the Tartars and to ourselves.' The author's knowledge
of the East was scanty, but his lifelong interest in its teeming
peoples shines out again and again. Far worse than the defeat of
the French army in Asia was the breaking of Lally on the wheel.
Stirred to the depths by such an atrocity he strove to clear the

memory of the unfortunate General, and the news of the vindica-
tion of his honour was brought to him long afterwards on his
deathbed. Scarcely less poignant was his grief at the execution
of Admiral Byng for his inaction at Minorca, which, foreigner
though he was, he had striven to avert. 'In vain Marshal Richelieu
sent the author a declaration justifying the Admiral. It reached the
King of England, and Byng dispatched his thanks to the author
and to Marshal Richelieu.' Voltaire's lifelong detestation of
cruelty, irrespective of the victim's nationality or creed, is the
most attractive feature of his character. He even spares a crumb
of sympathy for Damiens, who jabbed at the King when he was
entering his carriage at Versailles. It was merely a political demon-
stration, explained the assassin, without intention to kill. He
thought his action would be pleasing to heaven: that was what he
had heard all the priests say. 'This wretch was just a crazy fanatic.
The only accomplices of these monsters are the fanatics whose hot
heads unwittingly kindle a fire which consumes feeble and dis-
torted minds.' Though he only inflicted a skin wound Damiens
was broken on the wheel, while his innocent father, wife and
daughter were banished.

The real criminals in the case, as Voltaire saw it, were the
priests, of whom the Jesuits were the worst. They had always been
a danger to the safety of kings, and long ago Aquinas had proclaimed that the Church might depose unfaithful princes. Monks
had only possessed power owing to the blindness of the laity,
and with the coming of the eighteenth century eyes had at last
begun to open. A religious Order which had made itself hated by
so many nations deserved its fate. To the general surprise the
Protestant King of Prussia retained them for his schools. 'He
thought them useful and was not afraid of them. He regarded
Calvinists, Lutherans, Papists, Ministers of the Gospels and
Fathers of the Society of Jesus with equal disdain, while establishing universal toleration as an axiom of government. He was
more interested in his army than in his colleges, knowing that
with his soldiers he could control the theologians, and not caring
whether a Jesuit or a pastor taught Cicero and Virgil to the
young.' A chapter subsequently added on the suppression of the
Order warmly applauds the wisdom and courage of Clement XIV,
who had demonstrated that it was as easy to destroy monks as to

create them. 'It raises one's hopes some day to diminish this crowd, useless alike to others and themselves, who vow to live at the expense of workers and who, though formerly very danger-ous, are now considered merely ridiculous.' The thought of a swarm of idle celibates in states requiring a larger population and every available pair of hands filled him, as it filled Frederick, with contempt.

On reaching the closing phase of the reign the historian selects two topics for special treatment—the acquisition of Corsica and the conflict with the Parlement of Paris. Writing after the death of Louis XV he criticises that unworthy monarch as he would not have dared during his life. Choiseul, the greatest political figure of the reign, who had added Corsica to France, had been banished at the instigation of the du Barry. 'Louis XV was too much in-clined to regard his servants as tools, to be broken at his pleasure. Exile is punishment, and only the law should punish. It is deeply regrettable when a sovereign punishes men whose offences are unknown, whose services are known, and who had public opin-ion on their side, which is more than their masters can often claim.' Though he had no love for the Parlement of Paris, he denounced the banishment of magistrates as illegal. Though never a demo-crat he believed in the separation of powers as wholeheartedly as Montesquieu himself.

A chapter on Laws, added when the author was seventy-five, preached the humanitarian gospel of which he was the most elo-quent champion in Europe. He had welcomed Beccaria's epoch-making treatise on *Crime and Punishment*, and had earned the applause of the world by his protests against the savage treatment of Calas and La Barre. All the most cultivated men in recent times, he declared, felt the need for milder laws, yet no great nation had disgraced itself by assassination and major crimes more than his own. The horror of the trial of the Knights Templars had been staged by priests with the approval of the Pope. Men had been governed like wild beasts by wild beasts, except perhaps during a few years under St. Louis, Louis XII and Henri IV. The more civilised they became the more they detested barbarism, of which so much still survived. Torture, which had been abolished in England, parts of Germany and recently Russia, was worse than death, and should be reserved for the Chastels and Ravaillacs, since the whole kingdom was interested in discovering the accomplices of such monsters. The confiscation of a criminal's property, on the other hand, was an abomination, for it punished the innocent children. 'Everywhere we witness contradictions, severity, uncertainty, arbitrariness, and the venality of the magistracy in France is unique.' He returned to the subject in a closing chapter entitled 'Progress of the Human Mind in the Century of Louis XV'. There had been great advances in the science of government, of which jurisprudence was a vital branch. 'The bar has often recognised the universal jurisprudence, derived from nature, which transcends all conventional laws and mere authority, dictated as they often are by caprice or need of money.'

Writing in 1768 at the age of seventy-four, the sage of Ferney detected rays of light spreading across the sky. The Academies encouraged youth by competition for prizes. Disease was coming under control, the Duke of Orleans had inoculated his children, and when Louis XV died of smallpox his grandsons were treated. Man learned by experience, however belatedly. Scientific discoveries opened up new vistas. The *Encyclopédie*, in which experts in many fields had collaborated, was the glory of France; it would have been of still greater value but for the fetters imposed by authority and the persecutions its contributors endured. Living till 1778 he witnessed the dawn of a new reign and greeted it with applause. 'All that Louis XVI has done since his accession had endeared him to France.' Little could he foresee that the century of reason, of which he was the most celebrated spokesman, would end in a deluge of blood.

Voltaire covered a portion of the same ground and reiterated some of his political convictions in his sixth and last historical work, *Histoire du Parlement de Paris*, published pseudonymously at Amsterdam in 1769. It was an inflammable topic, and the author had no craving for a martyr's crown. The title page carried the words 'par l'Abbé Big . . .', but it was easier for a camel to go through the eye of a needle than for the most celebrated of European writers to conceal his identity. The book was written at the instigation of the Ministry, then engaged in open conflict with 'Messieurs', as the members of the High Court were called. Though it is no shrill indictment of a venerable institution, the factual record helped to undermine what little was left of its prestige. The Parlement tried to prevent its circulation, and the booksellers who sold it were threatened with dire penalties. Despite the attempt at suppression, an eighth edition appeared in the following year. The decision to burn the book frightened the author into a repudiation of his offspring by a letter to *Le Mercure*. To produce such a book, he explained, it would have been necessary to toil in the archives: this he could not have done, since he had lived far away from Paris for twenty years and had busied himself with widely different tasks. He never scrupled to lie when his physical safety was at stake, and he concealed the fact that friends in Paris sent him material.

The Preface contains reflections on the task of the historian. Students should shed all prejudices so far as human frailty allows. They should remember that no government and no institution remains unchanged: the Empire, England, France, for instance, were utterly different to what they had been. The science of history was the measurement of change. All that we know with certainty is that everything is uncertain. Very few laws, civil or ecclesiastical, had retained their original form; for instance, there were neither Prince Bishops nor Cardinals in the early Church. The administration of justice exhibited a similar record of change. No society could exist without laws and law courts, but after the collapse of the Roman Empire in Gaul there was no law except that of the strongest. 'The centuries from Clovis to Charlemagne are merely a tissue of crimes, massacres, devastations, the foundation of monasteries, which arouse horror and pity.' The thesis of the book is the same as that of the *Essai sur les Moeurs*: the instinctive struggle of mankind towards enlightenment despite the resistance of secular and ecclesiastical tyrants.

The larger portion of the book is devoted to the Middle Ages, and the subject is so broadly treated that it almost amounts to a history of France. The first Parlements were assemblies of fierce warriors in arms and had nothing in common with the modern tribunal except the name. When Hugh Capet followed the Carolingians the anarchy became even worse, every feudal lord seizing all he could. The country was divided into seigneuries, and the great lords reduced most of the towns to servitude. The Kings themselves were scarcely more powerful than the nobility which made such laws as they pleased for their domains. Hence the differ-

ence of local customs, all equally ridiculous. In this ocean of barbarism the Kings summoned Parlements of the upper barons,
bishops and abbots, which formed the Estates of the nation. The
mass of the people had no share, for most of the towns and all the
villages were in a state of slavery.

The historian wrings his hands over the tyranny of the few, the
exploitation and miseries of the masses, who were almost as helpless as dumb animals. The whole book is a plea for the reign of
law as the only barrier against misrule. It is above all the misdemeanours of the Church which excite his anger and contempt;
the more backward the population, the more power it gained. All
Europe, except the Eastern Empire, groaned under this misgovernment. How could so many different nations live in such degrading
servitude under about sixty to eighty tyrants who had other
tyrants under them, and who in combination made up the most
detestable anarchy? 'I can only answer that most men are imbeciles, that it is easy for the successors of the conquerors, Lom-
bards, Vandals, Franks, Huns, Burgundians, being in possession
of castles, armed from head to foot on armoured horses, to keep
the population under their yoke. The masses, possessing neither
horses nor arms and immersed in earning their livelihood, believed they were born to serve.' Since every feudal lord adminis-
tered justice on his domains according to his pleasure, all Europe
lived in anarchy. Spain was divided between Mussulmans and
Christian Kings, Germany and Italy were in chaos, the quarrels
of the Emperor Henry and Pope Gregory VII inaugurated five
hundred years of civil strife by a new Papal jurisprudence which
turned Christendom upside down in order to dominate it. The
Pontiffs profited by the ignorance and confusion to sit in judgement on Kings and Emperors, who often invited them to arbi-
trate. Amid this barbarism the bishops established a monstrous
jurisdiction, and the ecclesiastics, being almost the only literates,
controlled the affairs of Christian states. The barbarian invasions
brought terrible evils, but the usurpations of a greedy and intolerant Church were much worse. If a testator omitted a legacy
he was deprived of Christian burial, his will was annulled, and
the Church seized what it thought he should have given. The
most atrocious of its crimes was the trial of the Templars, in
which fifty-nine Knights were burned to death in Paris; though

the Church pretended to abhor bloodshed it evidently did not feel the same objection to fire.

The newly created Parlement played no part in this unique trial, an eternal witness to the ferocity of Christian nations almost till our own times. Anything was better than anarchy, and the Parlements, as Courts of Appeal, performed a useful service. The first of them, instituted at Paris by Philip the Fair in 1302, was followed by Toulouse and Grenoble, Bordeaux and Dijon in the fifteenth century, Aix, Rouen and Rennes in the sixteenth, Pau and Metz, Besançon and Douai in the seventeenth. The youngest of the family was instituted at Nancy only fifteen years before they were all swept away by the French Revolution. Taken as a whole their record was no more creditable than that of the Monarchy and the Church. For Voltaire the Middle Ages were a melancholy epoch of anarchy, suffering and superstition, a discreditable intermezzo between the glories of the classical world and the Renaissance when the goddess of reason returned to a benighted earth.

On reaching the sixteenth century the historian found himself on familiar ground. Mercenaries were hired, judgeships were sold, the wars of religion began. The horrible practice of condemning citizens to death for their beliefs, a grim legacy of the Middle Ages, continued; though there was no Inquisition, the Vaudois were burned and the horrors were no less than in Spain. France was a vast charnel-house. The Chancellor L'Hôpital, leader of the *Politiques*, a man after Voltaire's own heart, shone out like a beacon in the storm. He was almost the only member of the King's Council who sincerely desired peace; but scarcely had he issued an edict of pacification than Catholic and Protestant divines alike preached a gospel of murder and a call to arms. The Guises and their *Ligue* were too strong for him, the Duke and his brother the Cardinal were murdered, and Henri III, the last of the degenerate Valois, soon joined them in a bloody grave.

Once again Voltaire pays homage to Henri IV. Using the Memoirs of Sully, the voluminous journal of Pierre l'Estoile, and the copious narrative of de Thou, he pronounces him the greatest of French kings. The Prince of Orange, Gustavus Adolphus and Charles XII would have been more inflexible in their religion, but Henri of Navarre possessed more humanity, and more political flair. His conversion, though a sacrifice of pride, was the price of peace. The Edict of Nantes proclaimed that there must no longer be any legal discrimination between Catholics and Huguenots; all could be good Frenchmen. Though the Parlement of Paris accepted him as King it was deeply divided, and attempts on his life were made. He was the greatest man of the age, and the last decade of his reign was the happiest era the Monarchy had ever known. Yet the wisest of rulers was no paragon in his private life, and his attempt to seduce the Princesse de Condé, a married woman and a member of the Royal Family, tarnished his name.

The survey of his successors repeats the verdicts of the *Siècle de Louis XIV*. The Regency was a time of chaos, weakness and coups. Concini, the Italian favourite of Marie de Medici, was murdered with the young King's consent, and his widow was executed. There were a few wise men, such as L'Hôpital and de Thou in the political arena, Montaigne and Charron in the world of thought; but the flicker they had kept alight had gone out. Louis XIII—ailing, ignorant and lazy—had to choose between an unloved mother and a detested Minister. He chose the latter because the ship of state needed a pilot. The portrait of the great Cardinal is severe though not unjust. Ungrateful, ambitious and tyrannical though he was, he rendered immense services to France. Ignored by the Iron Cardinal, the Parlement became omnipotent when the authority of the executive collapsed after his death. Mazarin was an even worse financier than Richelieu, his knowledge being limited to the methods of piling up a fortune. 'He was the first man in the world for intrigue and the last for everything else.' His one merit was that he was less vindictive than Richelieu and never shed blood. Moreover he played a useful part in defeating the Fronde, that ridiculous revolt in which Condé became the bane of France. When the young King took the reins firmly into his hands the Parlement gave no further trouble for a hundred years.

Once again, under Louis XV, it strove to limit the power of the crown, and once again it deserved to fail. It had tried his patience for years, for it always seemed jealous of the royal authority. Voltaire was no friend of monarchical absolutism, but he preferred it to the selfish pretensions of the jurists. Their power was broken by Chancellor Maupeou, and new Parlements were nominated, the members being paid by the crown instead of buying their

H

place. The book closes on a cheerful note, like the *Siècle de Louis XV*, for a new ruler was on the throne. 'All the Parlements were reformed, and it was hoped, though in vain, to reform the jurisprudence as well. The changes should have gone further, but they honoured the King who ordered them, the Ministry which framed them, and the Parlement which accepted them, and France witnessed the dawn of a wise and happy reign.' Blissfully unaware of what was in store for his countrymen, Voltaire died a happy man.

III. *The Story of Civilisation*

THE *Essai sur les Moeurs* is the largest and the most personal of Voltaire's historical works. While the other histories and biographies provide only occasional glimpses of his ideology, the survey of world history vibrates with his personality. To use a convenient adjective, it is as Voltairean as *Candide* itself. All his writings, declared Grimm, breathed love of virtue and a generous passion for human welfare, but in none was this passion more articulate. He has no use for 'drum and trumpet' history, and the military spirit fills him with disgust. Unlike the Abbé Saint-Pierre he propounds no scheme for the prevention of war, for he was too much of a realist to expect radical changes in human behaviour. His hopes centred in the *élite*, those of Rousseau in the common man. All progress had been the work of gifted pioneers who followed the light of reason and humanity. Here we find not only his considered estimate of institutions, celebrities and world-shaking events but his interpretation of the human drama in all its length and breadth. It was the first attempt of the kind. Bossuet's *Discours sur l'histoire Universelle* was a majestic theological tract, its scope strictly limited as regards both time and place. Since God always arranged the programme and pulled the strings of the puppet show, history was merely the implementation of the divine will. Blindly accepting Ussher's dating of the Creation in the year B.C. 4004, he built the first stages of his edifice round the Chosen People and the second round the Catholic Church. Voltaire, on the other hand, embraced the whole world so far as it was then known, and traced the ascent of man from primitive times till the century in which he was born. He was the first to envisage the story of civilisation as a connected whole of enormous length and to map out the main stages. The barrier between sacred and profane history was broken down. The outstanding merit of the book is its majestic design. Mere annals no longer sufficed. Like the *Siècle de Louis XIV*, but on an ampler scale, it is a blend of politics and culture. Though an amateur by the side of such giants of erudition as Scaliger and Ducange, Mabillon and Muratori, he possessed a wider range of knowledge, a broader perspective and a more original mind. 'I wish to discover what society was like, how people lived, what arts were cultivated, rather than to renew the tale of so many miserable conflicts, the commonplace of human misdoings.' The Supreme Being, having created the world, left man to work out his destiny; history was the record of his efforts. The book anticipates both the spaciousness and the superficiality of Wells' *Outline of History*, but surpasses it in the recognition of the significance of great men. 'A great but most unequal work,' declares Faguet, and few readers will be inclined to dissent.

The 'only begetter' of the treatise was Mme du Châtelet, 'the divine Émilie', who enjoyed Voltaire's society and shared his intellectual pursuits in her quiet house at Cirey for thirteen years. Her masculine intellect turned to science and mathematics, and her translation of Newton's *Principia* revealed her as more than a Parisian bluestocking. She complained of being bored by the current manuals which provided raw materials without illumination. 'I have enjoyed the history of the Greeks and Romans,' she declared, 'but I was never able to finish a detailed record of our modern nations. I find little but confusion—a multitude of minor events without connection, a thousand battles which settled nothing. I renounced a study which overwhelms without enlightening the mind.' Here was a challenge which her friend felt unable to decline. It was for the journeyman to collect the materials, for the architect to plan the house. The growing demand for historical instruction was proved by the success of the *Universal History*, a co-operative enterprise in sixty volumes published in London 1736–65. The Preface claimed that it was by far the most comprehensive work of the kind ever offered to the public. The best known contributor was George Sale, the translator of the Koran, who wrote on the East, and the principal novelty was the inclusion

of Asia and Africa, not as a mere background to the history of
Europe but in their own right. Since there was no trace of national
bias or religious propaganda the enterprise was widely welcomed.
There were several translations and abridgements, one of them by
Heeren, the High Priest of the Göttingen historical school.

'You wish to overcome your disgust for modern history since
the decline of the Roman Empire,' wrote Voltaire in the Preface,
'and to form a general idea of the nations which inhabit and deso-
late the earth. You only seek in this immensity what deserves to be
known—the mind and customs of the leading nations illustrated
by facts. My object is not to record in which year an insignificant
prince succeeded a barbarian ruler in an uncivilised state. Just
as one should know the principal actions of the sovereigns who
made their peoples better and happier, so we should ignore the
common type of kings. We have to select. History is a vast store-
house from which we take what we need, but we must choose
wisely. The illustrious Bossuet stopped at Charlemagne, dismissed
the Arabs as barbarians, and attributed everything to the Jews.
He ignored the ancient East, the Indians and the Chinese, though
we were nourished by their products, clothed in their fabrics, and
instructed by their moral fables.' Voltaire had no intention of
immediate publication, and he constantly bore in mind what
seemed likely to appeal to his friend. A few copies were made of
the elaborate Introduction, which he called *Discours Préliminaire*.
One of them, found among the booty taken by the Austrians at
the battle of Soor in 1745, was published at The Hague under the
title *Abrégé de l'Histoire Universelle*. It was an old manuscript he
had given to Frederick in 1739, explained the author, a first draft,
and the edition was full of errors. The work was expanded when
he settled in Switzerland and was published in 1769 under its
familiar title which had been suggested by Montesquieu.

'You would like philosophers to have written ancient history',
begins the Preface addressing Mme du Châtelet, 'because you
wished to read it as a philosopher, seeking useful truths, and you
say you have only found useless errors. Let us try to enlighten
ourselves together, to disinter some precious monuments beneath
the slag heaps of the centuries.' The first task was to inquire
whether our globe, as we knew it, resembled its former state.
Probably it had undergone as many transformations as human

communities. The sea had covered immense spaces now occupied
by mighty cities and bountiful harvests. Everywhere the waters
had receded or advanced. Were not the sands of the North African
and the Syrian desert once the basin of the sea? Could we not
say the same of the southern shores of the Baltic? Was not Sicily
once a part of Italy? Had not parts of Frisia and Southern France
been under the waves? Ravenna had been a busy port. Perhaps
'Atlantis' had existed and disappeared. Passing from the earth to
its occupants, the historian suggests that the legends of satyrs and
centaurs, half man, half beast, may have embodied traditions of
sub-human types which had long disappeared. There had probably
been little change in the span of life. There is for once a touch of
Rousseau in the remark that life was healthier and happier before
the growth of large cities and powerful empires. Much time had
been needed to build a society, to construct a language, to frame
laws. Warm climes were the first to be inhabited because they
provided most food: in northern lands it would have been easier
to find a pack of wolves.

More important than material factors were the thoughts of men.
With the emergence of societies a few gained leisure to reflect.
Belief in hell and a future life originated in Egypt, and Plato first
conceived of an immaterial spirit. Wisdom was a plant of slow
growth. The knowledge of a God, creator, rewarder, avenger, is
the fruit of reflection. All peoples were once as they are today in
many parts of Africa, America and the islands—lacking the notion
of one God, omnipresent and eternally existent. Atheists they
were not; they could not deny the Supreme Being because no
such idea entered their mind. Some adored the heavenly bodies,
trees, even serpents. The earliest deities were invented as pro-
tectors against disaster. Primitive religion was the child of fear.
There were many varieties of belief but also much imitation. Sun-
worship was widely spread, and great men were held to be gods or
the sons of gods. The majority of mankind had been and would
long remain imbecile, and the most foolish were those who sought
to find some sense in their ridiculous fables. Nature being everywhere the same, men had necessarily adopted the same truths and
errors in the attempt to explain what their senses perceived: for
instance, thunder was attributed to a superior being in the air.
The world was full of mysteries and our ancestors groped about

for a key. The serpent was often a symbol of immortality, shedding its skin and thereby renewing its youth. Dreams seemed to lift a corner of the curtain. Since there were good and evil deities, the latter had to be propitiated. It was a gloomy picture of childish superstition and chronic fear. Man had been always much the same: the differences were less than the similarities. There was no need for a social contract since there had always been some embryo of society. Though God had provided an organ of reason we had made little use of it. Yet some progress there had been: one of the greatest achievements had been the development of language from the inarticulate cries of animals.

After this thoughtful survey of primitive man Voltaire passes to the earliest organised communities. In some respects there was certainly an advance, but the lot of man was little improved, for in most cases he set out on the wrong road. If anything could be worse than anarchy it was the yoke of priests. Most ancient states—India, Persia, Egypt—were governed, or rather misgoverned, by theocracies which abused their powers. 'When a nation has chosen a tutelary deity, it has its priests who control the mind of the community in the name of their god. Hence the human sacrifices which have disgraced almost the whole world. Theocracy has carried tyranny to the most horrible excesses to which human madness can attain: the more such a régime claimed to be divine the more abominable were its actions.' Nearly all nations have sacrificed children to their gods. China was a shining exception, for theocracy was unknown.

In the survey of ancient civilisations, their customs and beliefs —Chaldeans, Persians, Syrians, Phoenicians, Scythians, Jews— the latter receive the lowest marks. Everything was miraculous in the history of the Hebrews. The Chinese, who had no need of priests, were a far better model. 'Their religion was simple, wise, impressive, free from all superstition and barbarism. Confucius introduced neither new opinions nor new rites. He was neither inspired nor a prophet, merely a wise magistrate who taught ancient laws. We speak sometimes, very incorrectly, of his religion. He had none but that of all the Emperors, the tribunals, and the first sages: he merely enjoined virtue and preached no mystery. His countrymen were not atheists.' Voltaire quotes approvingly an inscription on the temples: 'To the first principle, without be-

ginning and without end. He has made everything, governs everything, is infinitely good and just, illumines, sustains, directs all
nature.' Not a word about survival, rewards or punishments, for
they had no wish to affirm what they did not know. The historian
believed that in China he had found the simple and sufficient
Deism and the doctrine of the good life which he had always taught.

In comparison with this satisfying faith there was little to
admire in Egypt. 'I do not challenge the story of the Hebrew
books, which I duly revere,' declares Voltaire with his tongue in
his cheek; 'I am merely surprised that Herodotus, Manetho and
the Greeks do not mention the passage of the Red Sea.' The Pyra-
mids were symbols of despotism and vanity, servitude and superstition. Egypt's most significant contribution to mankind was the
belief in survival. Greece, too, was a land of fables, almost every
one of which was the origin of a cult, a temple, a festival. The
philosophers could shed little more light than the priests. 'Plato's
reputation does not surprise me. All the philosophers were unintelligible—he as much as the rest, but he was the most eloquent.
There was much nonsense in his teaching but also some very fine
ideas.' The Greeks had so much intelligence that they abused it,
yet, to their honour, the governments did not interfere with
thought. Athens admitted all the foreign deities and dedicated an
altar to the unknown god. Like all the nations they recognised a
supreme God—Zeus—as others recognised the sun, moon or
stars. While China realised the limits of human knowledge Greece
revelled in futile speculation. 'Man only loves the extraordinary
and the impossible.' The more incredible the miracles the more
readily are they believed. Voltaire underestimated the Greeks as
much as he overestimated the Chinese, for all speculation seemed
to him mere waste of time. No *Philosophe* took less interest in
philosophy. He saw the surface of things with his sharp eyes but
did not probe far underneath.

No chapter of ancient history receives so much attention as that
of the Jews, but the idea that a race with such a record could be
the Chosen People filled the historian with anger and disgust. It
was in large measure a story of massacres and miracles. All peoples
have had their prodigies, but we are only expected to swallow
those of the Jews. 'Let us confess that, humanly speaking, these
horrors revolt reason and nature. But if we consider Moses as the

instrument of the Deity we can only adore in silence.' Such sentences were inserted like mascots to diminish the danger to life and limb in an intolerant age. Of Rome only a hasty sketch is supplied to the fall of the Western Empire and the centuries of gloom. Rome's best legacy was her laws. In all countries noble souls and good lawgivers were to be found and the latest of them was Peter the Great.

The larger work, like the spacious *Discours Préliminaire*, begins in the East. Why should we ignore the spirit of these nations whom our traders have visited? The East was the cradle of the arts and had given everything to the West. The picture of China is fuller than in the Introduction, and the appreciation no less generous. To her we owed silk, printing, paper. 'All the vices existed there as elsewhere, but they were better kept within bounds by the laws. Obedience to the laws and adoration of a Supreme Being was the religion of the Empire and the Intelligentsia. The ethics of Confucius were as pure, as austere, as human as those of Epictetus. Atheists they were not.' The vices of India, in like manner, were of a milder character than ours. The work of Mohammed is described as the greatest and the most rapid revolution in history, greatly superior to that of the Jews since the Arabs brought the arts and sciences to the West. Nothing was new in Islam except the Prophet himself. Simple monotheism and resignation to the will of God proved attractive in many lands. Its teaching had no need of mystery and it alone forbade games of chance. The Prophet was a formidable and awe-inspiring man who established his dogmas by his courage and his arms, yet his religion became tolerant. The divine institutes of Christianity preached the pardon of offences, yet that holy and gentle religion had become the most intolerant and barbarous of all. Voltaire admired the early Christians and their simple life. No hierarchy existed for over a century; Bishops began under Ignatius; there was no evidence that Peter visited Rome, and the early Popes were as legendary as the early kings of France. No Roman Emperor wished to force the Jews to change their religion, and the Christians enjoyed a large amount of liberty. Diocletian, a fine soldier and a just lawgiver, deserved a better reputation, for he only persecuted after twenty years of toleration and then only for reasons of state.

For Voltaire the history of the Christian Church was a tragedy of degeneration from the teaching and practice of its founder. *Corruptio optimi pessima.* 'Our holy religion' was disfigured by pious frauds and impudent inventions: the Bollandist *Vitae Sanctorum* swarmed with them. 'So many errors, so many disgusting absurdities, with which we have been inundated for seventeen centuries have failed to harm it.' Constantine cuts a sorry figure, and the biography of Eusebius, his Court historian, was full of fables. He murdered members of his family, and the transfer of the capital sacrificed the West to barbarian invasions. The triumph of Christianity was followed by vengeance and atrocities. The 'Donation of Constantine' was a ridiculous imposture, but it had been accepted for centuries. Julian was a far better man. If anyone could have rejuvenated the Empire or retarded its fall it was he, but it was beyond his strength. He was not a soldier of fortune, like Diocletian and Theodosius. He was liked by his troops and was a fine general. No Emperor, not even Marcus Aurelius, was a juster ruler, and no philosopher was more sober or more moral. He reigned by the laws, valour and personal example. But his task was impossible. The Empire was plagued by barbarians and torn by religious disputes. There were more monks than soldiers—70,000 in Egypt alone. Christianity opened the doors of heaven but destroyed the Empire. The sects fought each other and they all attacked the old religion of the state—false and ridiculous, no doubt, but under which Rome had marched from victory to victory for ten centuries. 'Passing from the history of the Roman Empire to that of the peoples who tore it to pieces in the West is like leaving a proud city for a desert. Twenty barbarous jargons succeeded the noble Latin tongue, wise laws were replaced by savage customs, the fine roads decayed. A similar revolution occurred in the human mind: Gregory of Tours, the Monk of St. Gall and Fredegarius are our Polybius and Livy. The most insensate superstitions prevailed. The monks became lords and princes, possessing slaves who dared not complain. All Europe submitted to this enslavement till the sixteenth century and only emerged at the price of terrible convulsions.'

The weakest portion of the whole work is the picture of the Middle Ages, which Voltaire approached with the same pitying contempt as Gibbon; the Ages of Faith were for both the Age of Darkness, though Voltaire managed to discover a few gleams of light. The Christian Church had made a good start, but its sublime moral precepts had been overlaid by speculations which no one could understand. With the ascent from the catacombs to temporal power simplicity was laid aside. Orthodoxy usurped the place of morals, and the priests imprisoned the mind of Europe in an iron cage. 'Notre crédulité fait toute leur science,' he had written in his early drama *Oedipe*, and he applied this sweeping condemnation to ecclesiastics of every age and creed. The Roman Church, wealthy, worldly and intolerant, unworthy representative of the gospel of love, was the worst offender. Natural religion was enough for him, and in his opinion it should be enough for everyone. Dogmas were not only superfluous but the worst foes of faith, for how could we hope to express the divine in formulas and ritual? The simpler a religion the more it appealed to him. For this reason he preferred Islam to Christianity and Confucius to both. The intellectual life was his province, and he ruled it like a king. The spiritual life was beyond his range.

The Eastern Church was little better than the Western, and it was torn asunder by the Iconoclastic controversy. Monasteries served a useful purpose as places of refuge for those who sought a quiet life. The reign of Charlemagne, like that of Constantine, was one of the greatest proofs that success is held to cover injustice and to confer glory. With his Thirty Years War with the Saxons, his massacres and his forced conversions, he could only be described as a brigand: Christianity was cemented by blood. While he founded the Vehmgericht, more abominable than the Inquisition, the Caliph, Haroun-al-Raschid, greatly surpassed him in justice, culture, and humanity. 'The Church has made a saint of this man who shed so much blood, who despoiled his nephew, and was suspected of incest.' The Franks had always been barbarians, and barbarians they remained after their conversion. Their laws were a blend of ferocity and superstition. 'Imagine deserts where wolves, tigers and foxes devour a few timid cattle: such was Europe for many centuries.' False Decretals found acceptance; Bishops were temporal lords with their lands and serfs, and sometimes they marched to battle. The only ray of light in this dark world was the Benedictine Order which preserved books by making copies. A new method of gaining power was invented when

Confession began in the sixth century, for priests thus learned secrets which they could turn to account. One of the most despicable institutions of the Middle Ages was the Ordeal.

The history of the great events of this world, laments Voltaire, is the history of crimes: there is not a century which the ambition of laymen and ecclesiastics has not filled with horrors. Nothing is so enduring as superstition. So obsessed was he with the barbarism of the Middle Ages that he failed to recognise that the Christian Church saved more than it destroyed and was the main civilising agency in Europe for a thousand years. The glories of Gothic art meant nothing to the eighteenth-century mind. The millennium from Augustine to Machiavelli was a lamentable interruption in the march of mankind which had begun in Asia and had been carried forward by Greece and Rome. Progress towards enlightenment and humanity had to be fought for at every inch of the way by an *élite* who dared to cast off the stifling yoke of tradition and to think for themselves. The age of authority was inevitably the age of darkness, for only the unfettered use of reason, man's noblest faculty, can guide us onward towards the light.

Voltaire breathes a sigh of relief when amidst these horrors he meets some great man who rescues his country from servitude. 'I know of no one more deserving of respect than Alfred the Great, if all that is told of him is true. He ordered books from Rome, could read Latin and studied history. His place is in the front rank of heroes useful to the human race which, without these extraordinary persons, would always have remained like wild beasts. The Normans were brigands and pirates, the Moors were cruel, but no more cruel than the Christians, and they fostered the arts and sciences. The Byzantine Empire of the eighth and ninth centuries was a scandal. Except Julian and two or three others, which of the Emperors did not disgrace the throne by abominations and crimes? The Eastern Empire was wider, had larger resources and was more powerful than that of the West, but on the moral plane there was little to choose between them. In the annals of the Papacy the sisters Marozia and Theodora were the dregs of humanity. Everyone carried arms and quarrelled over the spoils. The Albigenses, the Vaudois, the Lollards, were accused of heresy and vices as a pretext for seizing their property.

'You will notice that in all disputes between Christians since the birth of the Church Rome has always favoured the doctrine which most completely subjected the human mind and annihilated reason. I only speak historically, leaving aside the inspiration and the infallibility of the Church which are outside the domain of history. Yet its record was not wholly vile. It had often condemned savage customs, and despite all the scandals there has always been more decency and dignity there than elsewhere. There was scarcely a monastery in which good men were not to be found. When free and well governed it could give lessons to others. Among its merits was the recognition of talent regardless of birth. In the long line of Popes the proudest were the men of the lowest class.'

On reaching the Crusades the historian lays about him with a big stick. The Pope promised forgiveness of sins if men indulged their dominant passion of pillage, and though they carried the Cross the Crusaders were mere vagabonds. 'This epidemic fury proved that the human race was to be spared no curse.' Jews were massacred *en route*. Compared with this horde of undisciplined adventurers Saladin stands out as a pillar of light, chivalrous to his defeated foes. The sack of Constantinople in the Fourth Crusade, the crown of iniquity, opened the door into Europe for the Turks. Far the best of the Crusaders was St. Louis who receives unexpected and extravagant praise. 'He seemed destined to reform Europe, to render France civilised, victorious, the model for mankind. His piety did not unfit him for his royal duties nor did his wise economy prevent liberality. He combined deep policy with exact justice—perhaps the only sovereign to deserve such praise.' Prudent and firm in council, intrepid in war, merciful, no human being came nearer perfection. Yet this paragon had a bee in his bonnet: he longed to go on a Crusade and attacked Egypt with no other excuse than that it was not a Christian land. He was taken prisoner, ransomed, and spent four years in Palestine. Even now he had not enough crusading, and on his return to France he began to plan a new adventure which ended with his death in Tunis. The Crusades were the tomb of countless Europeans, the cause of vast expenditure, a crescendo of folly and fanaticism. Even more atrocious, though on a smaller scale, were the persecutions of the Albigenses, the establishment of the Inquisition, and the trial of the Knights Templars on vague charges with the unavowed purpose of seizing their property.

From the madness of the Crusades and the cruelties of the Church Voltaire turns with relief to Switzerland as a blessed island of peace, which had preserved the simplicity and poverty of primitive communities in a greater degree than any other land. Never had a people fought longer or better for its liberty which it seemed likely to preserve. Equality prevailed: not of course the equality of servant and master, artisan and magistrate, plaintiff and judge, but the equality by which the citizen is subject to the law alone and which defends the weak against the strong. They had no need of a professional army, no itch for aggression. Their mountains were their ramparts, every citizen a defender of the fatherland. There were very few republics in the world, and they owed their liberty to their rocks and the protecting sea. Unfortunately men were rarely worthy to govern themselves.

. With the fifteenth century Voltaire reverts to his usual whipping-boy, the Church. The Great Schism made it the laughing-stock of Europe, and the Council of Constance disgraced itself by a hideous crime. The authority conferred by superior culture gave the clergy and the Orders power which they used for their own interests. Yet the vices arising from opulence and the disasters which flow from ambition reduced most of them to the level of ignorance of the laity, and learning was left to the universities of Bologna, Paris and Oxford. The doctrines of Wycliffe, largely anticipating the Protestants in his attack on confession and indulgences, transubstantiation and ecclesiastical opulence, had reached Bohemia where the torch was carried forward by Hus and Jerome of Prague. The guilt of their death, which led to the fierce Hussite Wars, must be divided between the Emperor Sigismund, who violated a safe-conduct, and the Church which practised the burning of heretics.

If *La Pucelle*—a satire not on the Maid but on the superstitions which had gathered round her name—was the worst of Voltaire's literary offences, he made partial amends in the *Essai sur les Moeurs* which speaks of her with admiration and respect. France was in chaos. It was necessary to resort to a miracle. A gentleman of Lorraine, Baudricourt, believed that he found in a young barmaid in Vaucouleurs a person suited for the role of inspired warrior. 'This Jeanne d'Arc, generally thought to be a shepherdess, was a young inn servant, possessing sufficient courage and intelligence to undertake this enterprise which became heroic. She was examined by women who found her a virgin, and by doctors of the University and councillors of Parliament who declared her inspired. Whether she deceived them or whether they were clever enough to enter into the artifice, the crowd believed and that sufficed. The King was crowned, the foreigner driven out, the Maid wounded, taken prisoner and burned. A man such as the Black Prince would have honoured and respected her courage. The Regent Bedford thought it necessary to encourage the English. She feigned a miracle and Bedford pretended to believe her a sorcerer. Accused of heresy and magic, this heroine was worthy of the miracle she had feigned. Having saved her King, she would have had altars in the heroic times when men raised them to their liberators. It is not only cruelty which causes such deeds, but also the fanaticism of blended ignorance and superstition which has been the malady of nearly every century. Burnings for sorcerers were not uncommon. Let the citizens of the great city where the arts of pleasure and peace reign today, and where reason begins to prevail, compare these times and complain if they dare. That reflection is suggested by almost every page of this history.'

At the close of his survey of the Middle Ages, Voltaire pronounces judgement on their cultural achievements which, seen through the spectacles of the *Aufklärung*, he could hardly be expected to approve. The *Divina Commedia* is described as a queer poem but with natural beauties in which the author rises above the standards of his century and his subject. Petrarch is more to his taste. Scholastic theology, on the other hand, a bastard daughter of the philosophy of Aristotle, often mistranslated and misunderstood, damaged the cause of reason more than the Huns and Vandals. The Flagellants excite particular scorn. That there were no police tells its own story. Great virtues were to be found in all states, on the throne and in the cloister, among knights and ecclesiastics, but no nation can be happy without the reign of law. Liberty began in the towns, and when Philippe le Bel created the States-General and the Parlement of Paris the people began to count for more.

The fall of Constantinople in 1453 evokes no regrets. The

Byzantine Empire, shattered by the felon blow of the Fourth Crusade, had become a welter of cruelty, weakness and super-stition. Mahommed II, a good linguist and a lover of the arts, was wiser and more civilised than was generally believed, and the Sultans were no more cruel or despotic than many Christian rulers. He allowed the Greeks to choose their Patriarch and to retain some of their churches at a time when no Christian ruler would permit a mosque in his capital. A digression on the Jews in Europe combines a rebuke to their persecutors with dislike of their ways. 'This people should interest us, since we derive from them our religion and many of our laws and customs; but they had always been greedy moneylenders who regarded usury as a sacred duty.' Even the thieving gipsies have a chapter to themselves in this panorama of the fifteenth century.

On reaching the threshold of modern times Voltaire enters on more familiar ground. Since real civilisation, in his opinion, only emerged in seventeenth-century France he stresses the dark spots on the Renaissance sun. Florence and Milan under the Medici and the Sforzas were a hotbed of assassination and poison-ing, superstition and debauchery. He pronounces no opinion on the stories of incest and poisoning in the Vatican of Alexander VI, but he has no doubt that Caesar Borgia was a monster. The first Medici Pope, Leo X, possessed the merit of loving classical cul-ture, but the prelates lived like voluptuous princes and everyone was bent on having a good time. He is not impressed by Savona-rola, half impostor, half fanatic. 'We regard with pity these scenes of horror and absurdity to which we find no parallel among the Greeks, the Romans or the barbarians. It is the fruit of the most infamous superstition which has ever brutalised mankind and of the worst of governments. We have only recently emerged from this darkness, and light does not shine everywhere. Even the brain of Pico della Mirandola, that prodigy of learning, was con-fused.' France fared even worse than Italy for it could boast of little culture. The elaborate portrait of Louis XI, the first French ruler to call himself *Le Roi très Chrétien*, is darkly coloured. Yet, despite his cruelty, his iron cages and his superstition, he did some good, preferring little men to the nobility and effecting many improvements. His reign was the transition from anarchy to tyranny. 'Barbarism, superstition, ignorance, covered the face of

the earth except in Italy. It was the interest of Rome that the
peoples should be imbecile. The impudent charlatanism of the
doctors matched the imbecility of Louis XI, which in turn was
commensurate with his tyranny. But this was true of almost all
Europe.' The best energies of the sixteenth-century mind went
into literature. Guicciardini was the Italian Xenophon. *Orlando
Furioso* was in every way superior to the *Odyssey*, though both
exhibited the same fault—undisciplined imagination. Tasso's epic
on the Crusades possessed more interest, variety and grace than
the *Iliad*. In painting, architecture and music Italy surpassed the
Greeks, and in sculpture she was not far behind. In Shakespeare
there was far more barbarism than genius.

Voltaire's cool appraisement of the Reformation is equidistant
from that of both Catholics and Protestants: it was neither a disaster nor an emancipation of the mind. For their respective doctrines and controversies he felt nothing but contempt. Luther's
role is minimised, for the forces behind him were greater than the
man. 'If one had told him he would destroy the Roman religion
in half of Europe he would not have believed it. He went further
than he intended.' A vital factor in the Reformation was the dislike of the financial exactions of Rome. Though the historian has
no love for the Wittenberg reformer he applauds his courage.
'One can only laugh in pity at his treatment of the Pope—as if to
say: Little Pope, you are an ass.' He was right to reject sacerdotal
celibacy but wrong to condone the double marriage of Philip of
Hesse. The Anabaptist revolt arouses the detestation which the
historian felt for violence and fanaticism in every camp. Yet the
conflagration quickly burned itself out. 'The Anabaptists who
began with barbarism ended in gentleness and wisdom,' by
which he means that they became pioneers of religious toleration.
Since the sects were all equally mistaken there was no moral
justification for one to persecute another. 'The Papists ate God
for bread,' he sneers, 'Lutherans bread and God, the Calvinists
bread but not God.' Such hairsplitting speculations were unworthy of civilised beings. In an autobiographical fragment
written in the third person in 1776 he declares that 'M. de Voltaire
always fought atheists and Jesuits'.

Among the Reformation Fathers Zwingli finds most favour,
and the Zurich Senate wisely approved his rejection of the Real

Presence. 'Happy people which in its simplicity left the decision to its magistrates on a subject which neither they nor Zwingli nor the Pope could understand.' The magistrates of Berne, after listening to the debates, followed suit. Switzerland, to which the author owed so much, is described as the steadiest of nations. Calvin, on the other hand, was a tyrant by temperament, and the author's blood boils at the thought of the murder of the Spanish doctor Servetus who was passing through a foreign city. 'They differed about the Trinity, and theological hatred is the most implacable of all.' The austere fanatic who dominated Geneva would himself have been burned had he remained in France. If the same sanguinary spirit had always presided over religion Europe would be a great cemetery. Where Calvin burned one the Spanish Inquisition burned its thousands.

Henry VIII is denounced as a cruel tyrant, a barbarian, a slave of his caprice. The judicial executions under Edward VI and Mary were also a horror. Elizabeth soiled a fine reign by the murder of Mary Stuart. Yet to canonise the latter was a fanatical imbecility: she was merely the martyr of her adultery, the murder of her husband, her own imprudence. The Virgin Queen was a successful ruler but not a great character. 'Her people were her prime favourite; not that she really loved them, but she felt that their safety and glory depended on treating them as if she did.' Infinitely worse than the execution of Mary Stuart was the Bartholomew Massacre—'that abominable tragedy, half the nation slaughtering the other half, dagger and crucifix in hand', with Charles IX shooting at his subjects from the windows of the Louvre. That orgy of blood was followed by the chaos of the religious wars. The Court under Henri III was a sink of intrigue, debauchery and superstition. The King moved about with his minions. Catherine de Medicis brought an astrologer from Italy, sorcerers plied their trade, and wax figures were pricked in the heart to hasten the death of rivals and foes. The Protestants were at any rate austere.

Spain under Philip II was even worse off than France under the degenerate Valois, and the comparison of that besotted ruler to Tiberius was not undeserved. The gravest of his crimes was his treatment of his subjects in the Low Countries to whose courage and endurance eloquent tribute is paid. 'His bloody despotism

I

was the cause of their greatness. The Flemings are good subjects and bad slaves. The mere dread of the Inquisition made more Protestants than all the writings of Calvin, for this people is not prone to innovation or unrest. There are proud spirits whose quiet fidelity is stimulated by difficulties. Such was the character of William the Silent and of his descendant William III. He possessed neither troops nor money to resist a monarch such as Philip II, but the persecutions supplied his needs. The blood of Egmont and Horn was the cement of the Republic.' The fanatic on the Spanish throne rewarded the assassin of the heroic Prince of Orange. The morals, the simplicity and the equality in the Republic resembled Sparta. No episode in modern history except the reign of Henri IV excites the historian to such enthusiasm.

Voltaire's pulse always quickened at the mention of Henri IV. No Jesuit, he declares with Père Daniel in his mind, could write history faithfully: the King was amorous but not effeminate. Gabrielle d'Estrées, the most colourful of his mistresses, called him 'mon soldat'. Brave and generous, he was the only man who could save his country. His humanity after victory should win all hearts. He had only the justice of his cause, his courage, and some friends to sustain him. He had to fight Spain, Rome and France simultaneously. The *Ligue* was a gang of fanatics. Since they were taught that heresy is the leprosy of the soul, Henri III was a leper who ought not to rule. The conversion of the hero, recommended as it was by friends who remained Protestants, is approved for the sake of the unity and prosperity of France. 'If he had not been the bravest prince of his time, the most clement, the most upright, the most honourable, his kingdom would have been ruined. France needed a prince who knew both how to wage war and to govern in peace, who was acquainted with all the wounds of his state and could supply the remedies, and she found him in Henri IV. He wished every peasant to have a fowl in the pot on Sundays.' With the aid of Sully's wonderful finance he reduced taxes, paid off debt, repaired roads, reformed justice, instituted the lace industry. Above all, the rival religions lived at peace with one another. He was the greatest figure of the age, the arbiter of Europe. Yet several attempts were made on his life and he was wounded by Chastel in 1594. Regicide was approved by the Jesuits and their teaching was carried out by Ravaillac. The King only became dear to the nation after his death when his loss was increasingly felt. The more his career was studied in the Memoirs of Sully and others who had known him, the more he was beloved. The reign of Louis XIV was a far greater age but Henri IV was much the greater man. Each day added to his glory, and the love of the French people for the best of their rulers became a passion. 'By a mild and firm administration he kept all the orders of the state together, all the factions quiescent, the two religions at peace, the people in plenty. Thanks to his alliances, his treasure and his arms, the balance of Europe was in his hands.' All these advantages were lost under the Regency of his widow and their son Louis XIII, pious, mild, scrupulous, suspicious, but quite unable to stretch the bow of Ulysses. Of Richelieu there is only an unflattering sketch, and we are told that he was among the lovers of Marion Delorme. At this point the historian lays down his pen, for the story was continued in greater detail in *Le Siècle de Louis XIV*.

The significance of the *Essai* was promptly recognised at home and abroad. 'I have followed Voltaire,' testified Robertson in his celebrated survey of Europe before Charles V; 'he exhibited not only salient facts but the conclusions to be drawn.' The impact on the mind of the French intelligentsia is most eloquently described in Condorcet's *Vie de Voltaire*, written shortly after his master's death. 'The *Essai* will always delight for its range of subjects, the limpid style, the love of truth and humanity, the profound ideas. It is the record not of the centuries but of what one wishes to know. Few works are more useful for sound education. We learn to despise superstition, to dread fanaticism, to detest intolerance, to abhor tyranny. He was the brightest ornament of the *Encyclopédie*, the noblest monument ever designed by the mind of man. He was one of the very small number of men in whom the love of humanity was a veritable passion. We owe to him a conception of history vaster and more instructive than that of the ancient world. In his writings it has become, not a list of events or revolutions, but a picture of human nature itself, the philosophic embodiment of the experiences of all nations and ages. He introduced true criticism, showing that the natural probability of events must be kept in view, and that the philosophic historian must not merely reject miracles but assess the motives of belief in those which deviate from the common order of nature. We shall always remain his debtors for freeing history from the heap of marvels accepted without proof. He demonstrated that the absurdities of polytheism were never more than the faith of the masses, and that belief in one God, common to all peoples, did not require a supernatural revelation. He also showed that all peoples recognised the great principles of morality, becoming purer as men became more enlightened. The sentiment of active goodness and benevolence dominated him throughout life.'

Voltaire would have desired no other tribute. He had his failings and limitations but the core of the man was sound. He loved his fellows and strove for their happiness according to his lights. Far more than the elder Mirabeau he deserved the title *l'ami des hommes.* Since God has given us reason, 'as He has given feathers to birds and fur to bears', it was our duty to use it in the service of mankind. After the opening phase in which he lived for the delights of literature and society he became a reformer, preaching the gospel of enlightenment not merely as an intellectual luxury of the *élite* but as the guide to everyday life. To such enlightenment historians, scientists, and the great religious teachers made their specific contributions. The historian, like the statesman, worked with a practical end in view. Who before Voltaire, asked La Harpe, had conceived the sublime idea of demanding from the centuries what each had done for mankind, tracing, amid the chaos of revolutions and crime, the slow and painful steps of reason and the arts? No one else before the nineteenth century except Condorcet attempted such a task. Though the *Essai sur les Moeurs* cannot be classed with the *Decline and Fall of the Roman Empire,* the *Wealth of Nations,* the *Critique of Pure Reason,* and the *Reflections on the French Revolution,* among the supreme achievements of the eighteenth-century mind, it yields to none in the novelty and amplitude of its design.

IV. *The Philosophy of History*

In addition to his major historical works, Voltaire published a multitude of historical sketches and studies which form a large part of the four volumes of the *Dictionnaire Philosophique* and the ten volumes of the *Mélanges* in the latest edition of his writings. Many of them merely abridge or expand what he had said elsewhere, but there is also a good deal of new material. The first impression of the reader is the range of knowledge unapproached by any of his contemporaries, his vivid interest in every aspect of human activity past and present. The second arresting feature is that he is never content with the task of a recorder, and that he applies his measuring rod of reason and human welfare with confident assurance to each object in turn. Though not the earliest thinker to reflect on the processes and the lessons of the ages, he was the first to apply the scale of values elaborated by the *Aufklärung* of which he was the recognised oracle; and he was the inventor of the phrase 'the philosophy of history.'

His attitude must be studied against the background of European thought since the end of the Middle Ages. Though the word *Aufklärung* was a German invention the school which it denoted originated in France. The cult of reason, the pride in enlightenment, the buoyancy of spirit which dominated the middle decades of the eighteenth century, were the culmination of tendencies which dated back to the Italian renaissance, when the trend of thought began to shift from the theocentric to the anthropocentric approach. A new and vivid interest in the mind and body of man, his triumphs and his potentialities, came into being after the long and almost unchallenged reign of Augustine. The secularisation of thought which has coloured the modern era had commenced, but the process was not and could hardly be expected to be continuous. The sixteenth century was not the first act of a new drama but an intermezzo between two sharply contrasted eras. Luther's mind was as mediaeval as the approach of Machiavelli and Rabelais was empirical and modern. The world of today, in which the Christian Church no longer occupies the centre of the stage, dates from the scientific discoveries and the rise of the bourgeoisie during the seventeenth century. For the first time since the civilisations of Greece and Rome the state and the citizen moved into the front place, and man began to feel confidence in his power to shape his destinies. The rivulets of modernism were swelling into a mighty stream. 'The establishment of perfect liberty of thought and discussion', declares Bury in his *History of the Freedom of Thought*, 'may be considered the most valuable achievement of modern civilisation.' It was at any rate the mother of science and scholarship.

The various factors which contributed to the secularisation of thought provided the substructure for a philosophy of history. The classical world had produced historians of the first rank, but they knew too little of the past and present of any civilisations but their own to gain perspective. Ebb and flow, regional advances and retrogression, were a familiar experience, but even the greatest thinkers of the pre-Christian era failed to envisage a developing civilisation obeying ascertainable laws. Unable to peer far back or far around they lacked incentive to gaze into the future. The intellectuals of the Middle Ages had a longer span behind them, but they knew little about it and felt little desire to learn. The author of *De Civitate Dei* was more concerned with the salvation of a section of the human family in another world than with the fortunes of the whole of mankind on earth. The Middle Ages, of which Bossuet was the last majestic echo, visualised history as a succession of events shaped by the hand of God for the fulfilment of His purposes. So long as the notion of an all-controlling Providence remained without challenge, the idea of progress as a human achievement shaped by a combination of material factors and spiritual energies was impossible. Christianity had supplied history with meaning by teaching that it led up to a goal, but the process was regarded as the ultimate responsibility of God.

The crucial difference between the ideology of the Middle Ages and the climate of the modern world was that the latter entertained a loftier opinion of the powers of man, a deeper appreciation of the opportunities for self-realisation and happiness afforded by his life on earth, independently of another existence in another world. The substitution of a robust belief in man's progress towards perfection by the exercise of his mind and will for the traditional teaching of external control of his destiny could hardly take place before the eighteenth century, when the anthropocentric conception had had several generations to take root. Though the process may be broadly described as a shift from a supernatural to a natural interpretation of history, the new philosophy of progress—that mankind is advancing in the right direction and is likely to continue his advance—also contained an element of faith. How many assumptions there were in the philosophy of the

Aufklärung which transcended the bounds of pure reason or experience, how an exaggerated optimism in regard to the nature of man succeeded the pessimism of the Middle Ages, is more fully realised in the twentieth century than in the nineteenth, which has been labelled the Century of Hope.

The conception of an advance towards enlightenment, which formed the core of Voltaire's philosophy of history, was worked out by a succession of thinkers of the seventeenth century before it became the dominant creed of the Age of Reason. Bacon heads the list with the argument that the modern era was the old age of humanity and therefore possessed longer experience and riper wisdom. Descartes, mathematician and metaphysician, joined in the challenge to authority, proclaiming the supremacy of reason and the uniformity of nature, and Cartesianism has been described as a Declaration of the Independence of Man. Despite the transcendentalism of Pascal and Bossuet the empirical spirit continued its march, and Newton's discovery of the reign of law in the physical universe seemed to many to destroy the hypothesis of external intervention.

By the close of the seventeenth century reflection on the problem of progress had become general and gave rise to the celebrated controversy in France on the respective merits of the Ancients and Moderns. The tournament was opened by Perrault, who argued for the superiority of the latter on the ground that they inherited the wisdom of the ages and were continually adding to the treasure-house of mankind. Writing when Louis XIV was at the height of his prestige, he asserted that the race had advanced so far towards perfection that there were not many things for which he and his contemporaries need envy future generations. The man of letters was vigorously supported by Fontenelle, the man of science, who scouted the hypothesis of degeneration on the ground that as the modern world had moved beyond the limits of the ancient through the increase of experience so posterity would assuredly witness a further advance. Humanity had known a period of youth but would never experience the decline of old age. Admiration of the ancients in no way involved the thesis that man had reached the limits of his endeavour. Even more uninhibited in his championship of the doctrine of indefinite progress was the Abbé Saint-Pierre. Best known to posterity as

the author of the first detailed plan for the organisation of perpetual peace, he was regarded by his contemporaries as one of
the boldest thinkers of the opening decades of the eighteenth
century. If the seventeenth had been above all the age of science
the eighteenth was the age of sociology, inaugurated by Saint-
Pierre, developed by Montesquieu, Rousseau, and Adam Smith,
and culminating in Herder and Burke. Man had the right and the
duty to seek individual happiness and social well-being, and enlightened reason was his only guide. A Deist who did not believe
in the occurrence of miracles, Christian or non-Christian, the
Abbé never doubted the capacity of *homo sapiens* to work out his
own salvation. His *Observations on the Continuous Progress of Human
Reason*, published in 1737, reminded his readers that the race had had
only seven or eight thousand years to develop its powers. Civilisation was in its infancy and the future offered limitless possibilities.
Progress had begun with the Greeks, had been interrupted by
wars, superstition and intolerance, and was only resumed when
the broken threads were picked up during the sixteenth century.
Superstition was now declining and wars could be averted by his
proposals for perpetual peace. Give man a chance and he would
seize it with both hands. Living before Rousseau began to preach
democracy, Saint-Pierre taught that wise government and just
laws could mould society to a fairer pattern.

When Voltaire focused his attention on the study of history in
middle life, he inhaled the bracing air of the *Aufklärung*. The keenest intellects in France, with the exception of Rousseau, were in
general agreement that man was in large measure master of his
fate, that civilisation was a good thing, that conditions of life
could be improved, and that there were no insuperable obstacles
to a further advance. Humanists and humanitarians, the High
Priests of the Enlightenment, were thrilled by the thought of the
power of reason when the fetters of tradition were struck off and
the fear of penalties for new opinions was removed. No transcen-
dental philosophy of history was required, for there were no final
causes, no original sin, no need for a divine revelation, no
infallible Church. Man should use his wits, study, criticise, experiment, judging everything by its actual or potential service to
humanity. The Utilitarian approach proclaimed by Bacon was
adopted by the *Philosophes*, who in turn prepared the way for

Bentham. Their task was to create an intellectual atmosphere which would sooner or later compel governments to think only of the happiness of their people. Political revolution was not in their programme, for the age of democracy in France did not dawn till 1789. There was no objection to autocracy if the ruler was benevolent and understood his trade.

The message of the *Philosophes* was set forth at greatest length in the *Encyclopédie* planned in 1745, announced by Diderot in a prospectus in 1751, and published in seventeen volumes 1751–65. The first two instalments were denounced by the Church and suppressed as hostile to authority and religion. Booksellers were forbidden to sell them, but there was no veto on the continuation of the enterprise. A volume appeared each year, the seventh coming down to G in 1757. Beginning with 2,000 subscribers, the sales rose to 4,000, but the opposition waxed with the success. In 1759 the Government forbade the sale of the seven volumes and the printing of any more. At this stage d'Alembert withdrew, explaining to Voltaire that vexation had worn him out. The stout-hearted Diderot remained at his post as sole editor, contributing many articles himself. Offers of shelter arrived from Berlin and St. Petersburg, but the enterprise, with its large staff, was too big to transplant. The ten remaining volumes appeared *en bloc* in 1765, followed by ten volumes of plates. Yet it was not the *Encyclopédie* of the editor's dreams, for the timid Genevese printer had omitted or mutilated everything which seemed to him likely to provoke trouble. Owing to the ban the copies were privately distributed, but the purchasers were ordered to surrender their copies to the police. Despite official sabotage the work was reprinted at Geneva and Lausanne, and selections from the work appeared. No large-scale publication of the eighteenth century aroused so much antagonism or attracted such widespread attention.

The Bible of the *Aufklärung* furnished the first authoritative summary of human knowledge. The popularity of Bayle's *Dictionnaire Historique et Critique* had revealed the demand for information among the intelligentsia of Western Europe, but its significance pales in comparison with the *Encyclopédie*. The former was the work of a single brain, the latter of a brilliant team. The former virtually ignored natural science, the latter eagerly welcomed the latest discoveries. The former breathed a mild scepticism, the latter a militant rationalism. The former was primarily a book of reference, the latter primarily a manifesto. Leslie Stephen's description of the eighteenth century as an age of sound common sense may have been true of England, but it was a very inadequate characterisation of France. The *Philosophes* were men who dreamed dreams and saw visions, rationalists who proclaimed a rival set of dogmas, crusaders determined to sweep away the accumulated rubbish of the past. Never before or since has such an enterprise exerted so profound an influence on the thought of the time, for its comprehensiveness rendered it as indispensable to statesmen and civil servants as to scholars in every land. It helped to transform the authoritarian, aristocratic and traditionalist France bequeathed by Louis XIV into the bourgeois, critical and self-confident nation which carried through the revolution of 1789. Human nature was conceived as infinitely impressionable, as capable of responding to the inspiring guidance of the *Philosophes* as it had long obeyed the blind leaders of the blind.

Voltaire's article on History appeared in the eighth volume of the *Encyclopédie* in 1765, and his other contributions ceased in 1758. There were two reasons for withdrawing support from an undertaking which in its general purpose of spreading enlightenment commanded his entire sympathy. In the first place this knight of the spirit was always apprehensive as to his personal safety. The assertion in the article on Geneva that among the Genevese clergy were Deists and Socinians created an uproar in Swiss Protestant circles. It was wrongly attributed to Voltaire, for it was written by d'Alembert; but it was inspired by the veteran who had chosen Switzerland for his second fatherland. Having quite enough on his hands with his Catholic foes, he thought it wise to limit his risks by ceasing contact with the most explosive literary enterprise of the age.

The second reason for withdrawal was more plausible, for Voltaire was now busy with an Encyclopaedia of his own on a limited scale. The origin of the *Dictionnaire Philosophique*—in its final form the largest of his works—is sometimes traced to the supper-parties at Potsdam, when every subject in heaven and earth came up for review. The plan took shape in the little *Dictionnaire*

Philosophique Portatif containing seventy-three articles, published anonymously in 1764. The book grew under his hands till he was almost an octogenarian and eventually filled nine volumes. Its debt to the *Encyclopédie*, to which he frequently paid tribute, is obvious. In this vast medley of wit and wisdom, learning and prejudice, there is as much history as philosophy. Though many articles are abridged or expanded from his earlier writings, the *Dictionnaire Philosophique* is as essential for our understanding of Voltaire as a historian as his purely historical works.

To the contention of the Church that man had fallen and needed redemption the *Philosophes* retorted that he had risen by his own efforts. They formed a new church with a new gospel—humanitarian, optimistic, materialistic. The whole enterprise was planned as an attack on obscurantism and the dead hand of the past, a plea for the unfettered use of reason and the reign of law. 'You have no idea of the influence which Voltaire and his great contemporaries had in my youth,' remarked Goethe to Eckermann in 1830, 'and how they governed the whole civilised world.' Next to Diderot, the editor of the *Encyclopédie*, and d'Alembert, his chief of staff, the most eminent though not the most frequent contributor was Voltaire. There is no evidence that he had been consulted about the enterprise, and he was the guest of Frederick the Great at Potsdam when the first two volumes appeared. Diderot he had never met, and his acquaintance with d'Alembert was slight, but the editor needed the prestige of his name. A few articles from his pen on minor topics appeared in the fifth volume. Not till d'Alembert visited him in Switzerland in 1756 was his interest seriously aroused and his collaboration assured.

By far the most important of his contributions was that on History. 'Herewith the article,' he wrote to d'Alembert in 1756. 'I fear it is too long. It is a subject on which it is difficult not to write a book.' History is defined as a record of facts purporting to be true. There is also a history of opinions which is merely a collection of human errors. The history of the arts is the most rewarding when it stimulates further invention. The earliest attempts were the stories of fathers to children which are only to be believed if they do not affront plain common sense. With the passage of time the fable was embroidered and the truth was lost in a haze of superstition. All the stories of human origins which

had floated down the ages were absurd. Who could believe that
the Egyptians had been governed first by gods, then by demigods
for many centuries before their first king? The legends of the
Greeks and Romans, even of the Merovingians, were equally
ridiculous. Prodigies should be recorded, not as facts as by Rollin,
but as illustrations of human credulity. Since our acquaintance
with the ancient world was extremely limited imagination had had
full play. We must not always ask for what was mathematically
demonstrable and must content ourselves with the maximum of
probability. Marco Polo's account of the size and population of
China was disbelieved till it was confirmed by Portuguese navi-
gators and by the unanimous testimony of a thousand eye-witnesses since the sixteenth century. That some events which at first
sounded incredible had actually occurred was illustrated by the
most dramatic incident in the epic of Charles XII. 'If only two or
three historians had related how the King and his domestics
fought against an army of Janissaries and Tartars in his house at
Bender I should have suspended judgement. But having conversed
with eye-witnesses and receiving no contradiction of the story,
one has to believe it, for it contradicts neither the laws of nature
nor the character of the hero.' Probability and even improbability
could be turned into certainty by adequate evidence, but nothing
should find credence which plainly violated the ordinary course of
nature. Festivals, however ancient, medals and monuments, however imposing, did not guarantee the truth of what they were
designed to commemorate. The speeches attributed to ancient
leaders were obviously fakes, and a historian had no more right
to concoct orations than to invent facts. Faked memoirs, the latest
example of which was attributed to Mme de Maintenon, were
common, and of the '-ana' and anecdotes which were so popular
only one per cent contained a grain of truth. The first test to be
applied was inherent probability, the second the nature and
volume of the evidence. The historian should steer an even course
between scepticism and credulity.

If the first obligation was to sift the wheat from the chaff, the
second was to differentiate between the important and the unim-
portant and to search for the teachings and warnings of the past.
'If you have nothing to tell us except that one barbarian succeeded
another on the banks of the Oxus and Jaxartes, what is that to us?'

The story of errors, crimes and misfortunes was useful particularly for rulers and their advisers. Thus the catastrophe of Pultowa proved the folly of invading the Ukraine without supplies. Insensate ambition brought its own punishment. One advantage of the study of modern history had been to teach rulers that from the fifteenth century there had always been a rally against a predominating Power, a system of equilibrium unknown to the ancients. Another point to bear in mind was the usurpations of the Popes, the scandals of their schisms, the madness of their controversies, persecutions and wars and the horrors caused by this madness. If the young were not taught all these things, and if a few scholars were not aware of them, the public would still be as imbecile as in the time of Hildebrand, and the calamities of the past would inevitably recur since few precautions would be taken to avert them. 'Eliminate the study of history and we may see more St. Bartholomew massacres in France and new Cromwells in England.' Bayle had been blamed for criticising David, but the man after God's own heart deserved to be shown up as a criminal. Bad actions should never be concealed or excused. Constantine, Clovis and Henry VIII were monsters of cruelty. God had not compiled the history of the Jews, which was full of crimes. 'One must admit that if the Holy Spirit wrote this history He did not choose a very edifying subject.' The historian must be not only a recorder but a fearless judge.

Voltaire returned in 1768 to the theme of the duties and difficulties of the historian in a treatise entitled *Le Pyrrhonisme de l'Histoire*, which is included in the sixth volume of the *Mélanges*. Portions are reproduced from the article on History, but the detailed comments on historians, ancient and modern, which form the most valuable aspect of the work are new. 'I desire neither an unmeasured scepticism nor a ridiculous credulity,' he began. The main facts in a narrative or a tradition might be true though certain details might be false. The historian must use his own discretion. 'As children we are taught a chronology which is demonstrably false. We are taught everything except how to think. Even the most learned and eloquent writers have sometimes embellished the throne of error instead of overthrowing it. Bossuet is a conspicuous example in his miscalled *Histoire Universelle* which is only the record of four or five peoples, above all of the little Jewish nation which was either ignored or justly despised by the rest of the world. We should speak of the Jews as we speak of the Scythians and the Greeks—one race among many; nevertheless he relates everything as if a Cornish historian were to say that nothing occurred in the Roman Empire except in the province of Wales. We know that Providence extends over the whole earth and is not confined to a single race. Bossuet was like an artisan who systematically sets false stones in the gold. Heresies, he declares, were foretold by Christ. There is no mention of heresy in the Gospels, since the word dogma never occurs. Christ proclaimed no dogma. For instance He never said that His mother was a virgin, and there is not a word in the Gospels which bears any relation to the Christian dogmas we know. Fleury's *Histoire Ecclésiastique* was equally misleading, like a mud statue adorned with some gold leaf. I have thrown away the mud and kept the gold.' The bulk of his history was soiled by fairy tales which an old woman would nowadays blush to repeat, such as the miracles of Gregory Thaumaturgus, though he never says that he believes them. 'Is it to insult the human race, I had almost said to insult God Himself, that the Confessor of a king dared to relate these detestable absurdities?'

Passing from the moderns to the ancients Voltaire renews his campaign against the Jews. Were the historical books of the Old Testament inspired? Was God really the historian of the Jews? After citing with gusto a number of miracles and crimes he concludes with his customary grimace. Jewish history is the history of God and has nothing in common with the feeble reason of all other peoples. Since the history of Egypt was not the history of God, and since her religion was largely the worship of animals, we were allowed to make fun of it. With the Greeks we were on firmer ground. Herodotus was reliable on what he had seen, not on what he had heard. Yet the significance of the Greeks and Romans should not be exaggerated, since they were young in comparison with the Indians and Chinese, Chaldeans and Egyptians. The Romans deserved study chiefly because they were our legislators, and their laws, like their language, were still in use. After the dissolution of the Roman Empire came the Middle Ages—a barbarous history of barbarous peoples who, in becoming Christian, did not become better. Yet the Roman historians

must be read with critical eyes. Livy's stories were rightly treated
as fairy tales, but what of Tacitus and Suetonius? Were the atrocities attributed to Tiberius, Caligula and Nero true? 'Must I believe the report of a single man writing long afterwards that
Tiberius, nearly eighty years old, after a decent and strenuous life,
plunged into debauchery?' Similar stories of the Regent Orleans
and his daughter had circulated in his own time, but he never believed them. In relating such improbabilities the historian should
have said they were rumours and suspicions. How could we
believe that Agrippina frequently offered herself to her son at
midday and that Seneca saved the young Nero from incest by
introducing Acte? Is there any need to believe that he sent his
mother out in a leaky boat in the Bay of Naples? Was it not more
probably an accident? We should be equally prudent not to believe all the stories of Elagabalus.

That so many fables had become embedded in history was not
solely the fault of the historian: credulous human nature was
also to blame. 'If men were reasonable they would only ask for
histories which would stress the rights of peoples, the laws by
which a father can dispose of his property, events of national
interest, treaties which connect neighbouring nations, the progress
of the useful arts, the abuses to which the majority are exposed by
the few. But this method is as difficult as it is dangerous. It would
involve effort for the reader, not relaxation. The public prefers
fables, so it gets them. *Audi alteram partem* is the obligation of
every reader of the story of rival princes who disputed for a crown
or of religious bodies which anathematised each other. Nothing
succeeds like success. If the *Ligue* had won Henri IV would be
known as a little Béarn prince, debauched and excommunicated.
If Arius had won at the Council of Nicaea and Constantine had
taken his side Athanasius would now be regarded only as an
innovator, a heretic, a fanatic who attributed to Jesus what did not
belong to him. The Romans decried Carthaginian sincerity and
the Carthaginians suspected the *bona fides* of Rome. To judge fairly
we should have the archives of the Hannibal family. I should also
like the Memoirs of Caiaphas and Pilate and those of the Court of
Pharaoh; then we should learn how it defended itself for having
ordered Egyptian midwives to drown all the Hebrew males, and
what was the use of this order for the Jews who only employed

Jewish midwives. It affords us pleasure to read the writings of the Whigs and Tories. According to the Whigs the Tories betrayed England; according to the Tories every Whig sacrificed the state to his interests. Thus if we are to believe these advocates there is not a single honest man in the nation.' The recriminations in the Wars of the Roses were even worse. Voltaire was interested but not wholly convinced by Horace Walpole's *Historic Doubts concerning Richard III*, and wrote to the author. 'You seem to have a liking for this hunchback. I can well believe he was not so bad as he was painted, but I should not have liked to have dealings with him.' That Pope Alexander VI was poisoned and that Caesar Borgia prepared poison for several of the Cardinals strikes Voltaire as improbable. There were many fakes in very recent times such as the Testaments of Colbert and Louvois, and this should make us careful about the tales of antiquity.

Falsification was the deadliest sin. 'So many men of letters have been the worst calumniators, if one can give these fanatics that title. For they fear nothing when they lie. The Jesuits above all carried impudence to the furthest limit in the days of their power. When they were not writing *lettres de cachet* they wrote libels. It is these men of detestable character who brought on their *confrères* the blows which have destroyed them and have ruined for ever an Order which contained some men worthy of respect. This multitude of calumnies piously vomited over Europe from infected mouths who call themselves sacred is beyond comprehension. After assassination and poison that is the gravest and that has been the commonest crime.' It was characteristic of Voltaire that his treatise should close with a kick at the Order whose suppression by Clement XIII provided one of the keenest satisfactions of his later life. *Pyrrhonisme de l'Histoire* was a plea, not for wholesale scepticism, but for caution in dealing with statements outside the limits of our experience. He was right to stress the fact that a mass of primitive ideology had floated down the ages. His mistake—and that of the Century of Reason—was to draw the frontiers of experience too narrowly. To the *Philosophes* it was unthinkable that what seemed inconceivable to them would appear credible to any other thoughtful mind. Voltaire saw only what was visible to the naked eye and was convinced that there was nothing else, ignoring the truth enshrined in the most illuminating of Pascal's *Pensées*: *Le coeur a ses raisons que la raison ne connait pas*. The sub-rational and super-rational intuitions, ecstasies and torments of the soul were beyond his range.

In addition to the dissertations on *Histoire* and *Pyrrhonisme*, scores of articles in the *Dictionnaire Philosophique* are directly concerned with the events and problems of history, while many more employ historical illustrations to explain a point. There is a closer resemblance both to the *Dictionnaire Critique* of 'the immortal Bayle, the glory of the human race', than to the *Encyclopédie*, but it is more personal and therefore more interesting than either. Though ranging over an immense variety of subjects the author's ideology is simplicity itself. The philosopher, he declares, never claims to be inspired by the gods. The earliest and wisest of sages was Confucius who proclaimed rules of conduct which have never been bettered and who never attempted to deceive. Belief in a Supreme Being was the foundation of all the world religions, for how else could the world be explained? That was all we knew and all we could ever know. Everything else was guesswork and most of the guesses were bad. The article on Fanaticism concludes with a tilt against the limitless credulity of mankind. 'Someone declares that there is a giant seventy feet high. Then the doctors discuss the colour of his hair, the size of his thumb, the length of his nails. They shout, intrigue, fight. Those who maintain that his little finger is only fifteen inches in diameter burn those who argue that it is only a foot across. But, gentlemen, remarks a passer-by modestly, does your giant exist? What a horrible doubt! cry all the disputants. What blasphemy! What absurdity! Then they arrange a short truce to stone the passer-by, assassinating him with the most edifying ceremonial, and then resuming their conflict about his little finger and nails.'

Voltaire was academically interested in religious practices and beliefs, like Sir James Frazer and other anthropologists a century later, viewing them as a naturalist examines specimens in a glass case. Seen in broad perspective the story of mankind might be described as a duel between the philosophers and the priests. 'Poor creatures that we are! How many centuries were needed to acquire a little reason?' The article on the Jesuits written shortly after the suppression of the Order decides that they deserved their fate. There had been, and still were, men of rare merit in

K

their ranks. What then had caused their downfall? 'Pride. Their contempt was incredible for all the Universities in which they had no part, for all the books they had not written, for all ecclesiastics who were not *hommes de qualité*—of which I have been witness a hundred times. Nearly all their polemical writings breathe an indecent arrogance which estranged the whole of Europe. Everything could be forgiven except pride. Hence all the Parlements, whose members have usually been their pupils, seized the first opportunity of destroying them, and the whole world rejoiced in their fall. Under Louis XIV it was not considered good form to die without passing through the hands of a Jesuit.'

Voltaire's attitude towards marvels was conditioned by his philosophic and scientific beliefs. No eighteenth-century thinker was less of a sceptic, for there was no place in his brain for the penumbra of doubt which is the essence of scepticism. 'I believe in God—not the God of the mystics and the theologians but the God of Nature, the architect of the universe.' He fully accepted and continually proclaimed the argument from design: *tout ouvrage démontre un ouvrier*. As Paley was to argue in his *Evidences of Christianity*, if we found a watch we should conclude that there was a watchmaker. *Si Dieu n'existait pas il faudrait l'inventer*. Voltaire's deism, however, was as coldly intellectual as Rousseau's Savoyard Vicar in *Émile* was instinctive and emotional. When the *Être Suprême* had created the world and furnished it with the laws of nature man had to look after himself: there was no need for intervention by a subsequent revelation or recurrent miracles. Christ, who never claimed to be the son of a virgin, was a moral teacher, *un enthousiaste de bonne foi* like Socrates and George Fox. All experience, confirmed by recent scientific discoveries, pointed to the rigid uniformity of nature. Yet man was not a machine. The Divine Architect had provided him, not only with the material surroundings which rendered life possible, but with reason, the most precious of His gifts, to enable him to transcend the limitations of his physical needs.

The fullest exposition of his theology is provided in the article *Dieu* in the *Dictionnaire Philosophique*. 'Dans cet univers, composé de ressorts dont chacun a sa fin, on découvre un ouvrier très puissant, très intelligent.' Is this supreme artisan everywhere or in a particular place? How can we answer with our limited understanding? 'My reason indicates a Being who has arranged the matter of this world, but it cannot prove that He made the matter and created it from nothing. All the sages of antiquity believed matter to be eternal. So I believe the God of this world is also eternal. We shall never know more than Cicero. We feel we are in the hands of an invisible being; that is all, and we cannot advance a step further. It is insolence to wish to guess what this being is and how it operates.' Is the soul immortal? Here again we can only guess. The lengthy article on *Âme* reviews various hypotheses and concludes that no one can be sure.

Voltaire's theology is further explained in the elaborate dissertations on Miracles and Prayers. The Supreme Being is as distant and unapproachable as the stars. 'A miracle is a contradiction in terms; a law cannot be both immutable and violated. Why should God disfigure His own work? And why for particular individuals? Is it not the most absurd of follies to imagine that the Infinite Being intervenes in favour of three or four hundred ants on this little heap of mud? God's favours are vouchsafed in His laws. It would be a confession of His weakness, not His power. To attribute miracles to Him is to insult Him.' Since miracles are impossible prayers are futile and indeed irreverent: that they are as old as mankind is no proof to the contrary. 'We know of no religion without prayers. All men have invoked the help of a divinity. The *Philosophes*, more respectful towards the Supreme Being, only pray for resignation: that is all that seems suitable between the creature and the Creator. But philosophy is not made to rule the world, since it speaks a language which the crowd cannot understand.' The Eternal has His designs from all eternity. If the prayer is in accord with His immutable will it is useless to ask what He has already resolved to do. If one prays for the contrary of His intention, it begs Him to be weak, frivolous, arbitrary, inconstant. If you request something just He owes it to you and will do it; if unjust, it is an insult. 'We pray to God only because we have made Him in our image, treating Him like a pasha, a sultan whom one can irritate or appease. All the nations pray to God; wise men resign themselves and obey.' For Voltaire Newton was the greatest man who had ever lived, for he had discovered that the reign of law prevailed throughout the universe.

A further reason for believing that the task of the Supreme

Being began and ended with the act of creation was the human record, a sorry tale of cruelty and injustice, tyranny and superstition. If a benevolent God had been continually intervening, would not the picture have been very different, the sum of human agony vastly less, the tempo of progress far quicker? History reveals not the guidance and goodness of God but the struggles and the follies of man. Horror had succeeded horror, wars and massacres never ceased, and nature was as merciless as man. The Lisbon earthquake was the latest illustration of the blind forces at work. Was Lisbon with its 30,000 victims more wicked than Paris? The longer Voltaire reflected on the lamentable course of history the stronger grew his conviction that the Supreme Being, if indeed all-powerful and benevolent, could not be pulling the strings for it did not make sense. His philosophy of history is as clearly outlined in *Candide* as in the dissertations on History and Pyrrhonism.

Why the Creator had made so imperfect and suffering a world we could not guess; but man had been furnished with two precious compasses to help him on his tempestuous voyage—reason and conscience. The latter was indeed the voice of God. Voltaire accepted the conception of *Jus Naturale* formulated by the Roman jurists, adopted by the Christian Church, and retained by almost all modern publicists. The moral law, like the laws of nature, was immutable, since it was inscribed on the human heart. Though it was the least observed of laws it revenged itself on those who infringed it. Man was free to choose and he was punished if he chose wrong. 'It seems as if God has implanted it in man as a bulwark against the law of the stronger and the destruction of mankind by war, intrigue and scholastic theology. Morality comes from God and is everywhere the same: theology comes from man and is everywhere different and foolish.' Since a future state of rewards and punishments after death could neither be proved nor disproved it was wise to act on the assumption of its reality. Voltaire's advocacy of religious toleration halted at the preaching of atheism, since without belief in God it might be impossible to govern the masses. He would have chuckled over Gibbon's celebrated aphorism that to the people all religions were equally true, to the philosopher all equally false, to the magistrate all equally useful. Since man was born neither good nor bad, edu-

cation, example, the government, circumstances determined his
course towards virtue or crime. 'In morals', we read in the article
Athée, 'it is much better to recognise a God than not. It is certainly in the interest of all men that there should be a Divinity who
punishes what human justice cannot repress. But equally clearly
it would be better not to recognise a God than to adore a barbarian
to whom human beings are sacrificed as in many nations. Atheism
and fanaticism are twin monsters capable of devouring society.
But the atheist retains his reason while the fanatic is the victim of
chronic madness.' Theism, the middle way between atheism and
fanaticism, was the best and the most widely spread of religions,
for even polytheism did not exclude belief in a Supreme Being.
Confucius was a theist, and Mohammed, charlatan though he was,
proclaimed the unity of God and rescued almost the whole of Asia
from idolatry. It never occurred to Voltaire that his hypothesis—
that the world was created by a Supreme Being and then left to
sink or swim—was just as vulnerable as the rival ideologies which
he despised.

Voltaire was neither a determinist, an optimist, nor a pessimist,
but, to use an expression of George Eliot, a meliorist: things could
—but not necessarily would—be made better. His mind was far
too critical to believe in a golden age in the past, like Rousseau,
or in the future, like the utopians from Saint-Pierre to Condorcet.
Homo sapiens was a teachable but unruly animal. 'Every day the
question is asked if a republican government is preferable to a
monarchy. The dispute always ends with the admission that it is
very difficult to govern mankind.' The masses, he believed, were
unlikely to change. Progress had always been and would doubtless
remain an uphill fight waged by a minority of fearless crusaders.
History was above all the record of the swaying conflict between
reason and unreason. 'Reason survives despite all the passions
which war against it, despite all the tyrants who would drown it in
blood, despite all the impostors who would destroy it by superstition.' Reason was not the only instrument of progress, for the
urge towards greater material comfort and refinement of manners
was strong. 'Men have always asserted that the good old times
were much better than our own,' he wrote in the article *Anciens et
Modernes*. 'Happy is the man who, free from all prejudices, is sensible of the merits both of ancients and moderns, appreciates their

beauties and recognises their faults.' He might have said with
Molière, *Je prends mon bien ou je le trouve*—in China, in Greece, in
Rome, above all in Western Europe since the Renaissance. *Le
Mondain*, written in 1756, saluted the amenities of civilisation and
satirised the illusion of a simpler and purer age. 'Oh! le bon temps
que ce siècle de fer!' he exclaims ironically. Life in Paris, London,
Rome, was infinitely preferable to the Garden of Eden. 'Good
wine never tickled Eve's joyless throat. Our ancestors knew
neither silk nor gold. Is that a reason for admiring them? They
lacked industry and comfort. Was that virtue? It was pure ignorance.' Free from financial anxieties Voltaire was something of an
Epicurean, enjoying the good things which life in a cultivated
society could offer but without excess. He would have agreed
with the verdict of Talleyrand in old age that no one who had not
lived in France before the Revolution had known *la douceur de la
vie*. No one appreciated more fully the privileges of civilisation
and no one was more conscious how precarious were its foundations.

Voltaire's chief disciples in the sphere of historical interpretation were Turgot and Condorcet. When the former lectured at
the Sorbonne in 1750 on the successive advances of the human
mind he had probably read the portions of the *Essai sur les
Moeurs* which had appeared in *Le Mercure*. Though the work of a
young man these astonishing discourses presented a more profound and illuminating analysis of the story of man than Voltaire
was ever to achieve. He was more capable of understanding beliefs
which he did not share and he was more conscious of organic
continuity. For the facile teleology of Bossuet he substituted
the operation of innate energies and general causes. Historical
study must begin not with events but with societies, which were
shaped firstly by the nature, passions and reasoning faculties of
man, secondly by environment, geography and climate. Every
era was connected with all that had gone before, slowly moving
forward towards perfection, through alternations of repose and
confusion; the units did not move at the same pace owing to
differing circumstances. While Voltaire attributed progress
exclusively to reason consciously warring against ignorance and
passion, Turgot argued that man had moved instinctively in the
right direction without visualising the goal. History was a record

of crimes, follies and misfortunes, yet man had learned from his experiences. Even in dark times such as the Middle Ages there had been some advance. Christianity had been the agent, not the enemy, of civilisation. Turgot anticipated Comte's law of the three stages of intellectual development—theological, metaphysical, positive—the whole race moving steadily forward all the time. The Discourses at the Sorbonne steered a middle course between Voltaire's conception of haphazard advance and Condorcet's naïve belief in perfectibility. Compared with the wide vision of Turgot Condorcet was a doctrinaire. So strong was his faith that he composed his *Esquisse du Progrès de l'esprit humain* in prison while awaiting his summons to the guillotine. He was the last voice of the *Aufklärung*, of the Age of Reason, of the Century of Voltaire.

Before the Grand Old Man of eighteenth-century France closed his eyes in a blaze of glory at Paris in 1778, the Romantic Movement had begun with Rousseau, Richardson, and the young lions of the *Sturm und Drang*. The supremacy of reason was challenged, not from the angle of faith, but from the testimony of the human heart. The individual thinkers and lawgivers whom Voltaire had saluted as the principal agents of progress were dethroned in favour of the *Volk*, creating its laws and institutions, languages and beliefs as it went along. A new standard of values was worked out and applied. The technique of the Rationalists had been to produce their yardstick and to censure what failed to pass the test. The deepest urge of the Romanticists was to admire and give thanks. While the *Aufklärung* had looked back with disdain and forward with confidence, the Romantic school revelled in tradition and glorified the Ages of Faith. The *lumen siccum* recommended by Bacon—the cold, clear light of day—was replaced by stained glass windows resplendent with colour and symbolism. The Romantic Movement was above all the renascence of wonder. Our ancestors were not fools, declared Justus Moser, the champion of social continuity. Just as the critical empiricism of Voltaire constituted an advance beyond Bossuet, so the Romantic Movement, the foster-mother of the Historical School, represented an equally significant advance towards the reconstruction and interpretation of the past. Only by approaching the story of mankind without doctrinaire presuppositions could historians do justice to every type and every stage. In the nineteenth century the bed of Procrustes was removed to the lumber-room. If France had contributed the conception of progress, Germany inaugurated the evolutionary method, in which the historian exchanges the role of the advocate, the prosecuting counsel and the judge for that of interpreter. The scornful astonishment with which Voltaire would have greeted Ranke's celebrated aphorism that all the centuries are equal in the eyes of God is a measure of the deeper insight of the nineteenth. The Age of Understanding was to bury the Age of Reason as the Age of Reason had challenged the Ages of Faith.

Bibliographical Note. The most recent edition of Voltaire's writings is that of 1878 in fifty-two volumes edited by Louis Molland. Desnoiresterres, *Voltaire et la Société au XVIII Siècle*, in eight volumes, remains indispensable. Of subsequent major works that of Georg Brandes is the most important. Among the shorter studies those by John Morley, David Friedrich Strauss, H. N. Brailsford, Alfred Noyes, Gustave Lanson and Émile Faguet are of interest. J. Churton Collins, *Voltaire, Montesquieu and Rousseau in England*, and Raymond Naves, *Voltaire et l'Encylopédie*, contain new material. Reusch, *Der Index der verbotenen Bücher*, summarises the reactions of the Vatican. The best discussions of his philosophy of history are by Meinecke, *Die Entstehung des Historismus*; Sir J. F. Stephen, *Horae Sabbaticae*, Vol. II; J. B. Black, *The Art of History*; Paul Sakmann, 'Die Probleme der historischen Methodik und der Geschichtsphilosophie bei Voltaire', *Historische Zeitschrift*, Vol. 97, and Alfred von Martin, 'Motive und Tendenzen in Voltaires Geschichtschreibung', *Historische Zeitschrift*, Vol. 118. The best and most recent survey of philosophies of history throughout the ages is in Fritz Wagner, *Geschichtswissenschaft*. A new edition of Voltaire's correspondence, containing thousands of hitherto unpublished letters, is appearing under the editorship of Theodore Besterman.

For the political, social and intellectual background Cobban, *History of France*, Vol. I; Lough, *An Introduction to Eighteenth Century France*; Harold Nicolson, *The Age of Reason*; Spink, *French Free Thought from Gassendi to Voltaire*; Kingsley Martin, *French Liberal Thought in the 18th Century*, are useful.

7

THE GOLDEN AGE OF FREEMASONRY

THE Century of Reason was the golden age of Freemasonry. The cult had begun in obscurity, and after the French Revolution it almost ceased to count. Why did it flare up in the eighteenth century and spread like a rash all over Europe, cross the Atlantic and invade Asia? What was the secret of its appeal? Had it a message for the mind and heart of man? Did it exert any appreciable influence on politics? In a word, did it help to make history? The answer is that it was and still is above all a social phenomenon, a product of the gregarious instinct with a spice of romance thrown in. It derived not from the mystery cults of the ancient world but from the craft guilds of the Middle Ages, when the masons who built our cathedrals occupied an honoured place in our national life. Like the Trade Unionists of later date, members gathered to discuss their technical secrets and common interests and to enjoy each other's company. There was no esoteric doctrine and no impact on public life. Sixteenth-century records prove that the lodges consisted simply of artisans proud of their professional skill. Why then did some of them change their name from masons to freemasons? The latter word occurs as early as the fourteenth century, and the prefix was occasionally added to members of other crafts. Perhaps it merely denoted that they were free men in an age when traces of serfdom survived, or skilled artisans authorised to co-operate in the construction of some important edifice. The title may have had various interpretations according to time and place. The lodges, which were numerous in the seventeenth century, no doubt differed in membership, some of them admitting as honorary members men who never worked with their hands. Like similar associations they drew up rules, partly technical, partly general, such as exhortations to godliness, honest work, and mutual aid.

Under the Stuarts the mediaeval craft guild gradually moved away from a purely professional basis, and in 1717 four small London lodges united to form a Grand Lodge—the Mother Grand Lodge of the world—and elect a Grand Master. Here was the decisive break with the craft tradition and the inauguration of communities which had little in common with a mediaeval guild except the name. There was now a governing body, whose authority was soon recognised by a majority of existing and newly created London lodges, and Ireland and Scotland quickly established Grand Lodges of their own. Henceforth a lodge was a corporation which any suitable person might join, a blend of a club and a church, with ethical, social and religious ideals, secret ceremonies of initiation and secret signs of mutual recognition. Though the members who formed the new Grand Lodge were socially obscure and their resources were meagre, the vision and drive of a French refugee enabled it to develop beyond their wildest dreams. On the revocation of the Edict of Nantes in 1685 Desaguliers, a Huguenot pastor, escaped with his family and became a Minister of a Huguenot community in London. His son followed him into the Ministry after taking a degree at Oxford, where he was invited to lecture on 'experimental philosophy'. In 1713, at the age of thirty, he settled in London, became a member of the Royal Society, delivered popular lectures on science, conducted experiments, made inventions, and knew Isaac Newton who became godfather to his son. Invited to lecture to the King at Hampton Court, he was appointed Chaplain to the heir to the throne. Two years after the creation of the Grand Lodge he became its Grand Master and remained the soul of English freemasonry till his death in 1744.

The movement owed part of its success to its steady loyalty to the House of Hanover. George I had only been three years on the throne when the Grand Lodge was founded in London, and there were recent memories of the Pretender's attempt to seize the crown. The Huguenots had special reason to oppose the *protégé* of the Bourbons who had deprived them of their country, and the new dynasty was grateful for the support of a movement of increasing significance in high circles. The Duke of Cumberland became Grand Master, and on his death in 1790 he was succeeded by 'Prinny', afterwards George IV, who held office throughout the Great War. No one could accuse English Freemasons of disloyal deeds or subversive activities in Church or State. They were pillars of the throne from the start and have remained so ever since.

After founding the Grand Lodge and securing firm anchorage at Court and in society Desaguliers proceeded to draft rules of membership. Pleasant gatherings and good cheer in a tavern were well enough, but such a practical idealist wanted more. Since public and private morals were at a low ebb in the age of Hogarth he felt that England needed above all good citizens, and collaborated with the Rev. James Anderson, a fellow mason, in defining the duties of a community pledged to set a good example. The *Constitutions of the Freemasons* became canonical for all lodges and were translated into French and German. An American edition was published by Benjamin Franklin.

Article I. *Concerning God and Religion.*

A mason is obliged to obey the moral law, and if he rightly understands it he will never be a stupid atheist nor an irreligious libertine. But though in ancient times masons were charged in every country to be of the religion of that country or nation, yet 'tis now thought more expedient only to oblige them to that religion in which all men agree, leaving their particular opinion to themselves. That is to be good men and true or men of honour and honesty by whatever denominations and persuasions they may be distinguished, whereby masonry becomes the centre of union and the means of conciliating true friendship among persons that must else have remained at a perpetual distance.

This natural—or as we should say—undenominational religion required from the first members has remained an essential feature of English freemasonry, while the Continental lodges soon abandoned a theistic test.

Accepting doctrinal differences as a fact and rejecting all thought of proselytism, Desaguliers sought a common denominator in the moral law. His vision embraced the ultimate supersession of Christian dogma by the simple recognition of a Supreme Being, the 'Great Architect of the Universe'. Such

philosophic deism, free alike from superstition and atheism, without revelation and without dogma, had been proclaimed by
Toland and other English thinkers and was embraced by leaders
of the *Aufklärung* with Voltaire and Frederick the Great at their
head. Freemasonry, it was hoped, would build up a social and
intellectual *élite* transcending political, racial and doctrinal
antagonisms, and would raise the standard of conduct by con-
centrating on moral duties, respecting all creeds and Churches
while preaching and practising brotherly love. The ceremonies
with which freemasonry was identified in the public mind were
merely the picturesque trappings of a world-wide fellowship.

The Second Article of the Constitutions of 1723 presented
the political creed.

> A mason is a peaceable subject to the Civil Powers wherever he
> resides or works, and is never to be concerned in plots and con-
> spiracies against the peace and welfare of the nation, nor to behave
> himself undutifully to inferior magistrates. For as Masonry hath
> been always injured by war, bloodshed and confusion, so ancient
> kings and princes have been much disposed to encourage the
> craftsmen because of their peaceableness and loyalty, whereby they
> practically answered the cavils of their adversaries and promoted
> the honour of the Fraternity who ever flourished in times of peace.
> So that if a brother should be a rebel against the State he is not to be
> countenanced in his rebellion, however he may be pitied as an un-
> happy man; and if convicted of no other crime, though the loyal
> Brotherhood ought to disown his rebellion and give no umbrage
> or ground of political jealousy to the Government, they cannot
> evict him from the lodge.

Though toleration of a hypothetical rebel appears paradoxical
in a movement of such unfaltering loyalty we may remember
that in 1723 no further rebellion was in sight. The lenient attitude towards an erring brother suggests that members of a lodge
were often bound to mutual aid by the closest personal ties.
Similar consideration for potential rebels was adopted by the
statutes of foreign lodges with the exception of the Dutch who
decreed the expulsion of any member 'who sins against the chief
fundamental rule of our society, namely obedience and fidelity
towards his legitimate Sovereigns'. Though there was no thought
of rebellion or revolution in a movement sponsored by the

ruling classes, the general attitude to politics was one of mild liberalism.

Lodges on the English model sprang up in almost every part of Europe, mainly frequented by the aristocracy, the well-to-do bourgeoisie whose social importance was rapidly increasing, and in some cases by crowned heads. In the American Colonies widespread interest was aroused by the writings of Benjamin Franklin, printer and publicist, statesman and scientist, who paid his first visit to London in 1724 and joined a lodge in Philadelphia. The movement spread rapidly: among its members was George Washington, while in Prussia it could boast of Frederick the Great.

Nowhere was the appeal of freemasonry so powerful as in eighteenth-century France, where it became a partial substitute for the traditional religion. The removal of the dead hand of Louis XIV, the licence of the Regency era, and the anglomania fostered by Voltaire and Montesquieu prepared the soil for an enthusiastic welcome. The first lodges were founded by British refugees at the exiled Court at St. Germain, where the role of Desaguliers in England and Franklin in America was played by a Jacobite adventurer who, without any claim to nobility, called himself Chevalier Ramsay. Aspiring to integrate freemasonry with the Roman Church, to which he was converted, the disciple and biographer of Fénelon made an auspicious start by tutoring the sons of the Pretender; but his attempt to secure the patronage of the young King Louis XV was thwarted by Cardinal Fleury. Higher ecclesiastics agreed with the Vatican in regarding the movement with suspicion, and the Bull of Clement XII in 1738 forbidding the faithful to join masonic lodges on pain of excommunication inaugurated a conflict with Rome which has never ceased. Since, however, it was not registered by the Paris *Parlement*, the fortress of Gallicanism, it possessed no legal validity, and many Catholics both priests and laymen entered the masonic ranks. In the Age of Enlightenment some of the clergy were *Philosophes* or friends of *Philosophes*, and many laymen paid mere lip-service to the Christian creeds. The easy-going King was disinclined to interfere, Choiseul was a notorious anti-clerical, and condemnation by the fossilised Sorbonne in 1763 failed to raise a ripple on the flowing stream.

Though Ramsay's attempt to legitimise masonry by royal favour and ecclesiastical toleration was a failure, lodges sprang up like mushrooms throughout France and her colonies. They contained not only the *noblesse* and the professional classes but a few *petit bourgeois* who enjoyed meeting their social superiors on equal terms. Since this infiltration was not always to the taste of the latter, tension was eased by the invention of grades. The peasant and the manual worker, needless to say, never entered these select *Sociétés de Pensée*. The ceremonies of initiation delighted certain mystery-loving types in an age when the Rosicrucians and Illuminati flourished and St. Germain, Mesmer and Cagliostro found many admirers. The first French lodge was founded in Paris in 1731 with the Duc d'Antin as Grand Master. He was succeeded by Marshal Comte de Clermont of the royal house of Bourbon-Condé. By the middle of the century the country was dotted with lodges. *Le Grand Orient de France*, founded in 1772 with the Duc de Chartres—the future Philippe Égalité—as Grand Master, differed from the English Grand Lodge in omitting a declaration of belief in 'the Great Architect of the Universe' from its statutes. After protracted discussion the admission of women was authorised in 1794, with the Duchesse de Bourbon, of the Condé branch of the Royal Family, as the first Grande Maîtresse, to be succeeded by the ill-fated Princesse de Lamballe.

The prestige of masonry in France reached its height during the residence of Benjamin Franklin as representative of the newly founded United States. With the aid of the most influential of Parisian lodges, Les Neuf Soeurs, which had openly sympathised with the revolt of the American Colonies, he instituted what amounted to a free university. The most popular of its courses, to which women were admitted, was that of La Harpe on contemporary literature. Its *clientèle* included authors and artists, aristocrats and lawyers, among them Condorcet, Danton and the Abbé Siéyès. It campaigned for the reform of the judiciary and founded the Société des Amis des Noirs: and the example of the young republic beyond the seas was kept in the public eye by Brissot's Société Gallo-Américaine. Sympathy with republicanism in the new world, however, did not imply anti-monarchical sentiments. Never at any moment did masonic lodges in France or elsewhere become purely political, still less revolutionary, bodies. Ideas of equality and universal brotherhood were not a masonic invention, but their adoption by members of the nobility and prominent citizens helped to prepare the way for the Declaration of the Rights of Man. It was Aulard's memorable achievement to prove that there was scarcely a trace of republicanism in 1789.

Though the lodges avoided a direct clash with the Church, the fact that their members included men of all faiths and none accelerated the secularisation of thought inaugurated by the Encyclopaedists. The efforts of the youthful Savoyard mason, Joseph de Maistre, at all times a devout believer and in his later years the oracle of ultramontanism, to revive Ramsay's dream of cordial collaboration with the Church came too late and were abandoned.

When the storm broke in 1789 there were over six hundred lodges in France with perhaps between 20,000 and 30,000 members. The average membership was about fifty, and large towns required several centres to meet the demand. Though the timid bourgeois lawyer Barbier had noted in his journal as early as 1738 that the meetings were a danger, there is little sign of alarm before the Revolution. Recent French scholars differ widely in regard to their political significance. Right-wing historians like Madelin and Augustin Cochin believe that they exerted a profound influence, while Mathiez and Sée argue that their share in launching the Revolution was infinitesimal. In his majestic treatise *Les Origines Intellectuelles de la Révolution Française* Mornet sides with the latter, and supplies evidence from the membership lists for his verdict. Louis XVI himself, he believes, was a mason, and the lodges swarmed with the *noblesse*, members of religious orders, priests and *curés*. There were even lodges in convents, and excellent relations with the ecclesiastical authorities often prevailed. Protestants were sometimes accepted. Most lodges were a combination of clubs and literary salons, with banquets and the reading of poems playing a prominent part. Their charities grew with their numbers, and funds were provided for such purposes as dowries, scholarships and apprenticeships. Most masons, declares Mornet, were unpolitical, neither reformers, nor *Philosophes*, nor anticlericals. No doubt they talked politics in the months before the Revolution, but they were no more radical than their fellow-citizens. Diderot and Helvétius had been masons, and Voltaire was fêted in the Loge des Neuf Soeurs on his final spectacular visit to the capital in 1778. Masons thought of themselves rather as citizens of the world bound by a common tie than as social and political reformers, and in 1760 the Duc d'Antin, the first Grand Maître, spoke for the whole movement in the pregnant words 'Le monde entier n'est qu'une grande république'.

Dozens of masons were to be found in the States-General and the political clubs, among them such prominent members of the nobility as Philippe Égalité, Mirabeau and Lafayette. The notion that the lodges or any other semi-secret society played a deciding part in causing and guiding the Revolution is grotesque. The golden age of masonry closed in 1789. In the nineteenth century it lost its aristocratic *clientèle* and grew increasingly anticlerical as the ultramontane revival got into its stride. Though the Grand Orient became a nightmare of the Vatican, the movement as a whole was merely the ghost of its former vigorous self, and today its political importance is very limited.

8

CONDORCET AND HUMAN PERFECTIBILITY

THE last and noblest of the Encyclopaedists deserves the title
of *L'Ami des Hommes* far more than the elder Mirabeau, perhaps more than any other Frenchman of the eighteenth century.
Among the select class of Servants of Humanity the Marquis
de Condorcet holds high rank. Mathematician, sociologist,
statesman, economist, educational reformer, historian, biographer, he thought with his heart as well as with his head. His
outward reserve hid the fires within, and d'Alembert described
him as a volcano covered with snow. His ruling passion was to
help his fellow-men in every country and every class to a richer
life, and he was convinced that the beckoning goal could be
reached through wiser laws, universal education and the unfettered use of reason. Looking back with pride to the triumphs
of scientific discovery, especially in recent times, he perceived
no limit to the possibilities of further advance, not only in the
realm of mind but in the organisation of society after the elimination of war through arbitration. Everyone—women no less than
men—would have the opportunity of developing their capacities
to the full. Anchored in this robust conception of the dignity
of *homo sapiens*, he welcomed the American and still more the
French Revolution as a partial realisation of his dreams. When
the principles of 1789 degenerated into the Terror he spent the
last year of his threatened existence composing the *Esquisse du
progrès de l'esprit humain*, at once a record of human achievement
and a moving confession of faith. Among the innocent victims
of the Jacobin purge none had laboured more unselfishly nor
more constructively for the happiness of mankind. In so far as

the Encyclopaedists had sown the seed of the Revolution he alone lived to reap the whirlwind, yet in the darkest hours he never despaired.

Educated in a Jesuit school at Rheims and in the Collège de Navarre in Paris, Condorcet impressed his teachers by his mathematical ability, was elected to the Academy of Sciences at twenty-six, and appointed Secrétaire Perpétuel at twenty-nine. In the latter capacity he prepared sixty-one *Éloges* of deceased members, a task necessitating wide knowledge in many fields. His reputation spread quickly beyond the frontier, and in middle age he was a member of the academies of St. Petersburg, Turin, Bologna, Philadelphia, and the Royal Society. His major scientific publication, *The Theory of Probability*, was for the few, but he never shut himself up in an ivory tower. The practical bent of his mind was revealed in his plea for internal free trade in corn. At the age of twenty-six he accompanied d'Alembert to Ferney and maintained an affectionate correspondence with Voltaire till the end of his life. He was no less devoted to and equally appreciated by Turgot who, during his brief period of office, appointed him Master of the Mint. As the biographer of both he proclaimed the gospel of the Enlightenment of which all three were zealous apostles.

His fertile mind had turned to the problem of the destiny of man many years before he began to put his conclusions into a book. In an undated *Fragment of Justification* he recorded that he had long been convinced of the perfectibility of the species and that the process could only be arrested by some major physical convulsions of our planet.

The greatest benefactor, he believed, was Voltaire, who presented for the first time the model of a simple citizen embracing in his field of vision all the interests of mankind in every country and every age, standing forth against all error and oppression, finding and spreading all useful truths.

If the clergy in lands obeying the Roman obedience have lost their dangerous power and are about to lose their scandalous riches, if the freedom of the press has made some progress, if Russia and Poland, Prussia and the states of the House of Austria, have witnessed the disappearance of tyrannical intolerance, if the shameful survivals of feudalism and servitude have been destroyed in Russia and Poland, Denmark and France, if the need is everywhere recognised of reforming the laws and the law courts, if in Europe men have felt free to use their reason, if love of humanity has become the common language, if wars have become less frequent and the pride of sovereigns is no longer advanced as a pretext, if the imposture masks have fallen off everywhere, amid all these changes you will find the name of Voltaire either as launching or aiding the struggle.

In this eloquent tribute to his master Condorcet was giving utterance to his own deepest convictions.

The first public announcement of his belief in perfectibility was made in his discourse on his election to the Académie Française in 1782. 'Is there not a point where the natural limitations of our mind render further progress impossible?' he asked. As enlightenment grows the methods of instruction become more perfect, he replies, the human spirit seems to expand and the limits recede. 'A youth today leaves school with more knowledge than the greatest figures of antiquity or even of the seventeenth century could acquire by long study; and the moral sciences, almost the creation of our own time, which aim at human happiness will advance as steadily as the physical.' In an address to the Academy of Science in the same year he proclaimed that all men are members of the same family and have the same real interests.

Like Rousseau and unlike Voltaire Condorcet believed in the common man and advocated democracy as the only system of government capable of giving him his chance. He agreed with Fox that the fall of the Bastille was the best and happiest event in the history of the human race, and the Declaration of the Rights of Man might have come from his pen. Unlike Mirabeau, who would have been content with limited monarchy on the English model, he had no use for thrones which he associated with tyranny. He was one of the few republicans before the flight of the king converted masses of his subjects to the belief that the monarchy was superfluous. As a member of the Legislative Assembly and the Convention he devoted his chief attention to the framing of a constitution which was never even discussed, and to urging a comprehensive system of public instruction which he expounded in five memoranda, the most striking feature of which was the provision of equal opportunities for women. The only way to become happier, he declared, was to become better, and a sound education was the best approach to both these blessings. When the Terror was over and the author in his grave, Daunou secured a decree from the Convention for the purchase of three thousand copies of the Memoranda for use in the schools.

Though a lover of peace Condorcet supported the declaration of war in 1792 on the ground that the work of the Revolution was too valuable for France and the world to be trampled underfoot by the *Émigrés* and their allies beyond the Rhine. But when the September Massacres stained the record of the new masters of France, he realised that the Revolution had unleashed passions which it could not control. Though he condemned the conduct of the king in strong terms he was one of the minority who voted against the death penalty. He had never been an associate of the Girondins, but when they were struck down by the Jacobins he was charged with plotting against the new rulers and went into hiding in the house of an old friend who was prepared to risk her life for his sake. When, however, warnings reached him that a search of the house was imminent, he left without telling his hostess, wandered in the countryside outside Paris for a few days under a false name, was arrested on suspicion in an exhausted condition, imprisoned and found dead in his cell on the following day, whether by suicide or not we do not know.

His *Esquisse du Progrès de l'esprit humain* was the third major attempt to survey the story of mankind in broad perspective. Bossuet simplified his task by presenting it as the unfolding of a divine plan for shepherding all peoples into the sheltering arms of the Catholic Church. Voltaire's *Essai sur les Moeurs* covered a far wider field, and for the first time assigned their rightful place in history to Asiatic races. Condorcet's survey is much shorter, for it was undertaken when he had no notion how long he would be permitted to live. He had with him notes made before he was hunted off the public stage, and friends occasionally brought him books. The result of his frustration, however painful for the author, were beneficial to his readers, for he had to content himself with the broad outlines. He facilitates their task by numbering the phases of evolution, a precedent followed half a century later in Comte's scheme of three stages of human thought.

Have we reached a point [he inquires] where we have nothing more to fear, neither new errors nor the return of old ones, where no corrupting institution can be established by hypocrisy, ignorance or fanaticism; where no vicious combination can harm a great nation? Will it then be useless to learn how peoples have been deceived, corrupted and reduced to misery? Everything indicates that we are on the eve of one of the great revolutions in the history of mankind. What can be more suitable than to inquire what we may expect, to seek a sure guide through its movements? Our present stage of enlightenment guarantees that it will be happy, but only on condition that we make use of all our powers. If this promised happiness is to be purchased at a cheaper price, if it is to spread more rapidly and over a wider sphere, if it is to be more complete, is it not essential to study in the history of the human mind what obstacles remain and how to overcome them? The record would be presented in nine phases, and a tenth would scan our future destinies. History is the record of the progress of humanity towards truth and happiness. My book will show that nature has set no bounds to the perfecting of human faculties. Independently of any power which would like to stop it, so long as our globe exists the tempo will differ but we shall never go back.

Society began with the grouping of families into small nomad communities engaged in the task of satisfying the primary physical needs by hunting, fishing, the storing of food and provision for defence. The invention of language and the choice of some male to lead in case of conflict with another tribe was followed by the selection of male adults to discuss the interests of the group. Religion began with superstitions, medicine with the discovery of healing plants.

The second phase, *The Pastoral Peoples*, is treated with equal brevity, for the author was eager to reach the time when the human spirit was attaining the full stature. With the domestication of animals the community ceased to be nomadic, and with the assurance of sufficient food came leisure. Differences in possessions, measured in flocks and herds, led to social inequality, and prisoners taken in war relieved some women of their drudgery. As the communities grew in size certain rules, the forerunners of laws, were established. The study of the heavens began, and a few individuals claiming superior knowledge anticipated the arrogance of the priesthood.

The third epoch witnessed the growth of towns, the beginnings of commerce, and above all the invention of an alphabet; but the latter was not an unmixed benefit, for the earliest form was symbolic. The complicated hieroglyphs were in the hands of priests who used their new power to increase their authority over the ignorant by teaching them insensate rituals. Such was the origin of almost all known religions, to which the hypocrisy or extravagance of their inventors and their proselytes were to add new fables, which they ultimately came to believe themselves.

The fourth and fifth chapters are a paean to the Greeks, the people whose influence has been so powerful and so beneficial, whose genius has opened all the paths of truth, the benefactors of every land and every age, an honour hitherto shared by no other community. Perhaps France might inaugurate a similar revolution. In the absence of an arrogant priesthood everyone had an equal right to knowledge of the truth. While the philosophers constructed their castles in the air, scientists explored the secrets of nature. Democritus explained that the universe was a collection of atoms in motion, and Pythagoras taught that it was governed by natural laws. Socrates, Plato and Aristotle, the latter the most universal intellect of the ancient world, explored every province of the human mind. Even more important than their intellectual achievements was the victory of Salamis which saved Europe from domination by Asia. The fortunes of a single day decided for centuries the destinies of the human race, since without it Greek achievements, in the sciences, the arts and philosophy, would have perished with the loss of the liberty which made them possible.

Condorcet's picture of the rise and triumph of Christianity might have been signed by Gibbon. All the sects expected a Messiah sent by God to restore the human race, but a prophet said to have appeared in Palestine during the reign of Tiberius eclipsed them all, and the new fanatics rallied to the standard of the son of Mary. The more the Empire declined, the more rapid was the progress of the Christian religion. Despite their knaveries and vices the leaders were ready to die for their doctrines, formed a powerful party, and placed Constantine on the throne. The heroic Julian strove to rescue the Empire from this scourge, and his death removed the only dyke against the irruption of a torrent of new superstitions and barbarian invasions. The triumph of Christianity was the signal for the decline of the sciences and philosophy. If the art of printing had been discovered at this period the collapse might have been avoided.

After his attack on the Jewish and Christian Churches it is little of a surprise to read the tribute to Islam, in which there was less superstition because there was less theology, that disease of the human mind which had produced a few scientists at a time when Christian Europe was plunged in darkness. The author knew little of the Moslem world and its history, and was unaware that its record on toleration was no better than that of its rivals.

The sixth and seventh chapters cover the thousand years between the fall of Rome and the invention of printing, a disastrous period of ignorance and ferocity, corruption and perfidy, with only an occasional ray of talent, magnanimity or kindliness, a world of theological dreams, of superstitions, impostures, with religious intolerance as its sole moral principle. Europe, squeezed between sacerdotal tyranny and military despotism, awaited in blood and tears the moment when liberty, humanity and the virtues would reappear. Slavery ceased, but serfdom was almost universal. Rome strove to impose the fetters of a new tyranny, Popes subjugated the ignorant and credulous by forged documents, mingling religion in all transactions of civil life in the interests of their avarice and their pride, inflicting terrible penalties for opposition to their laws and for the least resistance to their insensate claims, possessing in every land an army of monks ever ready by their impostures to foster fanaticism, stirring up civil war, disturbing everything in order to dominate everything, commanding in the name of God treason and perjury, murder and parricide, making kings and warriors the instruments and the victims of their vengeance, a colossus with feet of clay. The people groaned under the triple tyranny of kings, military chieftains and priests. Absolution for crimes could be purchased from the priests according to a tariff. How vastly superior were the Arabs with their simple religion and their love of the sciences. Challenges came from the Albigenses, Wycliffe and others, and the growth of cities and commerce fostered the exchange of ideas. The fifteenth century witnessed the immigration of scholars from the Eastern Empire, carrying with them some of the

treasures of classical Greece. The nearest approach to praise of the
Middle Ages is an admission that Dante is often noble. The
author's contemptuous treatment of the Ages of Faith and his
complete inability to realise what a vital part the Church played
in millions of lives is the blind spot in a fine intellect. While
denouncing fanaticism in the Church he exhibited an intolerance
of his own.

The eighth and ninth acts of the drama carry the narrative
from the time when science and philosophy shook off the yoke
of authority. The dawn was overcast, but by 1789 the sun stood
high in the heavens. Reason had a new chance and proceeded to
make good use of it. The widening of the mental horizon was
matched by the discovery of the New World. The Reformation's
challenge to ecclesiastical authority led logically to a challenge
to monarchical authority. But the campaign for religious and
political liberty was long and arduous, for the Protestant sects
persecuted each other, and Protestant rulers tyrannised over
their subjects no less than Catholics. The discoverers of the
nature of the universe, Copernicus and Galileo, Descartes and
Newton, are the heroes of the eighth book. Of the two main
scourges of mankind, superstition and despotism, the former
began to wane, but the latter still cumbered the earth.

The ninth and last epoch claims the largest space and strikes
the most triumphant note. Reason and common sense were
battering at the walls of ignorance, prejudice, superstition, and
vested interests. Locke and Leibniz carried on the tradition of
independent thinking begun by Descartes. Despite their differences the philosophers of various nations, embracing in their
meditations the interests of the whole of humanity without distinction of race and sect, formed a phalanx against every form of
error and tyranny. Animated by a spirit of universal philanthropy
they fought against every injustice. Even more important than
any scientific discovery was the American Revolution, in which
little change occurred except the transfer of sovereignty, and
which inspired a revolution in France where a social no less than
a political transformation was urgently required.

Convinced that the hurricane would soon be over, Condorcet
passed in the tenth and final section of his book to the happy day
when the sun would shine on a world of free men recognising

no master except their own reason. The moral faculties listening to the voice of conscience would develop *pari passu* and were equally capable of perfection. Indeed the degree of virtue to which man might attain was as unimaginable as the achievements of genius.

Who knows if a time will not come when our private interests and passions will no more influence our judgements and our will than they do today our scientific interests? As they grow more enlightened the peoples will regain the right of disposing of their lives and their wealth, and will regard war as the most fatal scourge and the worst of crimes. Wars for pretended hereditary rights will cease. Peoples will learn that they cannot become conquerors without forfeiting their own liberty, that permanent confederations alone can maintain their independence, and that their aim should be security, not power. Commercial prejudices will gradually disappear, and a false mercantile interest will lose its sinister capacity to cause blood to flow, ruining nations on the pretext of enriching them. As the political and moral principles of peoples approximate, and as each for its own advantage invites others to share in the bounty of nature or in its industries, all the causes which degrade, envenom, or perpetuate national hatred will disappear.

This noble work, marred only by its pathological anticlericalism, closes on a note of optimistic serenity, a secular equivalent of the Hallelujah Chorus.

Freed from the enemies of his progress man will march with firm step along the path of truth, virtue and happiness, emancipated from the errors, crimes and injustices which continue to soil the world. This prospect is the reward for his struggles for the progress of reason and the defence of liberty. Here is his recompense for his lifelong constructive labours. Here is his refuge beyond the reach of his persecutors, of corrupting cupidity, fear and envy. Here is his real life, in the company of his fellows, in an Elysium which his reason has created for him and which his love of humanity adorns with the purest delights.

It is better to think too highly than too meanly of mankind, but it is better still to resist the temptation of wishful thinking. A large portion of Condorcet's tribute is well deserved, but it is not the whole truth. He died too soon to witness Napoleon's aggressions, the bloody struggles in the cause of racial integration and national independence, and the carnage of the twentieth century. With obvious reference to the Terror, though without mentioning names or places, he bids his countrymen not to despair when they see a free people falling back into corruption and ignorance, for it could not last long and servitude would never return. 'If the flame of philosophy is not extinguished, if it continues to burn among a few men of genius, if the enlightened are not exterminated, if the stars continue to shine in neighbouring lands, that will suffice to weather the storm and to keep liberty alive till the moment arrives when freedom of the press, triumphing over ephemeral tyranny, will restore the light of day. Did anyone believe that a system based on inequality and ignorance, corruption and ferocity, would long survive to degrade a nation? Ambitions and jealous mediocrities could send humanity to sleep at the expense of certain individuals who had rendered service to it, and could make their country groan. Whole peoples might be tricked and led astray, but they could not be corrupted and brutalised. Had Condorcet lived to hear Lincoln proclaim that all the people can be fooled part of the time and some of them all the time, all cannot be fooled all the time, he would have nodded assent. *Sursum corda.*

PART TWO

AFTER THE REVOLUTION

9

CHATEAUBRIAND AND THE CHARMS OF CHRISTIANITY

I

THE most shattering event in the life of Chateaubriand was the French Revolution which exploded with the force of a bomb when he was twenty years old. Though a member of one of the oldest families in Brittany, he was a child of the Enlightenment rather than of the *ancien régime*, fascinated by Rousseau, and casting envious eyes across the Channel at the system of limited monarchy. Unlike Burke and Joseph de Maistre he found much to approve in the opening phase of the drama. He was travelling in the United States when the news of the flight to Varennes brought him back to Europe. Though he disapproved of the *Émigration*, he explained that he thought it his duty to join his fellow-nobles beyond the frontier. 'I felt I ought not to be in the forests of America while my comrades were at the front.' On the outbreak of war in 1792 he shared the hardships of the first campaign and was gravely wounded. Stricken by dysentery and smallpox he lay in a ditch, was believed to be dying, was rescued, taken to Brussels and thence to Jersey. Directly he was well enough he crossed the Channel after the execution of the King, thus escaping the fate of his elder brother who was guillotined. Since he could no longer fight and was warned by his doctor that he had not long to live he resolved to write. Unknown, friendless and penniless in London, sometimes suffering from the pangs of hunger, he kept himself alive by giving French lessons and by translations.

After three years of hard work he published his first work in 1797, *Essai historique, politique et moral sur les révolutions anciennes et modernes considérées dans leurs rapports avec la révolution française de nos jours*. It was designed as the first instalment of a panorama of revolutions throughout the ages, a scheme that was never carried out, for shortly after launching his first effort a dramatic change in his ideology led to a new orientation. 'Who am I?' he began; 'people will say you were an actor in this astonishing tragedy, you suffered, you saw your fortune and your friends disappear in the abyss, and you are an *Émigré*. At this last word I see moderates and republicans throw the book aside. Please read on. I have never changed my political opinions. Suffering from an incurable malady I survey events in peace of mind. I bring you a heart as free from prejudice as a human heart can be. If my blood grows hot I drop my pen. If not always just, I am always sincere.' The claim to serenity is largely justified. The tone of the work is unemotional and there is little propaganda, for he strives to see his subject *sub specie aeternitatis*. Were any revolutions, he asks, like this one? What caused it? What was the present government of France? Was it based on true principles and can it last? If so, what effect would it have on other governments? If it were destroyed, what would be its result for the peoples of today and for posterity? Though much had been written on it each author had merely denounced his rival, so the theme was as fresh as if it had never been treated.

Republicans, constitutionalists, monarchists, Girondists, *Émigrés*, politicians of every sort, on these questions our happiness or unhappiness depends. The time of individual preferences is over, the petty ambitions, narrow interests of the individual giving place to national ambitions and the interests of mankind. In vain do you hope to escape the calamities of your century by solitude and obscurity. Friend is torn from friend, and the retreat of the sage echoes to the fall of thrones. No one can count on a moment of peace. We are sailing along an unknown coast in darkness and storm, so everyone has a personal interest in considering these issues with me because everyone's existence is involved. We must study the map in order, like a wise pilot, to discover where we are and where we are going, so that in case of shipwreck we may find some island beyond the reach of the storm. This island is a good conscience. In describing past revolutions I always bear in mind their relation to ours. I hope the book will be of use.

The larger part of the work is devoted to Greece, leaving Rome for the next volume. For modern readers the most interesting chapters are those which briefly discuss the causes of the French Revolution, the detailed analysis of which he was never to attempt. Of the *Encyclopédistes* he speaks with great severity.

Everything combined to favour the *Philosophes* and hurl France into a torrent of new ideas—the relaxation of morals, envy among the little, corruption among the great, the memory of monarchical oppression. The *Philosophes* produced scepticism and atheism. Clever men exploited the tendency to superstition and founded sects. As a believer in natural religion like Rousseau he deplores the religious decadence which began with the Crusades and the Schism. 'Popes, corrupted by luxury and intoxicated by power, plunged into every sort of vice. Some were atheists and led scandalous lives. The clergy were as depraved as their chiefs, indulging in every excess, and convents were haunts of debauchery.' The Renaissance and the Reformation struck blows from which the Church never recovered, and the Reformation was the prologue to the latest revolutions. 'When people begin to doubt religion they proceed to ask questions about the principles of government. After the Reformation the Vatican re-emerged, but in vain. The revocation of the Edict of Nantes was an act of fanaticism, and the Regency witnessed the almost total collapse of Christianity. The only legacy of the *Encyclopédistes* was the Revolution, for destruction was their aim. Voltaire laughed, wrote good verses and spread immorality. What did they wish to replace Christianity? Nothing. It was a fury against the institutions of their Fatherland which, in fact, were not very good. But whoever destroys ought to rebuild, a difficult task which should make us slow down innovations.' Though Rousseau escapes this indictment, *Émile*, we are told, contributed to cause the Revolution—a treasure for the wise but not for the many. It worked a complete revolution in modern Europe and formed an epoch in the history of peoples. Education was completely changed in France, and whoever changes education changes man by holding up the vision of the primitive man. 'Had I been his contemporary I

should have wished to be his disciple, but I should have advised
him not to publish, for his political and moral principles have
destroyed the governments of Europe, above all of France. Truth
is bad for bad men and should be buried in the bosom of the wise.'
The Court was no less responsible for the Revolution than the
Philosophes. The Duke of Orleans possessed genius, charm and
urbanity, but he was the wickedest man of his century and the
least fitted to rule the nation. The fiasco of Law's scheme shook
the morale of the people, and the press reported debaucheries
which would have made Suetonius blush. Contempt in the heart
of the citizen grew into indignation. People began to read, losing
their ignorance and their morals at the same time. The Court,
deaf to protests, plunged deeper into vice and despotism, and
lettres de cachet diminished respect for the law. The monarch dozed
amid his pleasures, surrounded by corrupt courtiers, evil or
imbecile Ministers, ignorant or vicious nobles, ecclesiastics a
disgrace to their calling. Who could wonder that after Louis XV
religion and monarchy had disappeared in the gulf of the Revolution? Among its causes Chateaubriand assigns a high place to the
decline of religion, and a series of chapters surveys the position
in Europe since the phenomenon was not confined to France.
The French clergy, he complains, were behind the times. The
Bishops retained much of the old spirit of their order and were
generally well-educated and charitable, but not up to the level of
their century. The Abbés receive lower marks and are described
as largely responsible for anticlericalism. The *curés*, on the other
hand, though ignorant and prejudiced, were generally simple
and saintly. In England, which he knew so well, he found not
hostility to religion but indifference. The Churches only opened
on Sundays and the clergymen were scarcely known to the
parishioners, for plurality of livings involved absenteeism.

Since institutional and dogmatic Christianity was declining day
by day, Chateaubriand wondered what would take its place.
Jupiter could not return, the Illuminati were unlikely to spread,
a new Mohammed would lack the military strength to conquer
Europe. If some prophet were to arise and preach a new gospel
the peoples would be too indifferent and too corrupt to trouble
about it, and it would perish by contempt. Yet some religion
there must be, else society would dissolve. 'The more we con-

sider the matter, the more alarmed we become. Europe seems to
have reached not merely a revolution but a dissolution of which
recent events in France were merely the prologue.' Another
possibility was that a higher level of culture and morality might
render a cult unnecessary.

Had not the invention of printing changed all the old assumptions?
Either the nations after a large dose of enlightenment will unite
under a single government in a state of unalterable happiness, or,
torn by internal stresses after bloody civil wars and fearful anarchy,
they will fall back into barbarism. During their troubles some peoples
less corrupted and more enlightened will first emerge from the
debris, to become in turn the prey of international strife and vice.
Then some nations will again emerge from barbarism in a sequence
of revolutions without end. To judge by past experience the latter
prospect corresponds best to our frailty. Who will destroy themselves
first? I answer the most corrupt, but unpredictable events may
force a nation to turn before the moment indicated by nature.

A detailed analysis of the French Revolution was reserved for
a future volume; but the author devotes a chapter to two of its
worst crimes, the execution of Malesherbes and Louis XVI. 'The
distinguished lawyer who at the peril of his life had defended the
unhappy king, and had always championed the oppressed, was
universally esteemed. It was reserved for our century to see the
venerable magistrate in a red shirt in a bloodstained tumbril
carted to the guillotine with his daughter and his granddaughter
at his side amid the plaudits of an ungrateful people.' Louis XVI
is saluted as one of the best kings of France, more innocent than
Charles I who had infringed the rights of a free people.

The *Essai* concludes with some general reflections on revolutions. Most features of the latest example which to the unin-
structed seemed so novel could find a parallel in ancient Greece.
The classical world knew all about them. Man had repeated himself unceasingly, revolving in a circle from which he vainly strives
to escape, confronted by recurrent situations which seem like the
play of fortune. Thus in the light of history it became possible
to outline a picture in which all conceivable events could be
predicted with mathematical accuracy. 'Everything is chance,
fatality,' the author jotted down in the margin of his copy of the
book. 'How can one believe that an intelligent God is guiding us?

M

Look at the rascals and criminals on top, decent folk murdered
and despised. Perhaps there is a God—if so, He is the God of
Epicurus, too mighty and too happy to trouble about our affairs
while we are left to gobble each other up.' These acid reflections
might have been signed by Voltaire himself. There was nothing
new in the rhythm of history. After the storm and the earthquake
man loses for a time the taste for innovations which plagues
the world. Enthusiasm arises from ignorance. Whether the new
system in France would take root nobody could foretell since
politics depended on morals, and the future of France would
depend on the wisdom or unwisdom of the nation.

A year after the publication of the book which declared that
the Christian religion was dying, Chateaubriand underwent a
conversion scarcely less dramatic than that of Saul into Paul.
Christianity, he was henceforth to claim, far from being on the
way out, was the only hope for the world. Like King Clovis, who
burned what he had adored and adored what he had burned, he
proceeded to denounce the *Essai sur les Révolutions* with merciless
severity. Reprinting it verbatim almost forty years later to form
the first two volumes of the collected works, he accompanied it
with notes on almost every page, correcting and regretting the
errors of his unregenerate years. 'Nourished in my early youth
on Voltaire and Rousseau, I thought myself a *Philosophe* and wrote
a bad book. I would suppress it if I could because it contains
some unsuitable chapters. As literature it was detestable and
ridiculous, a jumble of Jacobinism and Sparta, the Marseillaise
and songs of Tyrtaeus, praise of Christ and criticism of monks,
Robespierre and the Convention, fragments of Zeno, Epicurus
and Aristotle. The style was clumsy and pretentious, full of
foreign barbarisms.'

At this point the critic slightly relents, assuring his readers that
in addition to his juvenile delinquencies they would also find a
young man inspired rather than depressed by misfortune, devoted
to his king and the honour of his country. 'Young and unhappy,
my opinions were fluid in everything except politics, in which I
never varied. My Christian education had left profound traces
in my heart, but my brain was confused by books I had read and
the society I frequented. Like most men of that epoch I was a
child of the century and some of my indictments were too severe.

If I am credited with a lively imagination in my riper years, think what I was in early youth, without country, fortune or friends, knowing society only by the evils it inflicted on me.' That phase was over and he had learned the lesson that there is no real religion without liberty and no liberty without Christianity.

II

CHATEAUBRIAND thought with his emotions, and it was domestic bereavements not theological arguments which restored him to the faith of his fathers. Cut off from Catholic influences during his seven years in England, and at all times more attracted by literature and the arts, travel and politics, than by speculation, he drifted along on the tide of tolerant scepticism which had satisfied him in his youth. His religious indifference had been almost as painful as his physical absence to his pious mother and sister, and the death of the former in 1798 began the process of conversion which was to transform him into the principal champion of the Church in France. He was deeply moved by Julie's reproaches that their mother's closing years had been saddened by his incredulity, and when she followed her to the grave the battle was won. On his return to France in 1800 he brought with him the first version of his greatest book.

He was met by his friend Fontanes, a royalist who had climbed on the Bonaparte band-wagon, and as the lover of Eliza Baciochhi had ready access to the First Consul. Though no more temperamentally religious than Chateaubriand, he was anxious to reconcile the Church to the new master of France. For this purpose nothing could be more useful than a work which would find its way into circles beyond the reach of purely theological appeals. In *Génie du Christianisme ou les Beautés de la Religion Chrétienne* he found what he wanted, and he knew enough of the ruler's mind to feel certain that he would like it too. He was also enough of a *littérateur* to realise that no living Frenchman could write like his friend. 'No cult, no government,' he wrote to Lucien. 'Next to a victorious army I know no better allies than the people who direct consciences in God's name, and wise conquerors are never on bad terms with priests.' Lucien revived the official *Moniteur* with Fontanes as Editor, who commended the book as calculated to end the quarrel between philosophers and the friends of religion. Parts of the work were read to admiring listeners in the salon of Pauline de Beaumont. When at the suggestion of Fontanes and Joubert the story of Atala was detached from the major work and launched as a *ballon d'essai*, its success revealed the strength of the romantic movement and confirmed the conviction of Fontanes that *Génie du Christianisme* would be warmly welcomed. Published in April, 1802, one week after the Concordat, it took the world by storm. Read in proof by Lucien, reviewed by Fontanes in the *Moniteur*, and garlanded with compliments to the First Consul and his sister Eliza, it had the appearance of an official enterprise and the author was hailed as a restorer of religion second only to the ruler himself. As a result of its appearance, wrote the proud author many years later in his memoirs, religion was tinted with the colour of his religious pictures. Atheism and materialism were no longer in fashion and anti-religious prejudice relaxed. That the *Philosophes* frowned on his religious beliefs and intransigent royalists on his association with the usurper was neither a surprise nor an obstacle. The immense success of the work generated political ambitions. Perhaps, he wrote to Fontanes, he could be sent to Rome as Secretary to Cardinal Fesch. When he met the First Consul for the first time at the house of Lucien they were well pleased with each other. He dispatched a copy to the Pope with a flattering letter. The second edition, published in 1803, contained a fulsome dedication to Bonaparte who declared that he had never been better praised. The author was rewarded by an appointment to the French Embassy at Rome, and when he was received by the Pope he found his book on the table. Never had the picture of the Church as the mother of civilisation been painted in such brilliant colours. Though his conversion had no effect on his dissolute life—Sainte-Beuve, who knew him well, justly describes him as an Epicurean with a Catholic imagination—the magical style and vast scope of the survey won a multitude of readers. He woke up to find himself the brightest star in the literary firmament at a time when the throne long occupied by Voltaire was vacant. Frenchmen of all parties were proud of an authentic genius who ranked with Scott and Byron, Goethe and Manzoni.

The spirit and purpose of the treatise were explained thirty years later in a new preface when it appeared in three substantial volumes of the collected works. France at the dawn of the century, he recalled, was emerging from revolutionary chaos, and the book was composed among the *débris* of her temples. The faithful found salvation in a work which corresponded to their deepest sentiments. They felt the need of faith, a craving for religious consolation after years of deprivation, hastening to church as people run to a doctor in an epidemic or to a rock after shipwreck. 'Filled with memories of our ancient values, the glory and the monuments of our kings,' the book breathed the spirit of the old monarchy. The French learned to regret the past and hopes that were almost extinguished revived. A lengthy Introduction opens with a broadside against the Reformation as a schism leading to heresy and atheism. After Bossuet had destroyed the hydra of heresy, Voltaire introduced a new and even graver evil by rendering incredulity fashionable; religion was despised and its defenders were ignored. Perhaps France, after seeing where unbelief led, would listen. Approaching his task as artist and poet, not as a theologian, he set out to present the manifold beauties of Christianity. 'Will it be less true when it appears more beautiful? God does not forbid the flower-lined paths when they lead to Him.' Turning his back on the arid rationalism of the eighteenth century he salutes the Christian virtues—modesty, chastity, innocence. Religious sentiment was born in forests, the home of mystery. 'Everything in the universe is hidden, unknown. Is not man himself a strange mystery? All religions revealed the attraction of mankind for the mysterious—sacred caves, holy mountains, holy trees, sacrifices. God Himself is the great secret.'

Passing from Christian virtues to Christian doctrine he argues that all peoples believed in a state of primitive innocence followed by a fall which alone explained the nature and history of man. How else could we understand the misfortunes of the just and the success of evildoers? Reason alone never dried a tear: that only a Redeemer could do. Every doctrine, every ceremony, every injunction, the Incarnation, baptism, confession, confirmation, was an aid to the good life. Christ had made marriage a sacrament, and the Church rightly forbade divorce which rendered it insecure. The celibacy of the clergy is approved and extreme unction applauded as the beautiful consummation of a Christian life. As pride was the worst of spiritual offences, the sin of Satan, a challenge to God, so faith, hope and charity were the primary Christian virtues. Faith alone produced great achievements, and hope made our sufferings bearable. The Ten Commandments were applicable to all nations and for all time, for they were the laws of God.

Travelling far beyond the limits of his title Chateaubriand plunges fearlessly into the deep waters of theology. Assuming the literal truth of the Book of Genesis, he compares primitive men to animals without a sense of sin and therefore without sin. His fall was the penalty of his pride, the Flood God's vengeance on sinners. Far from contradicting the truths of religion, science revealed the grandeur and wisdom of Providence, for the clearest proof of the existence of God was to be found in the marvels of nature. 'There is a God. All nature, the animal world, proclaims it. Man alone has said: there is no God.' Can chance have produced so perfect an order? Think of the complex organisation of animal life and flowers. Everywhere design: all nature, the whole animal world, proclaimed it. Chateaubriand frequently draws on his American travels, marvelling at the instinct of migration and delighting in the song of birds. Why were such monsters as crocodiles created? He cannot answer the question, but he pleads in mitigation that at any rate they possess a wonderful maternal instinct. Plants and flowers were equally marvellous. Nothing was more conducive to piety than long sea voyages such as he had experienced alone with nature. 'I pity the man who with this spectacle before him has not felt the majesty and beauty of God and our human impotence in view of the infinite.' He had had the same feelings in the vast spaces of the new world. 'In Europe we are never far from human habitations, in parts of America the soul is alone with God. The loveliest nights in Europe cannot convey any idea of it.'

In rejecting the belief in a Supreme Being atheists were also renouncing the hope of another life, but at this point their own souls began to protest. If death is the end, how can we explain the craving for survival? The whole universe fails to satisfy the soul, for only the infinite can meet its needs. Everyone, secretly if not openly, aspires to an unknown happiness, and the hope was implanted in us by a merciful Providence to lessen the fear of death. Conscience is the voice of God with its phases of remorse for evil-doing, and its satisfaction in fulfilling the divine will was another pointer to immortality. Without such belief morality would collapse. Atheists were never happy, especially in old age, for their hearts were empty. All religions believed in rewards and punishments in another life, and the reward of the just would be a state of eternal admiration of the Perfect Being while they cried Holy, Holy, Holy in eternal ecstasy.

Christianity had left its mark on literature and the arts—think of Dante, Tasso and Milton. The author had brought back from England not only a thorough knowledge of English but an abiding admiration for *Paradise Lost* which he was later to translate. The main theme of great literature was love, and Christianity had helped to tame the passions of the heart by a heavenly wind which fills the sails of virtue, spiritualising the master passion by pacifying the heart. Christianity itself is a sort of passion with its ardours and sighs, its joys and its tears. Though well versed in the classics and a fervent admirer of Virgil, he maintains that the pre-Christian world can show nothing to match the ecstasy of martyrdom nor the sustaining conviction of an after-life as portrayed for example in Corneille's *Polyeucte*. Even purely as literature the Bible was superior to Homer. Christianity had always been the chief inspiration of the arts—far more favourable to painting than any other religion owing to its spiritual and mystical element and a tenderness elsewhere unknown. Sculpture could boast of the Moses of Michelangelo, architecture of Santa Sophia and St. Peter's, and of what are described as the three masterpieces, the dome, the campanile and the spire. A Gothic church inspired a feeling of awe and a vague sense of the divine.

The writing of history, like all other forms of intellectual activity, was indebted to Christianity, but here for once Chateaubriand awards the palm to the classical world. The only recent supreme achievement, Bossuet's *Histoire Universelle*, had received the compliment of an elaborate reply in Voltaire's *Essai sur les Moeurs*, but even Voltaire was conscious of the stature of St. Louis. The French had excelled in the writing of memoirs, which gave them freer scope in dealing with the passions, and de Retz was an acknowledged master of the craft. In pulpit eloquence the record was still finer, for Bossuet and Massillon were at least the equals of Cicero and Demosthenes, who, like all the ancients, knew only the eloquence of the agora and the law-courts and understood less of the human heart. Bossuet's *Oraisons Funèbres* were the supreme effort of human eloquence and caused at any rate one reader to shed tears of admiration. The atheist with his narrow vision, seeing nothing noble in nature, could never soar into the heavens like the Eagle of Meaux. Despite the great figures of Montesquieu and Buffon the eighteenth century was inferior to the seventeenth, for incredulity reduced the standard of taste and discouraged genius. The atheist confined his thought within a circle of mud. The common man was much wiser than the philosophers, more open to the inspiration of nature and sentiment, and the real believer never felt solitary. The anchorite in the desert was perfectly happy, for a good angel watched over him and he felt himself made for immortality. Church bells spoke to the heart; vestments, ornaments and incense appealed to his sense of beauty and stirred his religious emotions. Church festivals were a joy and prayers for the dead encouraged hopes of reunion. All races and religions had practised some form of cult of the dead and paid them honour by erecting tombs. In St. Denis he had shed tears amid the monuments of the kings of France.

The survey of Christianity closes with a poem to the hierarchy and the clergy and the marvellous organisation of which they formed part, the finest achievement in the history of institutions. 'When nations become civilised the Bishops reap the reward of the good they have done to mankind, above all in the maintenance of morality, works of charity, and the progress of literature. Their palaces became the centre of polite manners and the arts, and their talents aroused the admiration of Europe.' In France they had been models of moderation and enlightenment. There had been some exceptions, but recently over sixty had sought refuge in Protestant countries where they had won respect and veneration, the disciples of Luther and Calvin coming to hear the exiles preach the love of humanity and forgiveness of sins. The lower clergy were equally admirable; to them was due what survived of good morals in town and countryside. The peasant without religion was a wild beast without self-control, education or respect. His cramped life has embittered him and poverty destroyed the innocence of primitive times; he was timid, coarse, suspicious, miserly, ungrateful; yet by a striking miracle this man, perverse by nature, became excellent in religious hands. Where he was cowardly he becomes brave, his instinctive treachery turns into utter fidelity, his ingratitude into boundless devotion, his mistrust into absolute confidence. Contrast the impious peasants, profaning the churches, wrecking property, burning women, children and priest over a slow fire, with the Vendéans defending the cult of their fathers, the only free men when France lay prostrate under the Terror, and you will see the difference religion makes. What are the prejudices and the ignorance of the *curés* in comparison with their simplicity of heart and saintliness of life, their evangelical poverty, their Christian charity, which make them one of the worthiest elements of the nation? Many of them seem less men than beneficent spirits descending to earth to comfort the miserable. Often they refuse bread in order to feed the necessitous and part with their garments to clothe the penniless. Who among us proud philanthropists would be awakened in the middle of a winter night to minister to someone dying on a bed of straw? Which of us would wish to have perpetually before his eyes the spectacle of misery which he cannot succour, or live surrounded by sunken cheeks and hollow eyes which tell of hunger and uttermost need? Would we follow the Paris *curés*, those angels of humanity, to scenes of crime and grief and vice, shedding hope in despairing hearts? Which of us would be ready to turn his back on the world of happiness, spend his whole life among the suffering, to receive ingratitude from the poor and calumny from the rich?

Passing to the regular clergy Chateaubriand pronounces that the monastic orders are still needed for the care of orphans, the relief of the poor and unfortunate, as a retreat for solitary souls, to minister to the maladies of the heart as spas aid the maladies of the body. Think of the monks of St. Bernard succouring travellers lost in the snow, of their labours in hospitals, their crusade against slavery, their visits to prisons, the spiritual comfort they administer at the foot of the scaffold, their missions to China. The rigours of La Trappe are praised as a school of morals instituted amid the pleasures of the century, models of penitence in the midst of vice and prosperity. What a lesson is the spectacle of the

dying Trappist lying on straw and cinders in the sanctuary surrounded by his silent brethren, calling them to virtue while the
bell tolled for his approaching departure! Usually the living console the dying, here the dying man at the gates of eternity calls
them to penitence while he himself, despite his holiness, remains
in doubt as to his salvation.

10

JOSEPH DE MAISTRE AND THE VATICAN

I

COUNT JOSEPH DE MAISTRE was the ablest and most influential champion of the Catholic Church between Bossuet and Newman. The son of the President of the Senate of Savoy grew up in a family where order was regarded as heaven's first law. Order was clearly impossible without authority, but what sort of authority? The King, replied the French royalists. The *Tiers Etat*, argued the Constituent Assembly in 1789. Neither one nor the other, proclaimed de Maistre. Monarchy was not merely the best but the only stable form of government, yet a purely secular régime could not provide a satisfactory society. A quasi-mystical element was essential, and supernatural sanctions were only to be found in the Church. Unlike the Gallican Bossuet, he claimed authority over temporal rulers for the head of the only divinely inspired institution in the world; and authority, whether temporal or spiritual, was most effective if concentrated in a single hand. Hobbes himself had never affirmed more decisively the need of unchallenged sovereignty as the sole bulwark against the unruly passions of mankind. A century after his birth Sainte-Beuve, neither a royalist nor a believer, saluted him as a political thinker of the first rank and a Christian gentleman. He described himself as the most French of foreigners, regarded Paris as the capital of Europe, and saluted the King of France as the temporal Pope, French blood ran in his veins, for a branch of his family had migrated to Savoy in the seventeenth century.

Born in Chambéry in 1754, de Maistre, like Voltaire before him, was educated by the Jesuits from whom he learned the lesson of unquestioning obedience to authority. The young Savoyard carried the principle of subordination to the point of seeking permission from his father for every book he had to read during his law studies at the University of Turin. As he grew to manhood in the Century of Reason he was distressed by the impotence and lack of prestige of the Church. Freemasonry had spread all over Europe, and he, like his sovereign, joined a lodge after satisfying himself that it contained no threat to Church or State and despite the frowns of the local Bishop. Indeed in the truceless fight against three formidable forces, scepticism, Protestantism and Gallicanism, any potential ally was welcome. He had reached middle-age before anyone had heard of the conscientious magistrate outside his native city.

A new chapter opened in 1792, when the Duchy of Savoy, till then part of the Kingdom of Piedmont, was annexed by France, and his property confiscated. He spent the next twenty-three years in exile, first in Lausanne, Turin and Sardinia, and later as Minister of the King of Sardinia in St. Petersburg. His financial losses were the least of his afflictions, for he cared little for material things and was stirred to the depths by the mighty drama on the Seine. While Burke could thunder in the House of Commons against Jacobinism as 'an armed doctrine', de Maistre had no weapon but his pen. The Revolution transformed him into a publicist and filled him with a burning sense of mission. In 1796, when the Terror was over and the Directory was installed in Paris, he published anonymously at Lausanne *Considérations sur la France* which embodied his reflections not only on the Revolution but on government and society. The book fired a broadside against eighteenth-century France, its anarchic individualism, its naïve belief in perfectibility, its exaggeration of the power of reason, its hostility to religion and tradition. While the orators of 1789 proclaimed the Rights of Man it was his mission to proclaim their duties and to abate their pride.

During his exile he was fortified by a robust faith in an overruling Providence which neither public horrors nor personal misfortunes could shake. 'We do what we like, but that does not impair the general design; for Providence everything is a means, even obstacles.' Nothing like the French Revolution had ever been seen or would be seen again. Robespierre and other criminals had imposed the most odious despotism in history on a guilty nation and had justly suffered for their sins. The greater the offence the more speedy and exemplary the punishment, whether of individuals or nations: never had God shown His hand more clearly. If He employed the vilest of instruments it was in order to regenerate the community which produced them. Every nation had a mission. France had abused her trust, but one of the sternest of her critics never despaired of her recovery. She had long been the first country in Europe possessed of inspiring traditions, and her legitimate ruler was rightly called *Le Roi très Chrétien*. Since she had erred and had demoralized Europe she had to be redeemed by terrible means. Doubtless some innocent persons had suffered, but fewer than was generally believed, for responsibility for the Revolution was very widely diffused. 'I think the abominable revolution is the just and necessary conse- quence of mistakes everywhere, especially in your country,' he wrote to a friend in France. All who had shared in depriving the people of their religious belief, all who had exalted metaphysical subtleties above the laws of property, all who attacked the funda- mental laws of the state, all who approved violence against the King, all who had desired the Revolution, were quite rightly its victims. Some people grieved over the guillotining of illustrious *savants*, but divine justice was no respecter of persons, and too many *savants* had aided or approved the Revolution. The author was a stern judge and he was certain that God's verdicts were no less strict.

One of the worst crimes was the attack on sovereignty, since none produced more terrible consequences. The murder of the head of the state was the supreme atrocity, for the sovereign had not deserved his fate by any wrong-doing. Never had a great crime more accomplices—many more and with less excuse than the execution of Charles I. Not all Frenchmen desired his death, but for over two years the immense majority supported all the follies, injustices and conspiracies which led up to the catastrophe of 21 January. Every drop of his blood would cost torrents, perhaps four millions of lives. The longer the usurpation the more inevitable the counter-revolution, and here the Church had a vital part to play. The priesthood in France needed regeneration, for riches, luxury and the general tendency to laxity had lowered its prestige. The first attack was on its property, the second was the Civil Constitution. These outrages started the process of regeneration, and the crimes of the tyrants became the instruments of Providence. The French clergy were called to a great mission, all the more because human nature was full of faults. That war was the habitual state of mankind was illustrated from the history of France. Even here, however, there were compensations. When the human soul has lost tone, and scepticism and other poisonous vices bred by the excesses of civilisation are rampant, it can only be reinvigorated by blood. Moreover the arts and sciences, the great enterprises, lofty conceptions and masculine virtues are nourished by war. Nations never reach their full stature except after long and bloody conflicts. De Maistre, like the Crusaders, never thought of Christianity merely as a religion of meekness and love.

Would the French Republic last? Though his reply in the negative proved correct it was based on a false assumption. 'A great free nation cannot exist under a republican government.' Was it in the interest of the country to be ruled by a Directory and two Consuls instead of by a king reigning under the old forms? The provinces would be jealous of the capital. Every stable government rested on religious foundations, which in his case were totally lacking. Since philosophy was a disintegrating force, France would have to restore the *Roi très Chrétien* to his throne. Man could not create a constitution, merely transform existing institutions and embody ancient rights. The Constitution of 1795 was made for *man*, not for Frenchmen, and the seal of divine approval was not on it. Military victories were no assurance of longevity. The notion of a social contract was contrary to historical experience. No society had ever emerged from a consultation, and a written constitution was useless since attempts to alter it were inevitable. For Montesquieu's doctrine of the separation of powers he had as little use as for Rousseau's gospel of the sovereignty of the people. We might be listening to the voice of Burke in the plea for the continuity of society and the principle of organic growth. At this point, obsessed by his hatred of republics, he commits himself to a prophecy which helps to keep his name alive on both sides of the Atlantic. The Constitution of the United States, he declared, would not last. 'They have chosen a site for the new capital. One could bet a thousand to one that it will never be built and will not be called Washington and the Chambers will never settle there.'

How would the transition in France from the Republic to Monarchy occur? Very quietly is the answer. Apathy had succeeded to the hysteria of the years of revolution; less than half the people supported the Directory, and the return of the King would be generally welcomed. Would he then wreak vengeance on his foes? No, for he had promised an amnesty except for those who had voted for his brother's execution, and he was temperamentally averse to violence. His restoration would not be a counter-revolution but the contrary of a revolution. Apprehension that the returning Émigrés would assume control were baseless, for they no longer counted in official circles. There would, of course, be some restitution of confiscated national property, but that would be approved by all except its unworthy temporary owners.

In a final passage he appeals to his readers to take him seriously and hearken to his voice. 'I am a complete stranger to France which I have never seen, and I cannot expect anything from the King whom I do not know. My ideas may be wrong, but Frenchmen can read them without anger since they are wholly disinterested.' Every student of the life and writings of one of the finest spirits of his time will agree that he was not out for himself.

The book was read by his fellow exile, the future Louis XVIII, who expressed his gratitude for the tribute to the Bourbon dynasty, and sent a small sum which was respectfully declined.

II

THE main occupation and the principal solace of Joseph de Maistre during the dark and lonely years at St. Petersburg as Minister of the King of Sardinia was the composition of his most important work. Completed after his return and published in 1819, *Du Pape* may be regarded as his political testament, ranking among the classics of political and social philosophy with those of Locke and Burke, Rousseau and Marx, all of which were designed to change the outlook of Europe and have deeply influenced the course of history. Had the author returned to earth in 1870 to witness the proclamation of Papal Infallibility the father of modern ultramontanism would have concluded that he had not lived in vain.

A lengthy Introduction explains why a layman ventured to deal with a subject hitherto left to ecclesiastics. Why, indeed, should not the laity join the professional in the holiest of causes? Since a priest defending religion was regarded as merely pleading his own cause, the unbeliever was less suspicious of someone with no axe to grind. Himself the happy possessor of the truth he felt an indefinable urge to spread his ideas, so perhaps he had some right to believe that this sort of inspiration might not wholly fail to secure foreign approval. 'It is long since I wrote *Considerations on France* which did not arouse displeasure, for that country listened with good temper to the voice of a friend who belongs to her by religion, language, and the hope of a better order. Why should she not agree that she has taken a big step towards happiness and has regained sufficient poise to examine and judge herself wisely? Of course circumstances have greatly changed since 1796. If I did not feel myself full of goodwill and completely free from the spirit of contention, even with regard to men whose systems most offend, God knows I would throw down my pen. But this does not exclude the solemn expression of my belief, nor the clear and lofty accents of the faith, nor the cry of alarm in face of the enemy known or masked, nor the honest proselytism which precedes persuasion. Even when I find myself in direct opposition to other beliefs I shall be perfectly calm. I know what is owing to nations and their rulers, but I do not think it inconsistent to tell them the truth in a considerate manner. I have become convinced and should wish with all my heart to prove to others that without the sovereign Pontiff there is no real Christianity. Call this statement a paradox if you like but let no one call it an insult. Only one honourable vengeance is open to an opponent— to refute if he can.'

Special attention was devoted to France because only the realisation of her errors could save her. Certain privileged nations had a mission in the world, and hers was as clear as the sun. In

her national ideology there was a certain undying religious element, for the Frenchman needed religion more than anyone:
without it he was not merely enfeebled but mutilated. Look at
his history from the Druids to the Crusades! The satanic revolution would never be totally extinguished except by the contrary
principle. The priesthood should be the principal object of the
Government's attention, for priests had preserved everything
and taught us everything. Now was the chance for the nobility
to give their sons to the altar as in past times. Where great names
lead, others would follow. They owed France a debt, for the
Revolution was largely their fault. So long as a pure aristocracy,
exulting in the national traditions, surrounded the throne, the
latter was impregnable. Their apostasy would be its doom even
if it were occupied by St. Louis or Charlemagne. By its monstrous
alliance with evil principles in the last century it had ruined
everything, so now its task was to repair everything. That was
its destiny—an alliance with the priesthood.

The anti-religious fury of the last century against all Christian
truths and institutions was directed above all against the Holy
See. They depicted the Pope as the natural enemy of all thrones,
and their propaganda had found success in certain Catholic
states. Yet without him every Christian edifice would be ruined.
Protestantism, philosophies, and a thousand other more or less
perverse and extravagant sects, having emasculated the truth,
mankind could not remain in its present state. Now that France
was convulsively struggling against the torrent of errors, the
author hoped she would listen to him in a friendly spirit.

After this lengthy Prologue the curtain rises on the central
issue of Infallibility which is defined as the equivalent in the
spiritual order to sovereignty in the temporal sphere. 'When we
say the Church is infallible we merely claim for it the right common to all sovereignties which necessarily act as if infallible. No
government can be resisted on the pretext of error or injustice;
if it could it would no longer exist. Similarly the judgements of its
courts are absolute.' Equally preposterous was the contention
that his power must be limited by the Canons. Who indeed was to
decide if he had broken them, and who could compel him to obey
them if he refused? The only alternative to unchallengeable
sovereignty, in the Church as in the State, was anarchy. 'All we

N

say is that the Pope, speaking to the Church without pressure and *ex cathedra*, has never been and never will be wrong in matters of faith.' This formula anticipates the declaration of 1870, though no claim is made that he speaks with equal inerrancy on morals. The Church would never grow old. Neither young nor old, it was eternal. The Christian régime was the only institution which could not decay because it alone was divine. 'No society without government, no government without sovereignty, no sovereignty without infallibility.' It might be the voice of Hobbes, though the old sceptic never claimed a religious sanction for *Leviathan*. Monarchy, tempered by aristocracy, was a universal need. In describing the claim to Infallibility as modern Bossuet was mistaken, for Papal decrees on matters of faith had always been the law of the Church.

Passing to Church Councils the author pours scorn on the notion that they constitute the supreme authority. An intermittent sovereign functioning at long intervals was a contradiction in terms, for the sovereign must be available at any hour. The last Council was at Trent, and the Church had managed very well without another. Moreover it had become world-wide and a General Council was now impossible. 'I could never understand how the French could say that the decrees of such Councils had the force of law. If the Council were summoned and presided over by the Pope that of course was another matter.' To the Protestant complaint that a sovereign claiming infallibility would be a monstrous despotism fettering the human mind the author replies that the Vatican never claimed infallibility outside the sphere of dogma; thus no country need fear an affront to its pride or dignity, and despotism in the world of thought was impossible.

Having thus defined the power of the Vatican de Maistre proceeds in Part II to discuss the controversial problem of its relation to temporal rulers. He starts, like Hobbes, with the incurable imperfection of human nature. 'Man, by nature both moral and corrupt, just in intelligence and perverse in his will, needs to be governed, and sovereigns, like judges, are more often right than wrong.' Even with a dissolute ruler on the throne other evil-doers receive due punishment. To the old problem of how to restrain a very bad ruler without destroying the sovereign power there was no answer. Some argued for fundamental laws and constitutions, but who would make such laws and carry them out? Anyone who did so would be the sovereign. The history of popular revolts in the attempt to curb the sovereign was not encouraging, for the remedy had often proved worse than the disease. Constitutional monarchy had been a partial success in England, but look at France! Revolutions started by the wise are often continued by madmen. Their authors are often their victims and may well forge more chains than they break. 'I have never denied that absolute power has great disadvantages, but we are between two abysses.' Catholic dogma prohibited all revolt, while Protestants, who favoured the sovereignty of the people, regarded non-resistance as enslavement. Obedience to Nero, he admits, was difficult; yet disobedience to the legitimate ruler was always dangerous and sometimes fatal, for sovereignty was an emanation of the divine power. The Pope alone, who wanted nothing for himself, could relieve subjects from their allegiance, and then only in order to avert a revolution. Popes had struggled with sovereigns but never with sovereignty; they had never abused their power, and in their capacity as temporal rulers had never attempted to enlarge their territories by force.

In every sphere the Pope had been a stabilising influence, above all in proclaiming the sanctity of marriage, unlike the early Reformers who accepted the bigamy of Philip of Hesse. Hildebrand's challenge to the omnipotence of secular rulers was in the interest of the common man not less than of the Church. Did the Popes ever press their claims against secular rulers too far? Very rarely, for their weapons, such as excommunication, were purely spiritual, and citizens in every land needed some brake on the power of their ruler which only the Pope could supply. Rebutting Voltaire's dismissal of the Pope as a foreigner, the author declares that he was no more a foreigner within the sphere of the Christian Church than the King of France in Lyons or Bordeaux. He was usually wiser than Kings and Princes who were often at war. The mediaeval conception of all Christian states united by religious brotherhood under the supremacy of the Pope was better than any system of modern times, for nothing united people so much as religious unity. Had the rulers listened to his voice there would have been no Wars of Religion and no French Revolution, for he was the ideal mediator.

Book III analyses the record of the Papacy in the wider context of civilisation and human happiness. While their missionaries carried the Christian message to distant lands, the Protestants, separated from the Mother Church and from each other, were sterile. Equally noble had been the campaign against slavery beginning with the birth of Christianity. Women owed it even more than men, for the best method of improving the latter was to exalt the former. Insistence on sacerdotal celibacy earns the highest praise from de Maistre, who salutes Hildebrand as the saviour of priesthood since a married priest cannot give undivided attention to his flock. 'The unquestioned superiority of the Catholic priesthood derives solely from celibacy.' In a word the Pope was the natural head of mankind and the most powerful promoter of civilisation.

In Book IV, which deals with the separated Churches, the author lets himself go. The separation of the Eastern Church was a tragedy, for the Russians, among whom he had lived for years, were a fine people; but they were as far from the truth as the Protestants, with whom their only link was their common hatred of Rome. As a result of the Eastern schism and the Reformation half Europe was now without religion, and Protestant rationalists were steadily undermining the Christian edifice. Rome, on the other hand, had nothing to fear from the discoveries of science, a sort of acid which dissolved everything except gold. The Anglican religion was false because it stood alone, and its episcopacy was rejected by the nonconformists. 'Neither Catholic nor Protestant, so what is it?' Yet it was nearest the truth, for no separated Church had retained so many Catholic elements. Even now it was not too late to return to the fold. 'You noble English, you were the first foes of unity, and the honour belongs to you to restore it. What do you reproach us with? Everything invites Protestants to return to us, for no purely human institution could have endured for eighteen centuries.'

Regret warms into passion when the author thinks of Luther and Calvin. 'In an unprecedented access of frenzy, the immediate result of which was thirty years of carnage, these two mediocrities (*hommes du néant*) with the pride of sectaries, plebeian acrimony and the fanaticism of the cabaret, reformed the Church without knowing what they said or did. Their campaigns were in vain for they were fighting against God and every attack on the Church was an attack on Christianity. The only real Reformation was achieved at the Council of Trent.' The work closes with a rhapsody straight from the author's glowing heart. 'Oh! Holy Church of Rome, so long as I can speak I will sing your praises. I salute you, immortal mother of science and sanctity.' In his list of blessings conferred on mankind by the Church there is no mention of the Spanish Inquisition, but that topic had been dealt with in a series of *Lettres à un Gentilhomme Russe* in 1815 in which it received high marks for preserving the unity of the Church and the purity of the faith. Torture and the death penalty had been employed throughout history, so what country had the right to cast stones at Spain?

The onslaught on the Gallican Church designed as Part V of the treatise was written in 1817 and published as an independent work with a few additions and a Preface in 1820, the year before the author's death. Since *Du Pape* was written above all for French readers, many of whom would doubtless be shocked by the broadside against one of their well-established national traditions, he decided to hold it back till readers had had time to digest the larger work. In an earnest appeal to the French clergy he summons them to play their part in the great national recantation, great objects demanding large sacrifices, in this case the sacrifice of prejudices. Why was France so hostile to the Holy See? Firstly, owing to an exaggerated conception of her importance. She was a fine part of the Universal Church, but only a province of Catholic Europe. Secondly, Calvinists and Jansenists had struck rude blows against the Mother Church. Though France had spewed out the Calvinist poison it had left traces, for instance in the opposition to the reception of the Tridentine decrees. There was a good deal of Protestantism among the lawyers of the *Parlement* of Paris, at all times a stronghold of Gallican principles and a stubborn foe of all authority except its own.

Jansenism, which forms the subject of several chapters, is treated with no less severity than Calvinism, of which it is presented as merely a phase. It was the most extraordinary of heresies, the work of a few melancholy sectaries seeking solitude at Port

Royal who aspired to dominate France. Their reputation was largely undeserved and was mainly due to skilful propaganda. Its members were perpetually quarrelling and intriguing and caused only harm to religion. Their well-known textbooks on logic and grammar were largely copied from earlier writers. Pascal, their only outstanding figure, had been much overpraised, and the *Lettres Provinciales* owed much of their celebrity to the unpopularity of the Jesuits. Rome had deservedly condemned the Jansenists for their invincible contempt for authority, for they disobeyed the Sorbonne and the Gallican Church as well as the Pope. They boasted of their austerity, but what could be more dangerous for morals than disobedience to the Church? Bossuet had called the *religieuses* of Port Royal foolish virgins. De Maistre had no use for minorities, for truth was in its nature intolerant of error.

The second part of *L'Église Gallicane* deals at length with the Articles of 1682, the most celebrated and audacious challenge to Papal authority before the Revolution. No ruler since Philip the Fair four centuries earlier had given the Holy See so much trouble as Louis XIV. The chief culprit in that delirium of pride was Colbert, who advised him to summon a Council to define the limits of Papal authority. The whole affair was an inconceivable aberration which shocked other Catholic states no less than the Vatican. Though the Pope urged the King to repeal the offensive Articles, he feared that the Eldest Son of the Church might follow the example of England, and in consequence never formally condemned them. The chief interest of this long argument is the partial exoneration of Bossuet, the glory of the Church in France, who never wanted the meeting but accepted its findings since they did not touch the faith. It was absurd to speak of 'the liberties of the Gallican Church'. There were no liberties, merely a conspiracy to defraud the Holy See of its rights. In the words of Fénelon, the King was the head of the Church more than the Pope. That France was not wholly lost to the Church was largely due to the tact and patience of the Pope, and in a lesser degree to the moderation of the King who realised the value of his support. Spain was the best nation in Europe, for the Inquisition had kept it free from heresy, and Ignatius Loyola had founded the best of the religious orders.

III

AFTER moving around for several years in attendance on his master the King of Piedmont Joseph de Maistre was appointed in 1804 to the Embassy at St. Petersburg. Since the salary was too small to allow his wife and family to join him, and since his official duties were unexacting, he occupied his leisure in omnivorous reading, literary composition, and a voluminous correspondence. Some of his letters to his best friend Blacas, Secretary of the Bourbon claimant in exile, and to de Bonald, his ideological *alter ego* in France, are like treatises and reveal as much of his deepest feelings as his publications. In the spirit of a mediaeval Crusader he saw not only the French Revolution but every historical event in terms of black and white. Unlike Renan, who declared *la vérité est dans les nuances*, he abhorred compromise as heartily as he despised doubt. Every fight was a fight to the finish, and he believed that the good cause would triumph however long it took. Throughout the decades of exile his faith in the restoration of monarchy in France never waned. Compared with this man of austere character and burning convictions Chateaubriand was a light-weight. Burke launched the European counter-revolution and died while the struggle was at its height. De Maistre continued his work, lived to witness the emergence of ancient landmarks from the receding flood, and visited the restored Bourbon King in Paris. The stern Legitimist had never expected the parvenu Empire—a phase of the Revolution—to endure, and he rejoiced in the downfall of *l'homme infernal*, the monster, the brigand, the terrible usurper. Once again, as he felt sure would be the case, *la Providence c'est bien la maîtresse*.

While his treatise on the Papacy expounds his programme for the healing of Europe's wounds, the second of his major works covers many aspects of life and thought. Most of the eleven *Entretiens* which fill two substantial volumes entitled *Soirées de Saint Petersbourg* were composed in the Russian capital, and the series, which by its loose structure was capable of limitless expansion, was interrupted by his death at the age of sixty-seven. Modelled on Plato's *Dialogues*, the *Entretiens* grip the reader from the start. The curtain rises on a beautiful summer evening in 1809, when three friends, the Count (de Maistre), the

Chevalier, a young French *émigré*, and a scholarly Russian
Senator are boating on the Neva. 'If Heaven in its mercy', exclaimed the Count, 'granted me one of those rare moments when
the heart is flooded with an unusual and unanticipated joy; if a
wife, children, brothers long separated from me suddenly fell
into my arms, I should like it to happen on one of these lovely
nights on the banks of the Neva under the eyes of the hospitable
Russians.' The three friends were strangely moved by the peace
and beauty of the scene.

Chevalier: I should love to have here in this boat one of the perverse men born for the misfortune of society, one of the monsters
who cumber the earth.
The Others: What would you do to him?
Chevalier: Ask him if the evening seemed as beautiful to him as to us.
Count: Bad hearts never experience beautiful nights or days, for they
have no real delights.
Chevalier: You think evil-doers are never happy. I should like to
agree but every day I hear of their successes. If God punishes in
this world He is in no hurry about it.

At this point the Count invited his companions to continue the
discussion round his tea-table.

Senator: The happiness of bad men and the misfortunes of the just:
that is the great scandal, the mystery of divine metaphysics. Punishment in an after life does not satisfy me.
Count: That has never worried me. In war good and bad suffer alike.
An accident is a misfortune, not an injustice, for God cannot be
the author of evil. Moreover evil-doers do not flourish.

The host proceeds to remind his guests of the existence of the
executioner in the most notorious passage of the whole work.

Count: Though he is to be found everywhere no one can explain
why anyone chooses such a profession in preference to pleasant,
lucrative and honourable occupations. Are his head and his heart
like ours? They must surely contain some element foreign to our
nature. That such an extraordinary being should exist a special
decree of the creative power is required. How can he bear the
odium of his profession, shunned by everyone? Except for the
voices of his family he only hears groans. The victim arrives at the
place of public execution, greeted by cries of Poisoner, Parricide.

The executioner ties him down on a cross. Then amid a horrible
silence is heard the cracking of bones and the howls of the victim.
Then he is taken down and tied to a wheel; the broken limbs are
caught in the spokes; the head drops; his hair stands up, and the
mouth only utters a few agonising appeals for death. It is all over. The
executioner's heart beats for joy as he says to himself: 'No one can
do that like me.' Returning home he has a meal, goes to bed and
sleeps. Next day he is thinking about other things. Is this a human
being? He is not a criminal, but no one calls him virtuous nor
estimable. And yet all greatness, all power, all subordination rests
on the executioner. The scaffold is also an altar. He is at once the
horror and the cement of human association. Remove him and
order gives place to chaos, thrones collapse, society disappears.
God, the author of sovereignty, is also the author of punishment.
Since evil exists the sword of justice is never sheathed. Tribunals
rarely make mistakes.
Chevalier: What about the Calas case?
Count: The innocence of Calas was never proved.

In the second and third *Entretiens* the host proceeds from the
necessity of severe punishments to consider the nature of sin,
which he defines as the capacity to commit crimes dating from
the fall of man. Since that fateful parting of the ways our record
had been a disgrace. We could not look into our hearts without
a blush, for a potential angel had sunk into vice. 'We talk of
innocence but is there such a thing? Are we three good? Have
we the courage to look into ourselves with a lamp? We could
only claim virtue, justice, innocence with blushes. Let us start
by examining the evil in ourselves, and we shall turn pale as we
press into the abyss, for our transgressions are beyond computa-
tion. Our virtues are so few and are often the result of prejudices.
The only virtue is victory over oneself. I never think of this
without wanting to fall to the ground like a sinner asking pardon
and accepting in advance all evils as lenient treatment for the
immense debt I owe to eternal justice. And yet I am often described as a decent fellow. All sins are punished sooner or later
in proportion to their magnitude. Think how terrible they must
have been to necessitate the Flood.' The Count's Deity is a God
of wrath, the God of the Old Testament, not of the New. After
this thunderous broadside at fallen humanity it is surprising to
read that the just man has peace in his heart, an inestimable

treasure which makes up for everything, and a good repute is one of the most delicious of human joys. For once the stern author allows a ray of sunshine to penetrate a darkened world.

Little comfort is to be found in the discussion of prayer in the sixth *Entretien*. In the words of Saint-Martin it is the breathing of the soul, but its nature and purpose are misunderstood if we think of it as an almost mechanical device for obtaining what we desire. How often we want what is not good for us! All we know is that we do not pray in vain when we say His Will be done, in other words ask that evil should disappear. Instead of complaining that our prayer is not granted we should tremble for asking the wrong thing. Some prayers indeed may be a crime. The Count's dissertation, like all his utterances, is deeply coloured by his sorrowful conviction of the unworthiness of man who may think himself lucky that his lot is no worse.

The seventh *Entretien* deals with the place of war in the life of mankind and the divine plan. The author's views are put into the mouth of the Senator who starts with an elaborate survey of the moral issues involved. The soldier, like the executioner, is authorised to kill, and it is an honourable profession. He does not fight for glory, which is reserved for the commanders. Nor does he fight because the cause is just, for how many just wars are there, and what is the criterion? Most officers and privates are honourable, civilised, kindly, sometimes deeply religious persons, who would grieve if they killed their sister's canary; yet such a man is transformed in the heat of battle by the spirit of carnage as he climbs over a heap of corpses. The Chevalier confirms the picture of the two souls within the soldier's breast from his own experience of exaltation in the fray and reversion to the primordial instinct to slay. Despite its savagery, continues the Senator, there is something divine in war, and we are right to speak of the God of battles. Violence permeates all life, from the lowest animals upwards, and the earth is an immense altar of sacrifice. Since it is the law of the world as God made it there must be something divine about it—divine in its mysteries, its glory, its fascination, in the significance of morale, a factor even more important than big battalions. So deep and universal is the instinct that mankind has made no serious effort to pass from the method of savagery to the method of civilisation, though the relations between individuals have long been regularised by law.

The eighth *Entretien* returns to the theme which had started the discussions, the problem of the sufferings of the just. The Count's answer, however it may have satisfied himself, can have brought little consolation to his friends. Man suffers, he declares, because no one is just or even exempt from actual crime. To complain of disorder in the world is to admit the conception of order which in turn involves the existence of intelligence. The Count proceeds to belabour philosophers who have the audacity to complain that God is unjust, cruel, merciless, and that in consequence prayer is useless. On the contrary, we must pray to Him and serve Him with all the greater zeal than if His mercy knew no limits. 'The more terrible He appears to us, the more must we redouble our fear of Him, the more ardent and unwearying our supplications.' We know He exists, but we shall never fully know what He is. We find ourselves in an empire whose sovereign has announced once for all the laws which regulate everything. Generally speaking they reveal wisdom and indeed a striking goodness. Some appear hard, even unjust. But he asks grumblers what can be done. Leave the empire? Impossible, for there is nothing outside it. To complain, to fret, to write against the sovereign means flogging or death. The best course is resignation and respect, even love. As we are bound to serve Him is it not best to serve with rather than without love?

Whence come these insolent doctrines which cavil at God's decrees? They come from the large phalanx called the savants whom in this century we have been unable to keep in their place, namely the second place. Previously there were very few, and only a small number of them were impious. Today it is a profession, a mob, a nation. The exception has become the rule. Everywhere they have usurped a boundless influence. But if anything in the world is certain it is not for science to guide mankind. Nothing vital has been confided to them. One must have taken leave of one's senses to believe that God has commissioned the pundits to tell us what He is and what we owe to Him. It is the task of the prelates, the nobles, the great officers to be the guardians of traditional truths, to tell nations what is good or bad, true or false in the moral and spiritual sphere. The others have no right to reason about such matters. They have the natural sciences to amuse them, so of what can they complain? Anyone who speaks or writes to deprive the people of a

national dogma should be hung like a common thief. Why have we
been so imprudent as to give free rein to everybody? That is what
has ruined us. All the so-called philosophers have a certain fierce
and rebellious pride, and the eighteenth century had witnessed a
rebellion against God. They detest all the distinctions which they
do not possess, dislike all authority, and hate everything above
themselves. If you leave them alone they will attack everything,
including God because He is master. They are the same men who
have written against the King.

The Greeks had started the trouble by their audacious exaltation
of the faculty of reason.

The eleventh and last *Entretien*, even in its unfinished shape,
forms a fitting conclusion to a work of almost unrelieved austerity.
The Senator leads off with indications that the end of the world,
as foretold in the Book of Revelations, was at hand. There was
hardly any educated person in Europe, he declares, who was not
expecting some extraordinary event, precisely as the world sensed
something before the birth of Christ. No great events such as the
French Revolution had happened without being predicted. The
outlook was dark. The vast majority of mankind in Asia and
Africa had never heard of Christ, and in parts of Europe Christianity had been utterly destroyed by the insensate Reformation.
'Even in your Catholic countries [the Senator belonged to the
Orthodox Church] it only seems to exist in name. What prodi-
gious indifference! Think of the attack on the Jesuits. You have
no more Terror. You dare nothing while everything is dared
against you.' Protestantism was turning into Socinianism and
becoming the Islam of Europe. Such was the inevitable consequence of the Reformation, for both proclaimed the unity of the
Deity. Could such a wholesale apostasy endure? Was it not at
once the cause and the forerunner of some major judgement?

In the Count's unfinished comment on the Senator's survey
of the plight of mankind he associates himself with the prediction
of some great event. A fresh peril had emerged in the British
Bible Society which was selling copies of the Bible in many
languages. 'The whole enterprise rests on a capital error, for it
is not the reading but the teaching of the Scriptures which is of
value: read without notes or explanation they are poison. The
Bible Society is a Protestant enterprise, and as such you ought to

condemn it as much as many strange propagandists of the faith, while respecting the *bona fides* of the promoters. It embodies the insensate fundamental Protestant dogma of individual judgement.' There is something appropriate in the coincidence that the last paragraph of the *Entretiens* should reiterate in uncompromising terms the author's disbelief in the capacity of man to steer his course and his conviction of our dire need of guidance by an infallible Church.

I I

LAMENNAIS AND CHRISTIAN DEMOCRACY

I

LAMENNAIS stood much closer to Joseph de Maistre than to Chateaubriand, for religion was the main concern of his life. The author of the *Génie du Christianisme* was more interested in literature and society, travel and politics, than in the state of his soul or the sickness of society. To him as to millions of Frenchmen the Pope was little more than a dignitary in a foreign land whose authority was limited to the sphere of belief. For the impressionable Lamennais, on the other hand, the horrors of the French Revolution and the tyranny of Napoleon revealed the sinfulness of human nature and cried aloud for spiritual remedies. Fortunately for France and humanity a divine institution with an infallible head was available. In a world of low morality and religious apathy society was impossible without religion, and the Church could only exert its legitimate influence if it were financially independent of the State. A combination of secular and spiritual authority was required, monarchy humbly acknowledging the primacy of the Vatican. In the early writings of Lamennais, as of de Maistre, we approach so close to the ideal of theocracy that few of their countrymen were willing to march at their side.

Born at St. Malo in 1782, the son of a wealthy shipowner, Félicité de Lamennais was reared in a *milieu* where business counted for more than politics. Though his father had been ennobled for services to his native town he outwardly accepted the Revolution while keeping out of the firing line. Like other moderates, however, he disapproved of the Civil Constitution of the clergy and held private services in his house for a few friends under the auspices of an *insermenté* priest. Among his son's early memories was that of listening at the door for the slightest sign of danger. His love of images and the habit of kneeling before a statue of the Virgin earned him among his young companions the name of *le petit bigot*. The phase of precocious piety was soon over, for when he began to read he was enthralled by Rousseau's Savoyard Vicar. His incredulity shocked the priest whose task it was to prepare the lad of twelve for his first Communion, which was consequently postponed. As with Chateaubriand the phase lasted through the years of adolescence, outwardly conforming but inwardly wondering if all that he was expected to believe was true.

Visiting Paris with his father when the Terror was over, he was struck by the gaiety of the capital as if awakening from an evil dream. Since his elder brother desired to enter the priesthood he was drafted into the family business which had been badly hit by the storms of the Revolution, but his romantic soul was so bored by office routine that he dreamed of migrating to some French colony. The mood of frustration lasted till the age of twenty when he read Pascal and the *Génie du Christianisme*. His adored elder brother was ordained and persuaded him to make his first Communion at twenty-two. A new chapter opened two years later when he spent several fruitful months in Paris enjoying the lectures at the Collège de France and still more the teaching at St. Sulpice, then under the wise direction of Abbé Emery, who became his spiritual guide. Though the Concordat had ended the open quarrel between Church and State, a new danger had arisen in the resolve of the master of France to break all opposition to his will and to turn the clergy into a militia. Returning home, Félicité eagerly studied Bossuet and Bonald, whose doctrine of the vital necessity of authority captured his heart and mind. The revolt against authority, he believed, began with the Reformation. The right of private judgement had led through disorder to atheism under the cloak of liberty and to the multiplication of sects united only by their distaste for authority. Still more decisive was the influence of his brother Jean, and at last, at the age of twenty-five, all barriers were thrown down. 'Now I wish only for the cross of Jesus. What a happy life! The Cross and nothing but the Cross!' The dream of the brothers was realised as they worked in blissful partnership for many years.

Their first task was to set forth their programme, the elder supplying most of the inspiration and the material, the younger putting it into literary shape. *Réflexions sur l'état de l'église en France au 18ième Siècle et sur la situation actuelle*, written in 1808 and published in 1809, was submitted to and approved by the Abbé Emery. The little book of 150 pages opens with an attack on the Protestants, the Jansenists, the *Philosophes*, and the godless criminals of the Revolution who robbed the Church of its possessions. The Emperor—doubtless as a precaution—is praised for the restoration of the Church, and the political and social utility of religion, a consideration known to appeal to the Dictator, is emphasised. Even more deadly than overt hostility, in the author's eyes, was the widespread indifference, mainly the legacy of materialist teaching, though the tepid zeal of many clergy played its part. It is a dark picture and parts of the book read like a sermon.

The second portion proposes various remedies to restore the influence of the Church, among them a national council of the bishops to decide on important measures, synods of rural deans, retreats, doctrinal addresses, and a special body to supervise seminaries for the *curés*. To deal with academic attacks on the faith the brothers recommend a revival of Catholic scholarship, including the study of the Fathers and the technique of preaching. Passing to the laity they deplore juvenile immorality and demand Christian schools, missions and the use of the rosary. The Jesuits should be restored and new monasteries and convents founded. In their youthful zeal they hoped that the work might attract the notice of the Emperor, but despite the tribute to him it was seized by the police. Undiscouraged, Félicité now took minor orders and the brothers founded a training school for clergy at St. Malo in which the younger taught mathematics. Its career was brief, for church schools were suppressed in 1811.

The second act of the campaign against the Dictator as an enemy of the Church was the championship of the Pope's right to nominate bishops. Dynasties came and went, but the old conflict inherited from the sixteenth and seventeenth centuries remained. *La tradition de l'église sur l'institution des évêques* had to wait for publication till the fall of the Emperor. Once again most of the materials were collected by the more scholarly Jean who added notes to his brother's draft. The argument was familiar enough: the power given to Peter had never been and could not be surrendered, for to do so would destroy the Church. A survey of ecclesiastical history recorded the relations of the Papacy not only with the West but with the Patriarchs of the East, and asserted the derivation of the power of the Metropolitans from Rome. Throughout the treatise the authors strike an unflinching ultramontane note. The Church, they argued, was a monarchy, and its authority was indivisible.

No one rejoiced more heartily than Félicité at the restoration of the monarchy, partly because he was a royalist, still more because he expected the automatic renewal of the privileges and independence of the Church. It was a keen disappointment to discover that Gallicanism retained its grip and that, as he expressed it, no one cared about the Pope. He reprinted the *Réflexions sur l'état de l'église en France*, omitting the compromising tribute to Napoleon and adding notes disavowing certain opinions expressed in 1809. In those five years he had grown into a full-blooded ultramontane to whom any suggestion of chains on the Church was anathema. Since clergy paid by the State were not their own masters, they should live from the resources of the Church and receive instructions from the Pope alone. The argument was underlined by a tribute of admiration to Pius VII who had confronted the Dictator at the height of his power.

The lack of zeal among many of the clergy is contrasted with the dynamism of the Jesuits who alone could rescue religion from its plight. The sharpest arrows are reserved for the university system which survived the tyrant's downfall and functioned as an instrument of tyranny. Throughout life Lamennais detested the theory and practice of the omnipotent state not less than blatant atheism or indifference to religion. For such a notorious enemy of Napoleon there was no room in France on the return from Elba. He fled to England under an assumed name, recrossing the Channel after Waterloo. In the following year, at the age of thirty-four, he was at last ordained priest.

With his chronic ill-health and highly strung temperament

o

Lamennais was never fully at peace with himself, and even the downfall of the hated superman failed to raise his spirits. The new royalist broom, far from sweeping away the cobwebs of the interregnum, retained far too much to please him of the secularising spirit of the Revolution and the Empire, above all in the vital sphere of education. He wrote in bitter irony: 'Have you seen this beautiful ordinance drawn up by the Protestant Guizot and signed by *Le Roi très Chrétien*? Nothing is lacking in it except religion.' Even the news of Waterloo brought no joy to his heart. 'I foresee disasters, revolutions, endless wars,' he wrote to his brother-in-law. 'The king is good, but he accepts protection from murderers and demagogues, intoxicated worshippers of their own contemptible sovereignty. The whole human race seems to be rushing to destruction in its death agony.' Having been restored by foreigners, monarchy lacked prestige. The Organic Articles, which remained in force, created a state-controlled Church, a mere shadow of its great past. The clergy had become salaried servants of the state. Hatred of religion as manifested during the Revolution had given place to apathy which was as bad or worse. France, he believed, needed a prophet to proclaim that religion was the cement of society no more to be ignored than the law of gravitation, and he answered the call.

The larger part of his most important work, the *Essai sur l'Indifférence en matière de religion*, was completed when the publication in 1818 of Abbé Grégoire's *Essai historique sur les libertés de l'église Gallicane* gave the problem a touch of actuality, offending ultramontanists by its uninhibited Gallicanism and royalists by its contention that a national church required a liberal and republican state. Lamennais disapproved it on both grounds and resolved to present his own alternative. 'Perhaps', he wrote to his brother, 'Providence may cause a bad book to produce a useful result.' The main thesis of the volumes published at intervals between 1818 and 1823 is the need of society to rest on religious foundations provided by the Catholic Church. Part of the vitality of the *Essai* was the fact that it embodies the author's religious experiences. He had known indifference and self-disgust, had surrendered to Rousseau, and had groped his way out of the dark tunnel into the light of day. Saluted as the last of the Fathers, he was ranked with Bossuet and Fénelon.

II

THE note of urgency is struck in the lengthy introduction to the *Essai sur l'Indifférence*, for the temperamental author was always in a hurry. Disdainful indifference to truth seemed to him worse than error, for while men took any interest in religion there was always some hope. When, however, the pulse ceased to beat, when the chill reached the heart, a speedy and inevitable dissolution was at hand. No one could deny that society in Europe was rushing to its doom. Who could awaken it from its profound apathy and breathe life into its dry bones? Religion, morality, honour, duty, the most sacred principles and the noblest sentiments, were only a sort of dream, brilliant and fleeting phantoms at the back of the mind. Such a situation had never been known and could never have been imagined. A truceless war against reason and conscience had led to this brutal 'don't care' attitude; contemplating truth and error with equal disgust, man pretended that he could not tell one from the other. Such shameful degradation filled the observer with pity for mankind. Its primary cause was the supremacy of the senses, the paramountcy of the physical world. The pursuit of the physical sciences, which reminded him at every moment of his superiority to the brute creation, had focused his attention on material things and made him blush for his celestial origin. The horrors of the Revolution were the bitter fruit of the furious attack on every kind of truth. The history of Christianity and its martyrs was the record of the eternal struggle between the flesh and the spirit. At its coming it found the pagan world enslaved by the senses, without creed, pleasure its only god. How then could anyone maintain that the Christian faith had a natural origin? Struggling to victory through three centuries of persecution it had demanded more than fallen man could give, and the Church needed reform; but the Reformation had made things worse, striking at the roots of authority, leading logically through heresies to the militant atheism of the Century of Reason and the quasi-paralysis which followed the revolutionary tornado.

Having thus sketched the historical and psychological background of France under the restored monarchy, and agreeing with Pascal that opinion is the queen of the world, the author proceeds in the first half of the first volume to refute the three kinds of religious indifference. The first, envisaging religion as merely a political institution, believed it was only required by the common man. The second, while admitting the need of some form of religion for everyone, rejected the Christian revelation. The third recognised the necessity of a revealed religion but denied some of its truths. To the first Lamennais replies with Rousseau that all states had a religious foundation, adding that the latest attempt to dispense with it had only lasted a few months marked by bloodshed and spoliation. Religion was the sole basis of duties and duties the only cement of society: nothing could take the place of conscience. The Roman Empire began to decline when its citizens lost respect for the gods. The intellectual anarchy of the Reformation had produced a similar disintegrating effect, and England exhibited the monstrous spectacle of the true religion persecuted by heretics. Christianity had renovated mankind after the collapse of the Roman Empire; now it would do so again or society and the human race would disappear. Since philosophers blamed the multitude for not thinking, why should not they too think again and perhaps discover that they had been wrong?

Passing to the second school which taught that natural religion alone was true the author argues that Rousseau, who believed in God and immortality, was no more satisfying than the atheist *Philosophes* whom he despised. All the great religions, he declared, contained elements of truth and were deserving of respect; none possessed a monopoly and therefore people should practise the faith in which they were born. The best was that in which morality was the most pure, for nothing except the duties of morality was essential and they were independent of any formulated creed. To accept such teaching, comments Lamennais, was to despair of ultimate truth.

The third variant of indifference, which was found in the Protestant Churches, accepted revealed religion while rejecting some of its teachings. This application of the principle of private judgement to the fabric of belief led directly to deism and the toleration of errors. The Bible alone, declared Chillingworth in a famous phrase, was the religion of Protestants, but the Bible was often obscure. Since every reader claimed to interpret it for himself, rival interpretations led to the formation of a thousand odd sects attacking each other as bitterly as they all assailed the Catholic Church. Bossuet had told the lamentable story in his *Histoire des Variations*, to which no reply was possible since every statement was accompanied by a reference to its source. What was the good of revelation if men were free to pick and choose among its articles, classifying them as fundamental or non-fundamental according to taste? The Christian revelation was one and indivisible, every part of it essential. To reject a single item, as Jurieu felt entitled to do, was to deny the authority of the whole. To tolerate a single error was to open the door to a spineless latitudinarianism which allowed anyone to believe whatever he liked. Universal tolerance was only another name for universal indifference.

Having refuted to his own satisfaction the varieties of indifference the author turns to those who, instead of thinking wrong, did not think at all owing to lack of interest and laziness of mind, despising a religion which they had never troubled to explore. Everything was of interest to them except heaven, hell and eternity. Such people needed to be reminded of the importance of religion to the individual, society and God Himself. Pursuit of happiness was the deepest urge of man and could only be found by fulfilling the law of his being, for the fleeting delights of the senses could never appease the hunger of the heart. Without religion there was no hope of an after life, and the sceptic usually broke down on his death-bed. The believer knows his place in the scheme of things, knows God, knows himself, finds peace of mind and heart in contemplation of immutable truth. Aware of his duties and his destiny he knows all he needs to know. Nothing can trouble his tranquillity and his feeling of inexpressible well-being because they have their source in the depths of his soul, because he places himself unreservedly in the hands of the all good and all powerful Being who reveals Himself and unites to Himself all hearts which submit to His influence. Filled with a new light, estimating everything at its real value, man ceases to be the plaything of his passions and looks forward to an eternity of bliss as his reward.

The believer is naturally a good citizen. Untempted by selfish interest, his heart filled with pure and affectionate sentiments, he draws nearer to his fellows, sympathises with their troubles,

comforts them with tender love. Thus religion is as essential for
society as for the individual. Societies were not made, they grew,
their health depending on invisible ties, above all religious belief.
Societies, like private citizens, crave for happiness, which can
never be secured by force whether exercised by one, a few or in
the name of the whole community. History was full of proofs
that every irreligious philosophy tended to destroy social order,
the happiness of the peoples, and the peoples themselves. Had
not Voltaire declared that laws were required to prevent public
crimes and religion to prevent private sins? Christianity had
suppressed slavery, polygamy, infanticide and other abominations,
and had raised civilisation higher than the ancient world had ever
known. In view of the massive testimony of history and daily
experience, how could any rational being assert that religion was
of no importance to himself or the world?

The final chapter discusses the importance of religion to the
Deity Himself. Since man was made in the image of God his
Creator wishes him to co-operate in His designs. To decline such
partnership was to deprive the eternal Being of a portion of His
glory, a crime too grave for forgiveness except by God Himself.
How to fulfil our task had been revealed to us by His Son and by
the Church founded to preserve and apply His teaching. The
chapter closes with a denunciation of those whose perverted will
declined to listen to the divine word, to love the infinite good, to
obey the immutable order. The result was eternal war—first
among themselves, their minds like a silent and blood-stained city
where civil strife has destroyed every living creature. 'War in their
heart, war in the family, war in the state, war among the peoples
who will eat each other up, war against God, impious revolt of
man against his Creator by striving to usurp His place, war till
the day when the Eternal will grasp these feeble foes in His arms
and they will learn the truth of the words: It is a fearful thing to
fall into the hands of the living God.' No Frenchman since Pascal
and Bossuet had spoken with such moving eloquence and such
passionate conviction about religion and the Christian pattern of
life.

The *Essai* aroused so much discussion, both friendly and
hostile, that Lamennais returned to the charge in three more
volumes reinforcing his arguments with further details. Its

reception, he declared, proved how deeply people felt the need of the truth, and how easy it would be to restore its authority if the Government were to aid. This it had not done, for it asked for time as if unaware that the people were impatient. Monarchy had climbed down for fear of being thrown down, and its death certificate was being drawn up. The art of government, it was now believed, consisted in balancing between good and evil and in tolerating disorder. 'No more certain principles, no more fixed maxims or laws, no stability in our institutions, no firm basis in our ideas! Everything is true, everything is false. Who knows the doctrines of government or the belief of the peoples? All we see is a chaos of irreconcilable ideas, a violence in the peoples, a weakness in the sovereigns which bodes a sinister future. One moment the necessity of religion is felt and it is protected; the next moment, terrified by the furious outcry of its enemies, it is banished from the laws and God is disavowed as a disreputable ally. If the state declares itself Catholic, the tribunals decide it is atheist. What are people to believe amid such contradictions? While the good are overthrown, the bad boast of their complete triumph and redouble their activities. For some types of mind science is the only god, and the sovereignty of man is a revolt against God.' The last hope of recovery lay in the Catholic Church outside which Christianity was only a name. To strengthen the Catholic faith was the sole purpose of his book.

The second volume opens with a discussion on the existence of God, which is described as a fact more incontestable than our own existence, accepted by mankind from the earliest times as the only possible explanation of life and the universe; but this fundamental belief was not enough. The Jews are roughly handled. Obstinately shutting their eyes to the coming of the promised Messiah, they would always be strangers on earth; all peoples shuddered at their approach, and on their foreheads was branded a sign even more terrible than that of Cain—deicide. All that was true and good in the cults of the ancient world had been assimilated by Christianity, the only faith possessing universality, perpetuity and sanctity. The survey of religions concludes with an impassioned prayer for divine assistance in the author's missionary task. 'Oh God, deign to look down on a feeble mortal who tremblingly strives to defend Thy immutable truth against the error which attacks and the piety which blasphemes. By myself, I am nothing, know nothing, can do nothing. Shed on me a ray of Thy light. Fill me with strength to subdue rebellious souls and with the charity which touches and persuades. I ask not for myself but because Thou hast given me the desire to revive the faith languishing in some and almost extinct in others.'

The third volume illustrates by a mass of quotations the three unique qualities of Christianity: universality, perpetuity and sanctity. At the close of every chapter the author asks his reader: is it conceivable that you can set your doubts or your convictions against the testimony of the ages? The last clouds would vanish when death removed the garments of intellectual pride. To reject the testimony of Moses on the creation of the world would involve the rejection of all tradition and all recorded facts, for scepticism on a single point leads to scepticism on everything. Here, as throughout the whole of his treatise, the principle of private judgement is denounced as the most insidious foe of religion, the rebellion of fallen man against his Creator. 'Condemned by universal common sense, what does their particular opinion matter in face of the decision of the human race from which there is no appeal?' History was full of events no less surprising than the passage of the Red Sea. What better test of the inspiration of the Scriptures and the divine origin of Christianity could be supplied than the accuracy of the prophecies of the coming and career of the Messiah? The survey closes with one of the author's passages of rapturous eloquence in which the floodgates of his soul are opened. 'What can be more divine than a religion which fully satisfies all our needs, all the desires of our soul, revealing to us our origin and our destinies, which assembles before our eyes the past centuries and those to come in order to detach us from the present which is nothing, to inform us of our grandeur, to show in our fleeting existence the whole of eternity? For the Christian there is no such thing as time.'

The fourth and final volume adds the testimony of the miracles to that of the prophecies as further proof that Christ was indeed the Son of God. The Deists denied both their necessity and their reality, but ordinary human beings demanded something they could see for themselves. Miracles were merely divine acts, for the whole universe obeyed its Maker, and they were as well

attested as any occurrences in history. Hardly less miraculous was
the spread of Christianity from its humble beginnings despite
three centuries of persecution. Even Rousseau confessed that the
early history of the Christian Church was a continual prodigy.
Compare man under paganism with what he had become: the
humblest Christian faithful to his duties in chastity and humility
surpassed in perfection all the virtuous citizens of Greece and
Rome.

Lamennais was now the leading champion of the Church in
France. So wholeheartedly indeed had he identified himself with
the claims of the Papacy that he incurred resentment in royalist
circles by subordinating monarchy to the spiritual power; and
when Leo XII, after a flattering reception in the Vatican, proposed to bestow the Cardinal's hat the plan was opposed by
the French Government and dropped. When his brochure *La
Religion considérée dans les Rapports avec l'ordre politique et civil*
trumpeted ultramontanism in its extreme form he was charged
with ignoring the boundaries between the spiritual and the
secular by recognising the right of the Pope to depose princes
and release their subjects from their oath of fidelity. His counsel,
Berryer, the most eminent and eloquent of Catholic lawyers,
argued that a civil court could not deal with spiritual matters,
the author adding an expression of his unalterable attachment to
the unalterable teaching of the Pope. 'His faith is my faith, his
doctrine my doctrine.' When a fine of thirty-six francs, a purely
nominal sentence, was imposed, he exclaimed: 'I owe it to the
Church to fight to the bitter end and God gives me grace to have no
fear.' That the Bishops were issuing declarations demanded of them
in the name of the King excited his disdain: 'It could not be better
done in England. If you know any of these amiable priests,
remind them that there is a person called the Pope.'

Though Lamennais failed to obtain the support of the Jesuits
on which he had counted a few zealous young disciples rallied
round his banner. A new society, he proclaimed, was needed, for
the existing system was rotten and the restored Bourbons had
proved a disappointment. A brochure of 1829 entitled *Le Progrès
de la Révolution et de la Guerre contre l'Eglise* sharply separated the
cause of the Church from that of the monarchy, demanding
liberty for the former as promised by the Charter, liberty of

conscience, the press and the schools. Christianity had created liberty by providing an independent power capable of defying the omnipotent state. By establishing a royal despotism Louis XIV had prepared the way to the Revolution. Now priests and laymen should unite to render the Church independent and therefore able to survive the fall of the monarchy.

The campaign against state control was carried on with the aid of Lacordaire and Montalembert in the journal *l'Avenir*, which aspired to revive religion in France by severing the connection between Church and State and connecting it with democracy. Counting on the approval of the Vatican the three crusaders at Lacordaire's suggestion set off for Rome, where the new Pope, Gregory XVI, kept them waiting for weeks, and finally received them on condition that they should not mention the object of their journey. Worse was to follow, for on their way back they were staggered by the issue of an encyclical condemning their programme (without mentioning their names). Though *l'Avenir* had already ceased publication and had never had more than 1,200 subscribers, there was bitterness in Lamennais' heart as he saw his work in ruins, and he ceased to say mass. Catholicism, he declared, was his life, and he had wished to revive it from the depths into which it was sinking ever deeper from day to day. 'Since it did not suit the bishops I appealed to Rome, where I beheld the foulest cesspool which has ever sullied a human eye.' His old enemies the Gallicans rejoiced, Lacordaire left him at once, and Montalembert, who had deeply loved him, after an interval of hesitation.

Having always envisaged Christianity as above all an instrument of social regeneration, Lamennais transferred his dynamic energies from the Church to the cause of the people. The gulf widened when the most popular of his writings, *Paroles d'un Croyant*, described by Royer-Collard as 1793 going to Easter Communion, was condemned by Rome as small in size but great in wickedness since it attacked the authority of princes and preached radical democracy. 'The kings will howl on their thrones striving to hold on to their crowns against the wind, but they and their crowns will be swept away. The rich and the powerful will leave their palaces in fear of being buried in their ruins. They will be seen wandering along the road begging from those they meet a few rags to cover their nakedness, a morsel of black bread to appease their hunger and I do not know if they will get it. And in place of the dusk we call the day a pure bright light will shine from above like a reflection of the face of God. And everyone will love his brothers and be happy to serve them. And there will be neither small nor great, for love is the great leveller. And all families will be one family, and all nations one nation.' France had never heard such lofty accents from a Catholic priest and was never to hear them again.

Ceasing to regard himself as a member of the Church, and followed into the wilderness by none of his former disciples, he became a lonely man at the age of fifty. Sainte-Beuve compared him to a comet, lighting up the sky and traversing vast spaces in its course. Drifting ever further towards the left he welcomed the fall of the monarchy and took his seat in the Constituent Assembly on the proclamation of the Second Republic. His satisfaction was shortlived for democracy was speedily trampled underfoot by a new usurper. The old champion of authority and tradition now proposed allegiance to conscience alone, adopting the Protestant heresy of private judgement which he had once passionately denounced.

I2

MONTALEMBERT AND CHURCH SCHOOLS

Among the disciples of Lamennais at the height of his influence the most ardent and the most faithful was Montalembert. No more attractive figure was to be found on the French public stage during the four middle decades of the century than this knightly crusader for the causes of religion and liberty to which he dedicated his life. While the fiery prophet made as many enemies as friends, his aide-de-camp was made to be loved. The gods had showered their gifts on him in rich profusion—ancient lineage dating from the Crusades, an air of natural distinction, a melodious voice, unquenchable courage, the eloquence, as Sainte-Beuve testified, not of the advocate but of the believer, transparent purity of heart. Though he once thought of the priesthood and was pressed by Lacordaire to follow his example, he decided that his place was in the world. Though his revered master was a more original thinker and a more dynamic personality, his breach with the Church left him a lonely and embittered figure. Montalembert, on the other hand, bounded through life with a song in his heart, *persona grata* in society, the House of Peers, the Chamber and the Académie. The most eminent French Catholic layman of his time has been described as the French O'Connell and the modern Cid, *sans peur et sans reproche*. 'We are the sons of the Crusaders,' he exclaimed, 'and we will never retreat before the sons of Voltaire.' He announced himself as the first member of his family to fight with the pen alone and to use it as a sword. He was above all a man of action and his whole life was a campaign. As a liberal he detested violence and revolution, and feared that socialism and radicalism might threaten the moral foundations of society. He supported Louis Napoleon for the Presidency in 1848 but withdrew when the President established a dictatorship. All despotisms, whether on the extreme right or the extreme left, were in his eyes a degradation of human dignity no less than a deprivation of elementary rights.

Born in London in 1810, the child of an English mother and of a distinguished officer who had fought in the army of Condé and later under the British flag, Comte Charles de Montalembert was educated in England till the age of nine. This background exercised a profound influence on the precocious lad who retained throughout life an affectionate admiration for the home of ordered liberty. The most eminent of French anglophils was selected for the London Embassy during the Second Republic, but the appointment was vetoed by Palmerston whose policy he had at one time condemned. 'I love liberty,' he wrote from the Collège de Sainte-Barbe, but he adored his Church still more. He was horrified by the impiety and immorality of his schoolfellows, among whom no believer in the divinity of Christ could be found. 'I soon learned to know it was the same in the other classes of the College,' he wrote many years later to one of his old teachers. 'Never shall I forget the horrifying talk, the blasphemies at the approach of confession and Easter Communion. I still keep silence about the dirty language and dirty ways of the majority of these youths. You passed for a good deist, and you would have been less popular if you had been anything else. I never heard you say a word in your lectures which could encourage incredulity, but I must add that I never heard a word which indicated that you had any religious belief. Such a system sufficed for parents who did not wish their children to be more religious than themselves, but it was monstrous for believing and practising Catholics who think that this faith is the most precious heritage of their children. I spent two years at Sainte-Barbe where I was very happy. I walked at the edge of the abyss without noticing it, and my soul gradually absorbed the atmosphere which had poisoned everything around me. Had I entered earlier and remained longer I should surely have swum with the tide. When I was able to measure the depth of the gulf from which I had escaped my heart was filled with horror, which was followed

by a firm resolution to fight a monopoly which contemptuously
deprived the Church of liberty and Catholic parents of the faith
and innocence of their children.'

Visiting Sweden at nineteen when his father was Minister in
Stockholm he was pained to discover that there were only about
300 Catholics in the country. Happier emotions were aroused in
the following year by a journey to Ireland. The Irish, he declared,
loved France, and the clergy possessed enormous influence. A
call on O'Connell proved disappointing, and after hearing him
speak at a public meeting he dismissed him as a demagogue; but
the movement was greater than the man, and Ireland retained a
special place in his heart. 'My faith and my fervent attachment
to Catholicism', he wrote, 'have greatly profited by this journey.'
The Church, poor but free, was anchored in the hearts of the
people, whereas in France it was tied to the State and therefore
unpopular and powerless. A vision of his life's work rose before
him as he mourned over the contrast and drew the conclusion that
to fulfil its divine mission it must everywhere be freed from secular
control.

The revolution of 1830 which substituted the Duke of Orleans
for Charles X failed to revive the waning prestige of the throne.
The last of the elder line of the Bourbons had few devoted friends,
and Montalembert, though a royalist, was not among them.
Though no one had questioned the devotion of the fallen ruler
to the Church, he, like his predecessors, was a Gallican, and for
Montalembert Gallicanism, which amounted to state control, was
the enemy. The indifference of Louis Philippe, on the other hand,
was notorious, and when churches were sacked and crucifixes
broken during the July riots the Government looked on with
folded arms. Since no one could feel enthusiasm for the drab
bourgeois monarchy, Montalembert lost interest in thrones
without becoming a republican, dedicating himself to the uplift
of the masses with the Church as the principal agent of redemption.

At this moment when a born commander was looking round
for followers and a zealous recruit was craving for a leader,
Lamennais swept into his life like a tidal wave. After the revolution of 1830 the most dynamic figure in the Catholic world
turned his back on his authoritarian past and unfurled the banner

of Christian Democracy, pledged to reconcile the long-estranged Church with the proletariat. A new daily paper, *l'Avenir*, with its watchword *Dieu et la Liberté* and its policy of the independence of the Church, appeared in October, 1830, when Montalembert was in Ireland. 'Fine prospects for Catholicism at last!' he exclaimed. 'Freed for ever from its alliance with the civil power it will recover its strength, its liberty and its primitive energy, and I am resolved to consecrate my time and my studies to the defence of this noble cause. If they want me for *l'Avenir* I will scrap everything.' 'All I know and all I can do I place at your feet,' he wrote to Lamennais, who replied that he would welcome his aid in the noblest of causes, God and liberty; the columns of the paper would always be open to him, whatever his theme.

On the day after his return from Ireland Montalembert called on Lamennais in Paris and established a friendship which was to be his delight and inspiration for the next three years. The Abbé was equally impressed by the young enthusiast and each opened his heart to the other. 'What happiness!' wrote the visitor in his journal. 'My fair dreams are on the road to fulfilment. This is perhaps the most important day of my life.' On his next visit he met Lacordaire, already on the staff of the paper, and the two young men became friends for life. Thus was formed the celebrated editorial board which made *l'Avenir* a force and a ferment in the life of France. Never before or since has the Church in any Catholic country possessed a daily paper so brimful of reforming and challenging ideas. It was not to be plain sailing. Two consecutive issues were seized one month after launching the enterprise owing to an article by Lamennais complaining of the oppression of Catholics and another by Lacordaire criticising the nomination of bishops by the State. When the prosecutor spoke of priests as the ministers of a foreign sovereign, the author fearlessly rejoined: 'Sir, we are the ministers of someone who is nowhere a foreigner—God.' The charge was dismissed and the journal received encouragement from Chateaubriand, Victor Hugo, de Vigny and other celebrities. No one could accuse the editors of sailing under false colours. The Church, they believed, needed waking up; only thus could it serve the people. The first essential was to liberate it from secular control by ending State nomination of bishops and State payment of the clergy, for no one could be expected to fight in chains. The Revolution had failed for lack of religious inspiration. Thus emancipated, the task of the Church was to assume leadership of the democratic movement set in motion by the ideas of 1789 and developed by Saint-Simon and his school. Manual workers needed social legislation, and the wealth of the nation should be more justly distributed. Such reforms were in the interest of the whole community, for without them the masses would threaten public order when the spread of education led them to demand greater equality. 'That is why *l'Avenir* urges the Church to throw itself into the democratic torrent, not in order to arrest it, for that is impossible, but to guide it towards its goal without disorder. Then not merely the classes but the people would open their eyes and recognise that they were brothers with a common Father. Wearying of their old quarrels they would lie at the feet of the Father who stretches out His hand only to protect and opens His mouth only to bless.' The programme of *l'Avenir*, which may be defined as Christian Socialism, closely resembles the movement in England a few years later associated with the name of Kingsley and Maurice.

That a gigantic effort would be needed to reach the masses the editors were well aware, and their columns repeat the lamentations of the *Essai sur l'Indifférence*. 'In many places', wrote Lamennais, 'the priest finds himself alone in his deserted temple. His teachings are ignored, his words are sterile. While the strong man excites hatred because his domination is feared, the weak man moves through the throng under the shield of its indifference and contempt.' The simple explanation was that the priest had become the *gendarme* of royalty, an instrument of government. Archbishop Maury had declared that with a good police force and a good clergy the Emperor could always be sure of public order. Was it tolerable that bishops should be chosen by politicians who might be Protestants, Jews, atheists or freemasons? Was that the role which Christ had assigned to His apostles? Was it surprising that people witnessing servitude at the altar were afraid of God and kept away from the priest? To regain the soul of the people he must cease to appear as an agent of power and must break with the old parties; no doubt it would be a sacrifice but the gain would be worth the price. The editors had no objection to monarchy if it carried out the decisions of a representative Chamber and if there was no expensive Court.

The demand for the abolition of the Concordat and the Organic Articles aroused as much hostility within as without the Church. Since most of the bishops and clergy, like the Pope, were firm royalists who desired to continue the partnership of throne and altar, the chilly attitude of Lamennais towards the dynasty aroused deep resentment; but the more he was criticised the more violent he became. When asked how the Church could exist without funds from the State, he replied: How could it exist without liberty? It flourished in Ireland and America without subvention, for the people only loved the priest if he was as poor as themselves. Christ had been born in a manger. Back to the simplicity of the primitive Church! God would provide for its needs. With emancipation from its fetters the road was clear. The slave and the serf had been freed; now it was the turn of the working-man.

Montalembert fully shared the desire of his leader for social justice under Catholic auspices, but he was no less ardent a champion of the principle of nationality. His imagination had been fired by the struggle of Catholic Ireland and Catholic Belgium for independence. In this movement for national self-determination which was sweeping across Europe the Church should take the lead. The cause of Poland was particularly dear to his heart, and the insurrection of 1830 seemed to him as much a religious as a political movement and therefore a holy cause. He confessed to a longing to throw up everything and fly to Warsaw. 'At last', he cried as news of early victories poured in, 'Poland has shaken off her chains and defied her barbarous oppressors, this proud and generous Poland, so calumniated, so dear to every Catholic heart. Can she regain her place among the nations, this people which has for so long struggled for liberty and has kept unimpaired the faith of its fathers? Where is the heart which will not palpitate with joy at the news of this holy revolt? With what transports of happiness do we Catholics receive God's dramatic response to our prayers!' He drafted a petition to the Chambers in favour of the gallant insurgents, but the Government took no action and Russian troops marched into the capital. 'Catholics!' cried *l'Avenir*, 'Poland is vanquished.

P

Let us kneel beside the coffin of this betrayed people which has been great and unfortunate.' Sobieski had saved Vienna and the civilised world from the Turks, but now governments could no more be moved than bronze statues. For the simultaneous insurrection in the Romagna, on the other hand, *l'Avenir* had no sympathy, since the integrity of the Papal States was involved.

Encouraged by the interest shown in *l'Avenir*, Lamennais and his young lions founded an *Agence Générale pour la Défense de la Liberté Religieuse* with the object of marshalling ardent Catholics for defence of their rights against arbitrary acts in the Chambers and the Tribunals, for liberty of instruction, and for every other legitimate purpose advantageous to religion, the poor and civilisation. A programme of such amplitude mirrors the self-assurance of the little band which felt that nothing was beyond their grasp. Branches of the *Agence* were established in every diocese, and the crusaders carried the flaming torch into the provinces by speaking tours. The attack was concentrated on the state monopoly in the schools. A Government in control of education and the university was the fortress of incredulity, wrote *l'Avenir*, which 'could fashion to its taste the faith, the opinions, the morals of generations. To give it this power is to install despotism in the depths of the soul. Everyone for whom liberty is not an empty word must reject this monopoly of the mind as the most revolting yoke.' Parents and children, remembering with horror the education they had received, were urged to send petitions to the Chambers and thus arouse public attention.

Though the Charter of 1830 had promised liberty of teaching nothing had been done in 1831 when the *Agence* opened a school bearing a notice above the door: *Liberté d'Enseignement. Ecole libre.* 'We are assembled', declared Lacordaire at the opening ceremony, 'to claim the mother of all liberties, without which there is no liberty in the home, no liberty of conscience, no liberty of opinion, but sooner or later slavery, the subjection of all to the views of a single man.' The school in which Montalembert and Lacordaire were teachers was promptly closed, and its founders were charged with breaking the law. Montalembert, who at that moment succeeded his father in the family title, demanded to be tried by his peers as was his right. After making his confession to Lacordaire and receiving communion he pleaded the cause of liberty for the schools in a speech which revealed the youngest member of the Upper House as one of the finest orators in France. Since eight peers voted for his acquittal and the minimum sentence—a fine of 100 francs—was imposed, the trial was hailed as a moral victory for the defendants who had to wait twenty years for the triumph of their cause.

While Montalembert was campaigning in the south for the *Agence Générale* he received news that *l'Avenir*, after running for thirteen months, was to cease publication, as it had not paid its way and the bishops frowned on the policy of terminating the Concordat. 'We have sown seed', wrote Lamennais, 'which time will develop.' It was a bitter blow for Montalembert, who replied: 'God's will be done, I repent of nothing.' Was that to be the end of the story? 'We cannot fade out like this,' declared Lacordaire, 'we must journey to Rome to justify our aims. This dramatic step, proving our sincerity and our orthodoxy, will be a blessing to us and will disarm our enemies.' What if they were condemned? inquired Montalembert. 'Impossible,' replied Lamennais. He was soon to learn that their pilgrimage was extremely unwelcome to the Vatican, which could hardly approve their radical programme but wished to avoid public condemnation as desired by some of the French bishops, for *l'Avenir* had never challenged a single article of the faith. Their reception was as frigid as the winter weather. Instead of receiving them at once the Vatican requested a summary of their ideas. The document was drafted by Lacordaire and studied by the Pope, who replied to Lamennais through Cardinal Pacca that, while recognising his services and good intentions, he regretted that they had raised certain dangerous issues. The examination of their programme might take time, so they should return to France. 'This is the ruin of our hopes,' exclaimed Montalembert, 'but we must resign ourselves, though it does not arouse the slightest remorse in our soul.' Lacordaire took it calmly, but Lamennais declared his intention of remaining in Rome till the promised declaration appeared. Before it was ready the Pope granted them an audience. 'I was completely disappointed,' reported Montalembert. 'He is good-looking, but there is nothing lofty or spiritual about him, and he kept one hand in his pocket. For a quarter of an hour he talked to us in a very affable manner about various places and people, and dismissed us very graciously without having made the slightest reference to our mission and the situation of the Church.' While Lacordaire understood his silence and returned to France, Montalembert was still too much under the influence of *mon général*, *mon père*, and too convinced of the value of their labours to approve the caution of the Vatican.

After a visit to Monte Cassino and Naples and a second sojourn in Rome Lamennais and Montalembert travelled slowly north to Munich, the Mecca of German Catholicism, where, to their surprise, they were joined by Lacordaire. While the three friends were dining together the chief was called out of the room, returning with the words: 'I have just received an Encyclical against us and we must not hesitate to submit.' He proceeded to draft a declaration of submission, announcing that *l'Avenir*, provisionally suspended in the autumn of 1831, would not reappear and that the *Agence Catholique* would be dissolved. That, however, did not reflect his deeper mood, for he ceased to say mass, and returned to his Breton home with bitterness in his heart.

Lacordaire, then on the threshold of his career as the greatest French preacher since Massillon, left his old leader when he realised his determination to go his own way, and strove to carry Montalembert with him. 'I have tried to warn you against a fatal dominating influence, not from jealousy and personal dislike but from my infinite love for you, just as a mother attempts to cure her son of a taste which cannot bring him happiness.' The appeal was in vain, for his reverence for 'this great and holy man' was undiminished and he had not abandoned all hope of saving this dynamic force for the Church. What the arguments of Lacordaire failed to achieve was soon rendered inevitable by the caged eagle who beat his wings against the bars and longed to range the skies once more. 'At times', he confided to Montalembert, 'the yearning for the fray surges up in my soul and causes inexpressible anguish.' Convinced of a divine calling, he resolved to fulfil it outside the Church which declined its co-operation. 'I feel sure that all Catholic action which assumes the support or even the neutrality of the clergy is utterly impossible today, and will continue to be impossible till God effects an immense reform in the Church. The hierarchy obstinately desires everything that people do not want and rejects everything they desire. So let us leave the Pope and the bishops alone. Let us cease to concern ourselves with religious office and no longer approach any question from the theological point of view. Let us take our stand on the political and social plane and speak henceforth as Frenchmen and friends of humanity.' In his grief and disappointment he had adopted the broad distinction between the temporal and the spiritual which he had once denounced and thereby was more than half-way out of the Church.

At last even Montalembert was alarmed and begged his beloved master to avoid the dusty arena of politics. It was much more than politics that he had in mind, was the reply, for the transformation of society and the liberation of the human race were involved. Hearing that the Pope had written to an archbishop expressing doubts of his sincerity, Lamennais announced his wholehearted submission to all decisions on faith, morals and discipline, adding that he would no longer occupy himself with affairs of the Church. If this declaration appeared insufficient he begged to be told what form of words would be required. Since differentiation between the temporal and the spiritual, above all in a priest, was anathema in Rome, an unconditional formula was requested and promptly supplied. A new text was forwarded to Rome, but in a letter to Montalembert reporting his latest formula he added a few sentences which filled his favourite disciple with dismay. 'I renounce everything without exception which has filled my former life and shall try, however late, to start a new one. I shall not tell you my plans because I do not wish to associate anyone with my destinies. This prevents me from accepting your tender invitations. We shall meet again, I hope, above, but on earth we must follow separate paths.'

Montalembert could hardly believe his eyes as he read these ominous words and begged for an explanation. The Pope, replied the lost leader, was mistaken in confounding spiritual power with temporal, and thereby violating the tradition of the Church. An unconditional recognition of his authority, in his opinion, would mean recognition of his infallibility. To challenge the authority of the Pope, as the rebel was well aware, was to break with the Church, but he was convinced that he had no choice. Henceforth he was lonelier than ever, for Montalembert, whom he invited to stand at his side, reluctantly withdrew. When the

old leader published the *Paroles d'un Croyant* in 1834 explaining
his new faith the younger man publicly announced his adhesion
to the Encyclicals. In response to a final appeal Lamennais declared
that he could not act against his conscience, and when a friend
expressed the opinion that Catholicism was dead or dying, he
replied that he agreed. After reading the rebel's *Affaires de Rome*
in which he complained of the treatment he had received, Montalembert wrote to the Pope to express his disapproval, and on
his next visit to the Vatican was received with the words, 'Caris-
simo Conte de Montalembert'. The spell was broken at last. His
painful struggles were over. He continued to serve the cause of
the Church by his biography of Saint Elizabeth of Hungary, by
his massive survey of western monasticism, and above all by his
ardent support in the House of Peers and, after 1848, in the
Chamber, of the cause of confessional schools which triumphed
in the *Loi Falloux*.

The association with Lamennais was the most memorable
experience in the life of Montalembert, and twenty years after
the breach he felt that his early efforts had not been wholly in
vain. In *Les Intérêts Catholiques au XIXe siècle*, the most widely
read of his shorter writings, he contrasted the state of religion at
the opening of the century with the outlook in 1852. Pius VI
had died the prisoner of an atheistic republic, French bishops
were in exile, the clergy decimated by the guillotine and deporta-
tion, the religious Orders uprooted or destroyed. In the rest of
Europe religion was no longer alive. To the *Philosophes* Catholicism must have seemed a corpse awaiting burial. In the first
half of the nineteenth century the Church had resumed its place
in the front rank. In England the Catholics had been emancipated
and the Belgians had freed their country and their faith, but the
transformation had been most complete in France. The youth
had returned to Christianity, the leaders of thought professed or
at least respected religion. The Society of St. Vincent de Paul
and the Society for the Propagation of the Faith were flourishing,
the religious Orders were restored and increased, liberty of
teaching had been secured by the Church, and the Pope had been
restored to the Eternal City by French arms.

How had this incredible change occurred? Neither by Napoleon
nor the Monarchy; it was liberty, and the struggle rendered

possible by liberty, which had performed the miracle. Everywhere the same cause had produced a similar result. 'What I love and desire is ordered, tempered, moderate liberty which the great spirits and the great nations of all ages had won, or of which they had dreamed, liberty which, far from being the foe of authority, could only exist in association with it, while opposing the abuse of power.' Representative government was the only possible pattern in the nineteenth century. As a constitutionalist he disapproved of the Second Empire, but felt that there was no need for Catholics to oppose it and believed it would not last long.

The death of Lacordaire in 1861 caused a surge of memories, and in his touching memoir of his best friend Montalembert enshrined his final reflections on the thrilling experiences of his youth. Lamennais, he declared, had lost his temper and had been utterly wrong in breaking with the Church; happily he had not taken a single disciple with him. Lacordaire had been right to leave him after striving to keep him within the fold. He himself had misjudged Gregory XVI at the time, for the Vatican, he now realised, had displayed sympathy, patience and wisdom in dealing with the pilgrims who sought its approval. The long period of waiting in Rome before their reception was intended as a gentle hint that approval was improbable. How, indeed, could they have expected the fortress of tradition to approve such a radical proposal as the separation of Church and State in France? The appeal to Rome had been a grave error, and no Pontiff could have acted differently. Such a mistake was intelligible in young men without experience of the world and the Church, but how could one explain and much less excuse the illustrious priest who had once been received with distinction by Leo XII? While Lamennais never regretted his rebellion and Lacordaire had nothing to regret, Montalembert made peace with his conscience by a recantation as public and as wholehearted as the Vatican could have wished.

13

LACORDAIRE IN THE PULPIT

No member of the little group of friends who launched the Catholic revival in France directly influenced so many souls as Lacordaire. The greatest French preacher since Massillon impressed his friends by his sanctity no less than the crowded congregations in Notre Dame by his fervour. Though religion played an important part in the life of Chateaubriand and Joseph de Maistre, Lamennais and Montalembert, all of them had wider interests. With Lacordaire religion was the sole abiding concern. His success in the pulpit and his prestige at the Vatican left him as humble at the height of his fame as when, young and unknown, he joined the staff of *l'Avenir*. Everyone who approached him was struck by his modesty and sincerity. Though he never wrote a large book, and sermons need to be heard, he lives in the voluminous correspondence with Montalembert, Mme Swetchine and other friends in which he revealed the secrets of his heart. When his voice was stilled, his work was carried on by the preachers of the Dominican Order which he had revived after its abolition during the Revolution.

Born in 1802, Lacordaire displayed signs of religious fervour in his earliest years. His first confession at the age of seven left a deep impression, and he preached to his brothers and his nurse in a makeshift chapel arranged by his mother, as the younger Pitt had harangued the servants from the dining-room table in his father's house. His zeal caused the nurse to exclaim: 'Don't get so hot.' With his sensitive nature he found his rough schoolfellows a sore trial; yet the secular atmosphere left its mark.

Clouds of doubt gathered in the sky, since, in his own words, his intelligence and his conscience were at war. He left college, according to his later account, with his faith destroyed, but there is no reason to believe that he ever crossed the boundary between temptation and sin.

After studying law at the University of Dijon with little interest, he entered the office of an advocate in Paris and began to practise at the bar. With his gift of speech he would soon have made his name in court, for Berryer, the leading lawyer of the Revolution, heard and admired him. But his heart was not in his work, for at this phase his thought turned longingly towards the Church. 'Alas,' he exclaimed, 'I have said good-bye to literature though I am born to live with the muses.' He felt lonely and disappointed, but the clouds soon cleared away. Influenced by Lamennais' *Essai sur l'Indifférence* and other religious works, he cast aside his doubts, resolved to be a priest, entered the seminary of St. Sulpice and was ordained. 'He frequently declared that neither man nor book was the instrument of his conversion,' testifies Montalembert, 'but that a sudden and secret spark of God opened his eyes to the nothingness of irreligion. In a single day he became a believer.' Even now he was not wholly happy, for as a liberal he found himself out of sympathy with the royalist atmosphere of the place and he regretted the lack of apostolic spirit in the Church which he had hoped to find. The task of imparting religious instruction in a girls' school failed to satisfy a young priest filled with burning zeal and conscious of his abilities. An invitation by the French bishop of New York to visit the United States, where the Church was entirely independent of the State, was seriously considered but declined after consulting Lamennais, the oracle of French Catholicism in the 'twenties.

The revolution of 1830 opened a new chapter in the career of Lacordaire. Accepting with a kind of intoxication an invitation from Lamennais to co-operate in a Catholic daily which he proposed to launch, he threw himself heart and soul into the crusade for the revival of Christianity in France by a frank acceptance of democratic principles, by championing the cause of social reform, and above all by liberating the Church from the stifling embrace of the State. While Lamennais supplied the ideas and the dyna-

mism his principal lieutenant wrote most of the leading articles.
'We are paid by our enemies,' he complained, 'by those who
regard us as hypocrites and who feel that our life depends on
their money. Though they are our debtors they have come to
think they give us alms. Their attitude is so wounding that anyone who tolerates it is beneath contempt. It is like a debtor
meeting his creditor, who flings a few coins in the mud, exclaim-
ing "work, lazybones, work". That is how our enemies have
treated us for thirty years. Catholic priests are as poor as Job.
All we know of tomorrow is that Providence will rise before the
sun. We feel our servitude deeply, and consider poverty a hundred
times better than the insults of a Prefect Church. Have men ever
been treated with greater contempt? They mock at your prayers and
command you to sing them. If you disobey, you are seditious and
the Treasury will close its doors. If you obey, no words can
express what they think of you. We protest against these indigni-
ties, against this martyrdom of opprobrium.'

L'Avenir was in revolt against the Government, not against the
Vatican, for the editors were perfectly sound on Catholic doctrine.
Three months after launching the paper they issued a declaration
of loyalty and submission to the Holy See: 'If there is anything
in our policy contrary to the Catholic faith, we beg the Heart of
Christ to be good enough to warn us. That is the first and most
vital principle of our writings. We are immersed in obedience;
after a life of trials and conflicts we hope the words of Fénelon
will be inscribed on our tomb: "Oh! Holy Church of Rome, if I
forget thee may I be forgotten".' The reformers were before
their time, and the paper, frowned on by the hierarchy, failed to
pay its way and ceased publication after eleven months. In their
zeal for renovation and material sacrifice they had forgotten that
self-preservation is the strongest of human instincts, and that the
clergy could hardly be expected to dispense with State help without certainty whether the vacuum could and would be filled from
another source. Though man does not live by bread alone, even
a *curé* cannot live and work without it. By the radical nature of
their programme and the peremptory tone of their utterances they
had aroused more opposition than support, and they felt that if
their crusade was to continue the sanction of the Vatican must be
sought.

The cool reception of the pilgrims in the Eternal City has been described in previous studies. Unlike Lamennais, who regarded himself as a prophet with a divine mission to save the Church in France, and the youthful Montalembert, who saw everything through his leader's eyes, Lacordaire was profoundly impressed by the tranquil majesty and detachment of Rome, and was soon prepared for unconditional surrender to the superior wisdom of the Holy See. While writing for *l'Avenir* he had been as intransigent as his colleagues, and no shadow of doubt as to the utility of their campaign ever crossed his mind. When the Vatican, before granting an audience, requested a statement on the views expressed in *l'Avenir*, he was charged by his colleagues to prepare a memorandum. The tone, needless to say, was less polemical than that of the paper, but the main principles of Christian democracy were firmly upheld. He began by arguing the necessity of avoiding the identification of the Church with any political party and above all of dispensing with financial aid from the State. Only by such a drastic measure could a convincing answer be found to the popular charge that the clergy were functionaries of the State. The memorandum closed with a declaration of their loyalty to the Pope, docile to his voice as little children.

Though there was no sign of recantation in the memorandum the author was already a changed man, and a few years later Lacordaire described the transformation. 'Arriving in Rome at the tomb of the Apostles I knelt and said: "Lord, I am beginning to feel my weakness. Have pity on Thy servant. I have learned that the Church is the liberator. Oh! Rome, seated amid the storms of Europe, in you there is no faltering, no weakness. Your glance, directed to the four quarters of the earth, views the panorama of events with sublime clarity and in relation to the divine scheme.' After drafting a statement on the policy of *l'Avenir* and receiving the advice which he interpreted as a command to return to France while it was being considered, he left his impatient colleagues in Rome in expectation of an early declaration. Seemingly unwanted in Paris and temporarily unemployed, he found an outlet for his energies in visiting hospitals during a cholera epidemic and comforting the victims on their death-beds.

The Encyclical *Mirari Vos* reached the three friends in Munich, where Lamennais and Montalembert were staying on their way home and where, by chance, Lacordaire was visiting friends. Though neither they nor their paper were mentioned by name they joined in a declaration of submission; but Lamennais had no intention of abandoning his campaign. Lacordaire now spent three months with his old chief in his home in Brittany in a futile effort to secure unconditional submission to the Holy See. The effort was in vain. 'I am leaving this evening,' he wrote to Lamennais, 'as in honour bound, convinced that henceforth my life will be of no use to you, owing to our disagreements on the Church and society which have increased every day. Despite my sincere efforts to understand your opinions I believe that a republic will not be established in France or anywhere in Europe in my lifetime or long after that, and I could not take part in a movement with other principles. Without renouncing my liberal ideas I believe that the Church has had very good reasons in view of the deep corruption of parties in declining to move as quickly as we should have wished. Perhaps your views are more correct and more profound, and in view of your superiority over me I ought to have been convinced. But reason is not the whole of man; and since I cannot eradicate the ideas which separate us it is only right to end our association. My conscience compels me no less than my honour, for I must make something of my life for God. Being unable to follow you what can I do here except weary you, discourage you, sabotaging your projects and annihilating myself? You will never know, except in heaven, how I have suffered during the last year by the mere thought of causing you pain. I go to the United States or remain in France; wherever I am you will receive proofs of the respect and attachment I shall always feel for you.'

After burning his boats Lacordaire informed the Archbishop of Paris that the break with the past was final. 'No one has suffered more in mind and his dearest affections in the last two years than myself. For the peace of the Church and the tranquillity of my conscience I have broken sacred ties and added to the distress of a man who, despite his talent and his fame, had no other earthly consolation than the fidelity of his friends. I have placed the Church above everything in my heart. Convinced that we cannot do too much for the Church to which we owe our life and the truth, nor for the peace, glory, exaltation and love of the Holy

See, I have resolved to give a new mark of my obedience and my faith. I undertake to follow solely and absolutely the doctrine set forth in the Encyclical *Mirari Vos*, and to write and approve nothing which does not conform to it. I am happy to have the occasion of laying at the feet of the Holy Father the expression of my veneration and I transmit to him through you this my filial act.' The Church in France, he had come to feel, was stronger than Lamennais and his youthful associates believed. 'Five centuries have elapsed between the Papal sojourn at Avignon and the revolution of 1789,' he wrote to Mme Swetchine. 'This country has experienced religious ferments, Gallicanism, Protestantism, Jansenism, Cartesianism, and yet nothing has availed to eradicate or wither the Catholic roots. God does not seem to have abandoned France which may be destined to renovate Christianity in Europe. I have been charged with enthusiasm. But who has placed France so high, who has so confidently foretold her resurrection as M. de Maistre, and that at a time when there was none of the light on the horizon which we witness today? France has been expiating her crimes for fifty years, and words of encouragement would aid her convalescence.'

Though Lamennais and Lacordaire never met again, they crossed swords when the former published his version of the fruitless pilgrimage of 1831–2 in his brochure *Affaires de Rome*. Lacordaire replied in the best known of his minor writings, *Lettre sur le Saint Siège*, though without mentioning his old chief. While the elder controversialist confined himself to his unhappy personal experiences the younger ranged over a far wider field. Without any pretensions to erudition the brochure repeats the arguments of *Génie du Christianisme*, *Du Pape* and the *Essai sur l'Indifférence* that the Catholic Church, under the inspired guidance of the Holy See, had been the guiding light throughout the ages in a dark world, the source of the faith which was the best hope of mankind. One of the greatest and commonest errors in regard to the Church, he declared, was that it had tied itself to the State and frowned on countries with liberal institutions. On the contrary Rome, the mother of all peoples, respected all forms of government. God had chosen Rome, not Jerusalem, as its guardian and, if the nations of Europe were to have a future, they must turn their eyes to Rome. The Church stood for love, the only real value in the world, the beginning, middle and end of things. Love is knowledge, devotion, contentment. With one drop of love in the scales the whole universe would not weigh it down.

Lacordaire's hymn of praise was music in the ears of the Vatican, but the Archbishop of Paris advised postponement of publication on the ground that its political radicalism might provoke controversy. Its appearance a year later, however, caused no ripple on the surface of the waters, and his first comprehensive declaration of faith gave its author unbounded satisfaction. Rome, he had discovered, was his spiritual home. 'Never was I so tranquil and so happy,' he reported from the Eternal City. 'I feel I am in port. Nowhere is there so much liberty combined with a sense of security. Here the passions of the outer world vanish like grain on the beach. I have finished with Paris; my furniture is sold and Père Ravignan has worthily filled the pulpit of Notre Dame.' He accepted an invitation to preach at Metz but his mind was full of other far-ranging plans.

After the final break with Lamennais Lacordaire turned to the Archbishop of Paris, who received him with open arms like the prodigal son. Having had his fill of journalism he declined both the editorship of a new paper *l'Univers*, which Louis Veuillot was soon to make the leading Catholic organ of the century, and the offer of a chair of Theology at Louvain. After two years of controversy he longed for a period of solitude and study. An invitation to preach at the Collège Stanislas was more to his taste, and his success in the pulpit was as much a surprise to himself as to Paris. His fame quickly spread beyond the walls of the college to literary celebrities, among them Victor Hugo and Alfred de Vigny. He was rewarded by an invitation from the Archbishop to occupy the pulpit in Notre Dame where the triumphs of the college chapel were repeated. The preacher suddenly found himself a national figure, the most prominent Catholic in France since Lamennais had strayed from the fold. For the next two years believers sat at his feet, and unbelievers, attracted by reports of his eloquence, mingled with the throng. Though the salvation of souls was his central theme and purpose, he also proclaimed the social duty of the Church with a zeal recalling his articles in *l'Avenir*.

However gratifying his success in the pulpit, Lacordaire desired something more constructive and more permanent than the spoken word. The destruction of the religious Orders, it appeared to him, had impoverished the spiritual life of France, and the restoration of the Society of Jesus supplied a precedent for the revival of other communities. The foundation of the Society of St. Vincent de Paul by his friend Ozanam provided an opportunity for those who felt the call to social service. 'In Rome I saw the magnificent remains of the Orders founded by the Saints. I could not believe that this was all over, and I felt that the best service one could render to the Church would be their restoration.' That there were many obstacles in the path he was well aware, among them the widespread unpopularity of the Church and the notorious indifference of the Government.

His resolve was strengthened by a visit to the Abbey of Solesmes where the scholarly Dom Guéranger had revived the Benedictine Order. After prolonged reflection he decided to revive the Dominican Order of Friar Preachers. When his project was approved in Rome he served his novitiate at Viterbo, employing his leisure in writing a life of St. Dominic, a companion work of edification to Montalembert's life of St. Elizabeth of Hungary. He was appointed Provincial of the Order in France, and his share in the revival of the Orders provided the deepest satisfaction of his life. 'Those who had not lived through the two phases of incredulity and faith', he declared in the funeral tribute to his friend Ozanam, 'could form no idea of the change. Tears fill our eyes and we should give thanks to God.' When he resumed his sermons in Notre Dame, where he appeared in the white and black habit of the Order, he was recognised at home and abroad as the greatest ornament of the Church in France.

Lacordaire had genuinely admired Lamennais during the brief period of discipleship but had never been completely dominated and never really loved him. The two central friendships of his life, into which he poured all the treasures of his heart, were with Montalembert, to whom he stood in the position of an elder brother, and Mme Swetchine, a childless Russian lady old enough to be his mother. To her he looked up with filial affection and reverence not merely as a spiritual comforter but as something of an oracle. Born in 1782 into an old and wealthy Moscow family long connected with the Court and married to an elderly General, she had witnessed the closing phase of Catherine the Great. During the brief reign of the half-crazy Emperor Paul she had been a lady in waiting to his German wife while General Swetchine was Military Commandant of the capital. But the favour of the ruler never lasted long and the General was not only dismissed from his post but forbidden to live in St. Petersburg. All eyes, however, were beginning to turn to his eldest son Alexander, already a valued friend of the General and his gifted wife.

After the assassination of the Tsar and the accession of Alexander Mme Swetchine entered a new ideological phase. Hitherto religion had played no part in her life, for her father, like her husband, while outwardly conforming to the Orthodox Church, stood much nearer to Voltaire, Rousseau and the Encyclopaedists. She knew nothing of Catholicism till the arrival of Joseph de Maistre as Minister of the House of Savoy, bringing with him not only wider erudition but a rock-like conviction of the superiority of the Catholic Church. Her conversion was complete and irrevocable. In her own ecstatic words she threw herself into the arms of God, and began the serious study of theology and philosophy. Her keen interest in religion strengthened her ties with the Tsar whose attraction to spiritual things increased with advancing years and who found a sympathetic friend in the mystical Mme de Krudener.

When General Swetchine was appointed Russian Minister in Paris in 1816 his wife opened a salon for Catholic circles to which it was a privilege to be invited. Lacordaire was introduced by Montalembert, and for the remainder of her life he was regarded as her most intimate and valued friend who was grateful for her 'supernatural tenderness'. Her exceptionally wide culture and sympathetic personality secure her a place in the story of the Catholic revival, for she was more than merely the hostess to distinguished men. It was not till the Revolution of 1830 that she came into her own, and began to play an important part in the counsels of the young Catholics who looked to Lamennais as their leader and proclaimed their political and religious convictions in *l'Avenir*. The new friendships were the more welcome since her husband remained a member of the Orthodox Church. Lacordaire often said mass in her private chapel, and it was partly at her suggestion that the Archbishop of Paris invited the young preacher to occupy the pulpit of Notre Dame. It was a perfect relationship, cemented by a flaming devotion to the Church. 'Think sometimes of all you have meant for me,' he wrote, 'and through me perhaps for others.' Another grateful friend, Count Falloux, who was to write her life and edit her writings, testifies that her gift of understanding amounted to divination.

Lacordaire came to rely increasingly on her judgement. Her salon was not at all to the taste of Sainte-Beuve, who described it as a branch of the Church. She would have regarded the complaint as a compliment, for she had embraced her new faith with even more than the usual zeal of a convert. A salon, he declared pontifically, was a place where all opinions were allowed and represented, whereas in her drawing-room only believers were welcome. Since its special character was well known and there were other salons for other ideologies he had no reason to grumble. It was precisely the warm atmosphere which rendered it attractive to Catholics who regarded literature and politics as inferior in importance to the maintenance and propagation of their faith. Having never come under the influence of Lamennais, who was rarely seen in Paris, she wholeheartedly applauded Lacordaire's declaration of independence and urged Montalembert to follow his example without delay. The name of the intimate friend of de Maistre, Lacordaire and Montalembert cannot be omitted even in a brief survey of the Catholic revival in France.

14

OZANAM AND THE CLAIMS OF CHARITY

True religion and undefiled is to visit the fatherless and widows in their affliction and to keep oneself unspotted from the world.

Epistle of St. James

SUCH was the creed and such the practice of Frédéric Ozanam, founder of the Society of St. Vincent de Paul which has brought comfort and a ray of sunlight into many humble lives. If Lacordaire claims the first place in the Catholic revival as the shepherd of souls, the fame of Ozanam rests on his services to the poor and sick, the lonely, distressed and the disinherited. Speaking at the centenary of his birth Pius X compared it to a great tree spreading its leaves and branches in all directions. No work of mercy was outside its scope, it announced, and its record has proved it fully worthy to serve under the banner of the founder of the Soeurs de Charité and friend of the galley slaves. While Lamennais proclaimed the gospel of Christian democracy and a better life for the common man, he left neither disciples nor an organisation to bring his ideals down from the clouds. Though Ozanam served the Church by his lectures and his books on the religious glories of the Middle Ages, it is as the friend of the friendless that his niche in the temple of fame is secure. He agreed with Pascal that all bodies and brains and all they have done are worth less than the least act of charity which is of an infinitely higher and indeed supernatural order. The Church, like the Monarchy,

226

had lost its prestige before the Revolution and had never re-covered it. Now the laity must come to its aid, declared Ozanam, in the world but not of it, combining the practical idealism of the good Samaritan with the duties of professional life, preaching the gospel of love in the course of the daily round instead of from the pulpit. In the new era of democracy inaugurated in 1789 new methods were required, and here everyone could help.

Born in 1813 Ozanam grew up in the devout and cultured household of a doctor who had started his career as an officer in the armies of Napoleon. From his earliest years the precocious and sensitive lad was impressed by the self-sacrificing devotion of his father to his poorer patients in the slums of Lyons, and became aware of the grim contrast between affluence and poverty. After a brief phase of doubt he found in Catholicism all that the world needed for social as well as moral salvation. The writings of Saint-Simon and his school had called attention to social questions, but the creedless *Nouveau Christianisme* failed to satisfy believers. When a noisy band of Saint-Simonians, more radical than their master, invaded Lyons he published a brochure entitled *Réflexions sur les doctrines de Saint-Simon*. Socialisation of the means of production, and the slogan 'from each according to his capacity, to each according to his needs', were reasonable enough; but some members of the sect were virtually communists and others allowed sexual licence. Though he recognised that there were some sound and generous ideas in the system, he believed it would retard rather than advance civilisation since it ignored the Christian Church. He was to look back with a certain pride on the work of the eighteen-year-old student, in which he had pleaded for the uplift of the poor. Man did not live by bread alone. Spiritual renovation was as essential as economic better-ment, for materialism was no less an evil than poverty.

Ozanam's ideology shortly before his eighteenth birthday was set forth in a long letter to a college friend, which foreshadows the apostolate of the years to come.

Material order, moderate liberty, bread and money, that is all the people want here. Like you I feel the past is falling to pieces; the foundations of the old edifice are shaken, and a terrible convulsion has changed the face of the earth. What is to emerge from these ruins? What the shape of the new order will be I cannot guess; but

I believe in Providence, and the first need of man and society is some form of religion. The human heart thirsts for the infinite. Religious truth which society needs I have found. I wanted something solid, something to cling to, in order to resist the torment of doubt. And then my soul was filled with a great joy, a great consolation, for I discovered by the sheer force of reason that this something was the Catholicism taught by my mother, with all its grandeurs and all its joys supported by science, human and divine, with the rays of wisdom, glory and beauty. I clasp it with fervour and will point to it as a beacon of deliverance to those tossing on the sea of life. Happy shall I be if a few friends rally round me. Then we will unite our efforts, and perchance the day may come when mankind will be gathered beneath the same protecting shade. Catholicism, in its eternal youth and strength, would then rise suddenly on the world and, placing itself at the head of the age, lead it on to civilisation and happiness. The work is magnificent, I am young, and I have great hopes.

The same ideas were being proclaimed by Lamennais and his disciples, above all the renovation and ennoblement of society under the auspices of the Church. What was new was the plan of a youth organisation, with a special mission to the poor. Far from desiring the support of the state, the reformers wanted leave to go their own way, subject to no secular authority and making their own rules.

Migrating to Paris at the age of eighteen to pursue his studies at the School of Law, Ozanam felt at first as if he had been torn up by the roots. 'Here am I in a stupid and sensual crowd,' he reported to a friend. 'It is like an enormous corpse to which I am tied. Paris is freezing and killing me.' His anxious mother had extracted a promise to avoid the theatre which, despite his passion for literature, was loyally kept. The disdainful attitude of Jouffroy, the leading teacher of philosophy, to the Christian religion provoked a written protest from him and some of his fellow-students, but it seemed like a voice crying in the wilderness.

Among his comrades at the Ecole de Droit he discovered only three Catholics, the others being sceptics or Saint-Simonians. A second shock was their scoffing at Christian morals. 'Here am I,' he wrote in his first letter to his mother, 'quite unprotected, cast into this great capital of egotism, this vortex of human passions and errors. I have no one but you, dearest mother, to whom I can unbosom my heart—you and God, but these two are all in all to me.' The dark clouds soon melted, and in his later life he looked back on his university studies as golden years. He was invited by Ampère, the leading French physicist, to share his Catholic home, and he gradually came to know some of the pundits of the literary and academic world, among them Chateaubriand and Ballanche, Cousin and Montalembert, the latter coming to his Sunday *soirées*. He also belonged to a discussion circle of various parties and creeds called the History Society, where a chance remark led directly to the foundation of the Society of St. Vincent de Paul. After the Catholic view had been expressed by himself and other members with juvenile ardour a Saint-Simonian interjected: 'You are right to sing the praise of your religion in the past, but today it is a dead tree. What fruits of charity does it bear?'

Walking home with a friend Ozanam remarked that believers did no more than unbelievers for the disinherited. 'Yes, there is one thing we lack, works of charity.' 'Well,' replied his companion, 'what is to be done?' Ozanam was silent. Having climbed to the room they shared, his gaze fell on their store of logs. 'Let us give them away,' exclaimed his friend, and the youths proceeded to carry them to a working man with an empty grate in a garret. 'Such was the spark which was to kindle the divine flame of charity of the Society of St. Vincent de Paul,' commented Frédéric's brother, Abbé Ozanam. 'A few days later the two friends, joined by two other members of the Société d'Histoire, explained their plan of a society for religion and charity to a priest who undertook to be their adviser. Four more students, one of them a converted Saint-Simonian, joined them. The first meeting of the eight, or the *Conférence de Charité* as they called it, took place in May 1833 in the office of *La Tribune Catholique*; and at a subsequent meeting one of the members proposed that they should adopt St. Vincent de Paul as their patron. In the autumn of the following year Ozanam reported that they had distributed about 2,400 francs, some books, and a large quantity of old clothes. Before long their activities embraced the care of orphans and discharged prisoners and many other social needs of large cities. Having made several friends among Catholic

students who shared his ardour for social service, he decided to
form a community called the Society of St. Vincent de Paul.
Each member undertook to visit a poor family, and the members
met weekly to discuss how to help them without further pauper-
ising them by indiscriminate alms-giving. Beginning with seven
the society grew like the grain of mustard seed, and soon counted
several groups in Paris, the provinces and overseas. Though
Ozanam disclaimed the honour of originating the idea, his
personality rendered him from the outset the leader of the little
band of dedicated apostles aflame with the love of God and
man.

His first case was the rescue of a woman with five children
whose father spent most of his slender earnings on drink. Since
they were not married, it was easy to liberate them, a solution
which the poor sufferer through ignorance of the law had never
ventured to dream. Urgent material needs in the form of bread,
meat and coal were supplied from a common fund provided by
themselves and others from their own meagre resources. Though
the sacred flame within him needed no external sustenance, he
found fresh inspiration towards the Christian life in Lacordaire's
sermons. Social questions, he declared, were more important
and more urgent than political. Between the haves and the have-
nots, between the power of gold and the power of despair, he
believed a struggle to be imminent and Christians must mediate.
'A new *Conférence* has been formed of students of the Ecole
Normale and the Ecole Polytechnique,' he reported to Lacordaire. 'Fifteen young men have asked as a favour to work two
hours every Sunday, their only free day, for God and the poor.
Next year Paris will have fourteen *Conférences* and the provinces
the same.'

Ozanam, like his comrades, had to earn his living. He was
never attracted to the law, which he had only taken up at his
father's wish; but whatever he did was done with all his might.
He started practice in Lyons, took his doctorate in law, and was
rewarded by appointment to a chair of Comparative Law. His
heart, he declared, was in literature, and he proceeded to earn a
doctorate of letters by a thesis on Dante in which he proclaimed
his loving admiration for the Church and the Middle Ages. 'His
faith', he declared, 'is my faith.' His ambition was soon realised

through a call to the Sorbonne as Assistant Professor and before long successor to Fauriel in the chair of Mediaeval Literature. Henceforth his studies were devoted to the early Christian centuries, in which he found not, like Gibbon, 'the triumph of barbarism and religion', but the victory of love over force. His lectures and books rank him with Montalembert among the little group of Christian scholars who followed the lead of Chateaubriand in calling attention to the immense services to civilisation rendered by the Catholic Church. While Michelet and Quinet were denouncing the Jesuits at the Collège de France, Ozanam lectured to equally crowded classes at the Sorbonne on the Papacy, the Holy Roman Empire, and Monasticism. That he was more than a propagandist was recognised by his election to the Académie des Inscriptions. It was a novelty for the students at the Sorbonne, where the atmosphere since the Revolution had been predominantly anticlerical and rationalist, to hear lectures on history and literature strongly coloured by Catholic sentiment. As the only authentic Catholic voice in the university he occupied an exposed position, but the applause of his fellow-believers made up for the arrows of the majority. Realising that there was a great deal of lost ground to be regained and that he was working for the future, he was unafraid. His *History of Christian Civilisation* gave him particular satisfaction. To serve the cause of the Church while discharging the duties of a conscientious scholar filled his mind and soul with joy.

A visit to Italy in 1847 soon after the election of Pius IX strengthened his conviction that the Church was on the upgrade, for no papal accession had been greeted throughout the Catholic Church with such exhilaration and expectation. After the static Pontificate of Gregory XVI, here was a man of energy and initiative who won friends by his benevolent expression and warmth of heart.

I never saw so much nobility, innocence and sweetness combined [he reported]. Easter Mass in St. Peter's was the grandest act of faith I have ever witnessed. At a private audience he spoke to us of France, of the youth in our schools, of the duties of a Professor, with a nobility, an emotion and a charm that are indescribable. When I said that the deserved popularity of his name would hasten the return of public opinion to Catholicism he replied: 'I know that

God has worked this miracle and that prejudice against the Holy
See has suddenly given way to respect and love, but what utterly
astonished me is that He should have made use of a wretch like me
to work this change.

At a second private audience his enthusiasm reached new
heights.

The first, the strongest, the dearest of my hopes rest in the Pope
himself. When God wishes to bring forth some great evolution in
the Christian world He begins by sowing the seed of saints. Lacordaire had cried aloud from the pulpit of Notre Dame: 'Oh, God!
give us Saints! It is so long since we have seen any.' Let us
rejoice, Heaven has granted more than we asked. It has seated on
the Chair of St. Peter a saint such as the world has not seen since
Pius V.

Returning home via Assisi he received inspiration for one of the
most attractive of his works—*Les Poètes Franciscains*.

Ozanam who, like Lacordaire, had always ranked as a mild
liberal, welcomed the revolution of 1848. Though he declined
invitations to stand for the Assembly, for which he felt unfitted,
he advised those who sought his counsel to vote for Christian
Republicans and co-operated with Lacordaire in founding a
journal *L'Ere Nouvelle* to reconcile democracy with Catholicism.
For Lacordaire it was a return to the programme of *l'Avenir*, for
Ozanam an opportunity of shepherding the common man towards the Church from which alone, in his belief, social justice
could come. 'If more Christians, above all more priests, had concerned themselves more with the working classes during the last
two years', he wrote to his mother, 'the future would be more
secure. Occupy yourself as much with servants as with masters,
with workmen as well as with employers. That is the only possible
solution for the Church in France.' 'Priests of France,' he cried
in the *L'Ere Nouvelle*, 'do not take offence when laymen appeal to
your zeal as citizens. Have no doubt of the power and popularity
of your ministry. The time is come when you must go and seek
those who do not send for you, who have perhaps never known
the Church or the priest or even the sweet name of Christ. Your
fathers saved Europe by the Crusades; save her once more by the
Crusade of Charity.'

Turning to the rich he exhorted them to share their super-
fluities with the poor and to provide work as well as alms, while
members of the Assembly were urged to go and see for themselves how the people lived. 'Do not plead lack of time. Climb
those dark stairs, enter those wretched rooms, see how your
brothers are suffering utter destitution, do not plead want of
money but trust to the generosity of France. Open a national
subscription for the unemployed, not only of Paris, but of the
whole country.' Patrolling as a National Guard in 1848 he witnessed the social revolution at close quarters. It was at his suggestion that the Archbishop of Paris walked in his robes as a peace-
maker to the barricades in the Faubourg St. Antoine where he
met his death. Though the revolt was suppressed the social
danger remained, for there were 300,000 unemployed in the city.
Busy though he was with his lectures and his journalism, Ozanam
devoted part of every day to visiting the distressed.

> My heart is torn to pieces by the sight of the misery [he wrote to a
> friend]. Here the Society of St. Vincent de Paul has grave duties,
> and perhaps God may have permitted its rapid growth so as to be
> ready for this task. It is good to see in their homes these poor
> fellows one has met on the barricades. It is astonishing how much
> Christianity exists among them and therefore how much there is to
> work on. Let us not fancy that the end of France has come, for that
> would be the end of the world. Where is there a sound spot? Where
> is there a nation less gravely diseased than ourselves? Yet can we
> believe that God has nothing more to do with the world except to
> sit in judgement?

L'Ere Nouvelle, for which he wrote leading articles several
times a week, revealed him as a first-rate journalist; but it was not
his *métier* and when it ceased publication he returned to his academic duties and authorship.

Scarcely five years of declining health remained and he passed
away at the age of forty in 1853.

> None of us will leave such a void as you [declared Lacordaire in a
> touching tribute]; none of us will carry away so many hearts. You
> were the master of many, the comforter of all. Chosen by God after
> long years of humiliation to revive the prestige of the camp of
> truth, you fulfilled this mission to your last day. The poor man
> found you at his bedside, the tribune and the press saw you in

action. Our greatest joy will be to imitate you from afar if God permits.

Many petitions for his beatification have been addressed to the Vatican, and one of the latest of his Catholic biographers expresses the opinion that it will one day be granted.

15

LOUIS VEUILLOT AND THE PRESS

Among the major oracles of the Catholic revival Louis Veuillot alone was a son of the people. The most influential Catholic journalist of the nineteenth century grew up in the household of a manual worker and never forgot the hardships and frustrations of his youth. Educated in the rough school of life the lad formed his own opinions, felt an irresistible urge to write before he was out of his teens, and learned his trade in the provincial press. Converted from religious indifference to militant ultramontanism during a visit to Rome at the age of twenty-five, he spent the rest of his career in proclaiming that Christianity was the only hope for the world and Catholicism the sole authentic voice of Christianity. Personally disinterested and steadily refusing to limit his independence by association with any party or régime, he made *l'Univers* a force to be considered by friend and foe. Wielding his pen like a flaming sword, ready for any sacrifice on behalf of his principles, even imprisonment and the loss of valued friendships, fighting with the gloves off and rejoicing in the fray, the fiery crusader was rewarded by the admiration of a large section of the Church and the smiles of the Vatican. Though the Lacordaire of the press was occasionally rebuked by fellow-Catholics with cooler blood for intemperance of language, the twelve volumes of his correspondence reveal him as a loving son, husband and father and a faithful friend.

Born into the family of a Paris cooper Louis Veuillot grew up in an age where the lines between the working-class and the bourgeoisie were sharply drawn. Little was done for the former before Guizot laid the foundation of elementary education in 1833, and opportunities for secondary education lay far ahead. Throughout life he was mainly interested in raising the welfare and happiness of his class, and social reform seemed to him far more important than any purely political advance. 'Constitutional government is good, and we must love and defend it,' he wrote in 1844. But the July Monarchy, the golden age of the well-to-do bourgeoisie, took little interest in the toiling masses and he shed no tears over its fall. Since the Second Republic seemed no more humane he welcomed the Empire, not because he approved the principle of autocracy, but as the régime most likely to concern itself with the needs of the working-class.

Making up for his lack of education by his eager interest in public affairs, Veuillot began his journalistic career at the age of seventeen in the provincial press and quickly attracted attention by the vigour of his style. The Catholic revival was only beginning and religion meant little to him. There was little in the Gallicanism which had survived the Revolution to inspire the young, but he was never an anticlerical. One day, indeed, in a mood of dejection he entered a church in Toulouse, knelt down and repeated such of the prayers he had learned as a child as he could remember. Though he possessed a few young Catholic friends he felt no temptation to discuss matters of faith with them.

An official mission to report on education and charities took him to Rome in Holy Week 1838, where the most important event in his life occurred. He was overwhelmed by the atmosphere of the Holy City and its sacred shrines. He recalled in later life that he was suddenly converted at the corner of a street like Saul on the road to Tarsus. The tempo was not quite so rapid as it seemed in retrospect. In June 1838 he wrote to his brother Eugène:

> You told me to study Italy, and it is Italy more than anything else which has made me a Catholic. This country is so full of works of faith, and Catholicism produces so many men of genius that we must bow the head and bend the knee. That time is over, but as many simple faithful souls as ever pray before the altar.

His friends were assured that 'in getting a little religious' he would not be a worse son or brother. It was not a sudden resolution but the result of mature reflection. 'I have been having long talks with a French Jesuit which have moved me profoundly and I cannot predict the result. In any case I hope to escape from uncertainty. That would be a blessing, as for the last year I have been torturing myself.' He admits that the spectacle of a girl in fervent prayer in a church was one of the determining factors in his decision. At the age of twenty-five he was already a person of sufficient distinction to be congratulated and received in private audience by Gregory XVI. Thus began his contacts with the Vatican which were to form one of the happiest chapters in his life. Though proudly and passionately independent, he fed out of the hand of the three successive Pontiffs during the remainder of his life. Completely uninterested in philosophy and dogmatic theology, he envisaged the Papacy as above all the infallible guide to the moral, political and social problems both of individuals and nations. Henceforth his programme was the Church and France, not France and the Church. With the exception of Joseph de Maistre, none of the Catholic crusaders of his time fought with such fanatical zeal against Gallicans, Protestants, *libres-penseurs*, and other enemies of the Church. Indeed he went so far as to deny the title of Frenchman to those of his countrymen outside the Catholic fold.

After spending some months on the staff of Marshal Bugeaud, Governor of Algeria, he expressed the wish to return to Paris. 'What do you want to do there?' exclaimed the Marshal, who desired to retain his services. 'To make a revolution,' was the reply, and he felt he could do it, 'marching forward Cross in hand.' The only happy and indeed the only possible society was Christian and Catholic. 'When the Church is attacked I feel like a son who sees his mother being beaten.' His creed was simple enough. The Christian Prince has the right and duty to punish crime against the unity of religious truth, the greatest of all crimes. He denounces 'the cowardly sovereigns' who had the power to suppress the conflagration of the Reformation and failed to use it.

They allowed the greatest social crime which man can commit. Better permit poisoners and murderers, war, plague or famine than to allow heresy to enter a nation. Pestilence, war and famine are reparable and of brief duration, but the results of heresy last for centuries and destroy souls for ever. The only subject of regret about Hus is that he was not burned sooner and that Luther was not burned too. I regret that no Christian Prince was found in Europe pious and wise enough to organise a crusade against the heresy of Hus which cost 300,000 lives, that of Luther millions, and the list of the victims is not yet closed. These millions died without the slightest benefit to mankind. They bequeathed a legacy of hatreds, confusions and sophisms, seeds of crime and dissolution enough to ruin the world if God in His mercy was not watching over us.

When this scream was thrown in his teeth he roughly replied that if he were ever to disavow it they would have a right to think of him as he thought of them.

Veuillot's name is as closely associated with *l'Univers* as that of Delane with *The Times*, but the paper to which he was to render conspicuous service when he began his contributions under the title *Faits divers* was in a precarious condition at the time. Founded in 1833 as *L'Univers religieux, politique, scientifique et littéraire*, it announced that it was intended as much for men of the world, thoughtful youth, and sincere people of all opinions as for the Catholic clergy at home and abroad. Started and edited by Abbé Migne, the first number opened with an article by Abbé Gerbet, a former disciple of Lamennais. France, he declared, was the child of Christianity and would become Christian once more. Ozanam was a contributor and Montalembert helped with money. Veuillot's articles quickly attracted new subscribers and earned his appointment to the editorial chair. A temporary disagreement with the management led to a brief retirement, but his services were indispensable and he was quickly back on his own terms. On assuming full direction of the paper in 1843 he announced that it stood for the Church and the country.

In the flow of events and ideas we embrace the only things and the only ideas which do not pass away, the Church and the country. Free from prejudice against all opinions that are loyal and permissible, convinced that everything honest and legitimate in the present disorder will find its place in the new pattern, we oppose nothing except the radical source of disorder—impiety, the degradation of doctrine, the decline of morals. Just towards all, loyal to the laws of the country, and devoted to the ideas of the Church, we reserve our homage and our love for the authority, worthy of us, which, emerging from the present anarchy, will proclaim that it is from God, marching towards new destinies for France, the cross in our hands.

No French journalist before Rochefort and Clemenceau possessed such a power of holding the reader's attention by unexpected phrases and deadly thrusts. Steadfastly rejecting all invitations to serve under the banner of any party or to accept favours from any régime, he regarded his independence as his capital, only less a source of strength than his religious faith. His reward was the recognition of his sincerity by friend and foe. That his journal soon turned its back on financial anxieties was a further proof that the editor had come to stay.

The most burning question for Catholics during the later years of the July Monarchy was that of the state monopoly of secondary education exerted through the University of Paris and the Ministry of Cults, then occupied by Villemain, an acknowledged authority on the history of literature. Though liberty of education was promised in the Charter granted on the change of régime in 1830, it had not been implemented. Montalembert, whom Veuillot admired and regarded as his leader, warmly welcomed the ablest journalist in France in his campaign to break the monopoly of higher education by an authority whose indifference to religion was notorious. An Open Letter to Villemain, published as a brochure, set forth his case.

The system of which you are the head involves such intolerable burdens and prepares such subtle poisons that Catholics would think it a crime to keep silence. You can only reduce us to silence by doing us justice or by force. You will either let us open schools or you will open the prison doors to receive us.

Montalembert warned Veuillot against close relations with the Legitimists, who were glad of every opportunity to attack the régime.

One month's imprisonment and a fine of 3,000 francs came to him at the age of forty-four for disobedience to and disrespect for the law. From the Conciergerie he reported: 'I am well off. With a little more air it would be a pleasure. Able to read and write. God is good and knows exactly what He is doing.' The passing of the *Loi Falloux* in 1850 would have proved impossible without the parliamentary support of Thiers, but Veuillot's labours in the press were of scarcely less importance than those of Montalembert in the political arena. With his usual scorn of minor sacrifices to secure great benefits, he criticised the men who realised that in a nation of divided loyalties a price has to be paid for everything. He scorned Bismarck's definition of politics as the art of the possible, for in his eyes nothing that the Church required was ultimately beyond its reach. Though he owes his place in history above all to the conduct of *l'Univers*, he found time to write several books which enjoyed a wide sale. The first, published shortly after his conversion, described places of pilgrimage in Switzerland and Italy. The second contained studies of leading *libres-penseurs* whom he flagellated as the sons of Cain and the corrupters of youth.

The most popular of Veuillot's writings were *Parfums de Rome* and *Odeurs de Paris*, the titles of which sufficiently explain their propagandist purpose. He detested big cities in general and Paris in particular—the home of immorality, infidelity, materialism and the ruthless exploitation of the poor by the wealthy bourgeoisie. Among religious publications of his fellow-crusaders Montalembert's *Life of St. Elizabeth of Hungary* and his *Monks of the West* were particular favourites. In Joseph de Maistre's *Du Pape* he found all his beliefs presented with a learning to which he never aspired. Veuillot neither played nor desired a part in politics. He was far more interested in social reform than in forms of government. He welcomed the Second Empire as heartily as his friend Montalembert opposed it, and the Emperor's concern with the fourth estate confirmed his conviction that enlightened autocracy was best fitted to France. Though his tactics varied his strategy never deviated, and the charge of opportunism is unjustified. He approached every party, every school of thought, every régime, with a measuring-rod in his hand. Unlike Montalembert, who opposed absolutism as a thing degrading in itself, he disliked it only in so far as it clipped the wings or threatened the territorial possessions of the Church. Democracy was anarchy, universal suffrage madness. God sent dictators to punish mankind, he declared, when it forgot its elementary duties. Liberalism and above all the right of private judgement were the arch-enemies, and the issue of the Syllabus of Errors in 1864 was welcomed with a cheer. He looked back to the Middle Ages with their partnership of throne and altar as the happiest era in the annals of mankind.

Since a European theocracy was unfortunately impossible he regarded a Catholic Monarchy as the best available alternative. During the Ages of Faith all men were brothers since they were children of a common mother. The chief aim of government, he declared, was to give men something to love.

During the opening phase of the Empire Veuillot welcomed the friendliest relations between Church and State which France had known since Charles X, and the Crimean War was approved as an opportunity to transfer the custody of the Holy Places from a schismatic Church to Rome. When, however, the autocrat supported 'the monster' Cavour and the cause of Italian nationalism in 1859, and part of the Papal States passed under control of the House of Savoy, the editor unhesitatingly took the side of the Pope and his unflinching attacks led to the suppression of the paper which was only to reappear in 1867. Secure in the approbation of the Vatican, he was ready to criticise the dignitaries of the Church if he disapproved of their actions. When criticism of what seemed to him a culpable spirit of tolerance on the part of Sibour, Archbishop of Paris, led to the exclusion of the paper throughout his diocese, he appealed to the Pope, who expressed approval of the work of the paper and desired its continuance. Fresh conflict within the Catholic ranks arose when the use of unexpurgated texts of the Greek and Latin classics was attacked by Veuillot as endangering the morals of youth. He was defended by Bishop Dupanloup, himself a lover of ancient literature. Other dignitaries of the Church took the editor's side, and a compromise was reached by the introduction of expurgated versions.

Writing in 1855 at the height of his influence Veuillot lifted a corner of the veil on what the campaign had cost him. 'The happiness of defending the faith is worth any price. All wounds in God's cause are a pleasure. I speak from my heart in all sincerity after an experience of fifteen years. Had I known at the outset of my association with *L'Univers* the trials which lay ahead I might have drawn back. Now I know I would start again. Of course some blows are cruel. The enemy knows all the intricacies of the mind and heart and strikes at the most sensitive points. I

R

cannot boast of having reached total impassibility. I have suffered more for the Church than for myself though they have even insulted my mother. With the experience I have so painfully acquired I might make some changes in my language but nothing in my line of conduct. I have written about fifty volumes in the last twenty-five years, and now in the sixties I have dealt with various subjects and employed different methods, but I have only had a single idea, a single love, a single object of wrath. I have loved the Church which is the supreme justice, and hated impiety, which is the supreme social iniquity.'

In 1866, when the forces of Ultramontanism were gathering for the trial of strength at the Vatican Council four years later, Veuillot launched a broadside against Liberal Catholicism and Gallicanism. In his *Liberal Illusion* we might be listening to Joseph de Maistre, for there were no minced words or ambiguities in the attack.

Ultramontanism and its message was the only true Christianity, and its opponents within the Church were worse than its critics outside. Christian society existed, and must always exist, under the protection of two swords, that of the Pope and that of a secular power, and the former was by far the more important. The liberty to which man was entitled was to seek and find union with Christ. Christianity recognised, and indeed approved, the use of force in the service of the Church, which teaches publicly the words of God, while Liberal Catholicism would allow Christians to choose their way. The Ultramontanes proclaimed that all decisions must be made by the Pope, the only supernatural authority on earth. Stout arms are as necessary as stout hearts. No man knows anything except he who possesses the thought of God. We must lock arms round the Sovereign Pontiff, follow his inspired directions, and affirm with him the truths which alone can save our souls and the world. When he has made a pastoral decision no one has a right to add or suppress a single letter. What he affirms is true for ever.

Dying in 1883 at the age of seventy Veuillot could look back on the four decades of his campaign with the conviction that he had not lived in vain. The task of recalling his countrymen to the faith of their fathers was beyond the power of any individual, however inspired and inspiring, or of any group of men, as the opening years of the Third Republic, the era of Gambetta, Jules Ferry and Clemenceau clearly proved. Yet there was more interest in religion and more vitality in the Church than when he girded on his armour in 1838. In officially proclaiming the supremacy of the Pope in 1870 the Vatican Council set its seal on the Ultramontanism of which he had been the foremost champion in France, and in which he saw the only substantial hope of a better world.

BISHOP DUPANLOUP,
FRIEND OF CHILDREN

No one made such a substantial contribution to the Catholic revival in France as Dupanloup, the most influential and the most beloved figure in the French Church since Fénelon. An inspiring leader of youth, an eloquent preacher, a voluminous author, a capable administrator, a Member of Parliament and a shepherd of souls, he fought in the first line in the campaign to re-Christianise his country, and none of his fellow-crusaders touched life at so many points. Combining the spirit of the apostle with the tenderness of a woman, he attracted and retained the affection of those with whom he came in official and unofficial contact in an almost unique degree. Neither a scholar nor a profound theologian, he won his way into the hearts of young and old, Catholic and non-Catholic, rich and poor, by his sympathy with suffering, his gentleness, and his saintly life. His greatest joy and perhaps his supreme achievement was to train children for the battle of life, imprinting the Christian message on their minds and hearts.

Born in 1802 in Savoy, at that time temporarily annexed to France, Dupanloup was reared in humble circumstances. His illegitimate birth is not mentioned by his official biographer, Abbé Lagrange; he was baptised in the name of his father and it never interfered with his career. After starting school life at Annecy he moved at the age of seven to Paris, where he won golden opinions above all as a Latinist. His first Communion at the age of thirteen, for which he was prepared at St. Sulpice, made a profound impression, and a vision of the priesthood invaded his mind. After completing his studies in that historic seminary and after his ordination he was appointed to the Madeleine, with the special assignment of preparing boys and girls for their first Communion. It was here that he found his feet, for he transformed the humble duties of catechist into an apostolate. Children, he declared later, were his first and last love. He loved them with maternal affection and he possessed the secret of arresting their attention.

His first publication was a *Handbook of Catechism*. Since many parents attended the classes his name became known in ecclesiastical circles and reached the ears of Archbishop Quélen, through whose influence he became Almoner to the Duchesse d'Angoulême, daughter of Louis XVI, and catechist to the youthful Comte de Chambord, grandson of Charles X and heir to the throne, and to Princess Clémentine, daughter of Louis Philippe. His work at the Madeleine was interrupted after many happy years by his *curé* who disapproved of his methods or resented his popularity; but the change from the teaching of youth to the pulpit of St. Roch revealed him as a preacher second in eloquence to Lacordaire alone. Appointed Director of Studies at the Seminary of St. Nicholas in 1834 and three years later as Superior, he was at last his own master since he enjoyed the affection and confidence of the Archbishop.

He proved an ideal head of the Christian School, and many sons of the nobility were among his pupils. 'An incomparable awakener,' declared Renan in his *Souvenirs d'Enfance et de Jeunesse*, 'a great and good heart.' It was in these happy years that he learned the lessons which he was to expound in his longest and most famous work, the treatise on education. On his first visit to Rome he was greeted by Gregory XVI as 'the apostle of youth'. He was less happy during the two years as Professor of Theology at the Sorbonne, partly because he had little interest in doctrinal matters, partly because there was little opportunity for the intimate contacts between teacher and pupil in which he excelled. After being hissed by the class in consequence of a disparaging reference to Voltaire he resigned his post.

The name of Dupanloup became known to Europe in 1838

when he was summoned to facilitate Talleyrand's reconciliation with the Church. Feeling at the age of eighty-four that the end could not be far away, the former Bishop of Autun, who had shown little respect for Christian morality either in private or public life, invited the Superior of the Seminary of St. Nicholas to dinner. It was a preliminary reconnoitre, for other guests were present. No intimate talk was possible nor did the host desire it, but the old man liked the perfect manners and naturalness of his visitor, and when the shades began to fall he sent for him again. Only a few hours before the end when he realised that there was no hope of recovery did he announce his submission to the Church. Dupanloup was present at the signing of the document, described by Talleyrand's biographer, Duff Cooper, as his passport to heaven, and at the final scene on the same evening. One of the most attractive features of Dupanloup's personality was that he showed himself exactly the same in all human contacts, high and low.

As a bosom friend of Montalembert and Lacordaire he watched the experiment of *l'Avenir* with interest but without identifying himself with the campaign. The revolt of Lamennais against the declaration of the Pope moved him to indignation, since he believed that the Vatican was the voice of God. He disclaimed all ambition and declined flattering offers from abroad, among them the King of Piedmont-Sardinia's offer of an Archbishopric, for he had no wish to leave Paris. He was often consulted by Archbishop Affre, the successor of Quélen, was glad to accept a canonry of Notre Dame, and defended the Jesuits against their foes. 'I am a man of peace,' he declared, and his methods of controversy were widely different from those of Louis Veuillot, whose violence he deplored.

Though Montalembert and Veuillot have received most of the laurels for smoothing the path for the *Loi Falloux*, Dupanloup's share in the campaign was no less important, and as a member of the Commission appointed to draft the law he displayed exceptional gifts of negotiation. His greatest triumph was winning the support of Thiers. Though religion played no part in his personal life, and though he disapproved every form of clericalism, the old statesman feared socialism, communism and revolution far more. Haunted by memories of the fighting at the barricades in 1848, he came to realise that Catholic teaching in schools might form a measure of social security. No one knew better than Dupanloup that without Thiers' support no Bill acceptable to Catholics would have a chance. Both men realised that nothing more could be obtained from the Ministry or from the Chamber of the Second Republic, and Thiers generously acknowledged his debt. 'You know my feelings towards you since we had the happiness of sitting together on the Education Commission. But for you I should very often have lost patience. I have found few men with your clear insight, impartial reasoning and conciliatory character. We have come into port without much damage. I should have liked to satisfy you on all points, but that is impossible.' The same realisation that politics are the art of the possible enabled Falloux as Minister of Education to pilot the unanimous draft through the Ministry and the Chamber. Here for the first and last time Dupanloup helped to make history on a large scale.

In 1849, before the Falloux law reached harbour, Dupanloup was appointed Bishop of Orleans. His abilities no less than his character so deeply impressed Thiers, the most influential of politicians, and Cousin, the most authoritative spokesman of the University of Paris, that they urged Falloux to make him a Bishop. When a vacancy occurred at the city of the Maid Dupanloup declined the honour on the ground that he wished to remain in the capital to continue his preaching, and considerable pressure from Montalembert and other friends was needed before his *Nolo Episcopari* was withdrawn. That he brought new life into his diocese and won its affection confirmed the conviction of his closest associates that his new post would form the crown of his career. Busy though he was with his episcopal duties, he found time to complete a comprehensive treatise on education which embodied his experiences as a teacher. The book is much more than a treatise on pedagogy for it embodies his philosophy of life. Education, he insists, is primarily a shaping of character, a school of virtue, which can only be based on a definite religious doctrine. He speaks with scorn and horror of Rousseau, whose Émile is brought up without definite religious instruction. The sophists who contended that dogma is not only unintelligible to a child but unnecessary for the good life are denounced as enemies of God and man. His three volumes form the most complete manual of education on Christian lines ever produced in France. A notable feature of the book is the recognition that girls have as much right to a good education as boys, an attitude never so firmly maintained within the French Church since Fénelon's *Education des Filles*.

Dupanloup's political preference was for a Constitutional Monarchy on the English model. He had no fear of democracy for he believed in the common man. Though he never went so far as Lamennais in demanding the separation of Church and State he asked nothing except permission for the clergy to perform their educational and pastoral duties in their own way. Though he expressed neither approval nor disapproval of the *coup d'état*, he welcomed the friendly attitude of Napoleon III to the Church and recognised his sincere interest in the welfare of the manual worker. When, however, the Emperor's train passed through Orleans and the ruler addressed a few friendly words to the Bishop on the platform, the latter bowed without speaking and no private interview ever took place. When the Emperor's Italian policy led to the destruction of the temporal power of the Pope the Bishop shared the grief and anger of Catholics throughout the world.

Dupanloup's closing years were darkened by catastrophes and disappointments—defeat and invasion, the nightmare of the Commune, the failure of his efforts to effect a reconciliation of the two branches of the Bourbon family, and the inauguration of the *école laique* by the Third Republic. By the time of his death in 1878 the Catholic revival, in which he had played a leading part, had lost a good deal of its momentum, and no commanding figure appeared to continue his work.

SAINT-SIMON AND THE INDUSTRIAL AGE

THE collapse of the *ancien régime* left the ground free for rival projects of reconstruction. While Catholics demanded a return to religion, Saint-Simon argued that such a throw-back was impossible, and that nothing less was required in the dawning industrial age than a new society. Feudalism had vanished with the rise of the bourgeoisie and science had dethroned the dogmas of the Church. While the eighteenth century had been an epoch of demolition and revolution, the nineteenth would be an era of peaceful reorganisation—affairs of state would be directed no longer by kings and aristocrats but by a new *élite* of captains of industry and technological experts, intent on increasing the prosperity of the country and thereby raising the standard of life of the neglected manual worker and ensuring social order by removing the causes of discontent. Science had already fashioned a new ideology and was capable under wise direction of inaugurating an era of prosperity, political stability and international harmony. The answer to revolution was production.

Since material well-being was insufficient for human needs, leading figures in the sciences would assume the former functions of the clergy and become the lay apostles of the new religion of humanity based on mutual aid and brotherly love. Christian metaphysics had melted away but Christian ethics would remain as the foundation and inspiration of the new social order. Political self-determination was of infinitely less significance than the increase of well-being and happiness. His banner bore the words:

Everything for the people, nothing by the people. There is no trace in him of Rousseau, scarcely any of Voltaire, and nothing whatever of Karl Marx. Faguet's description of him as a feudal philanthropist fits him infinitely better than that of socialist, an adjective coined by Robert Owen, or even a forerunner of socialism, for he thought of social reform in terms of ethics rather than economics. In a word, he was a sociologist. Inheriting a good deal of the spirit and teaching of Condorcet, Saint-Simon believed that history justified the expectation of a far happier and more peaceful future for mankind. He had plenty of private faults, but no Frenchman of his time devoted such energy and ability to the problem of human betterment than the Bentham of France. 'The golden age lies in front of us,' he cried, 'not behind us, and our children will witness it some day. Our task is to find the way by perfecting the social order.' 'My mission', he added, 'is to tell the whole truth, to flatter the captains of industry as little as the princes, nobles and the bourgeoisie.' Wise leadership, popular education and hard work were the prerequisites. There were only two species in the community, the bees and the drones, and in the coming society the latter would be eliminated. Political and social institutions must be judged exclusively by their results. Comte coined the word sociology but Saint-Simon laid the foundation stone of the new science. He was a madman, declares Faguet, madder than Rousseau, but a very intelligent specimen of the tribe, for he instinctively anticipated the main preoccupation of the nineteenth century. He was like a seed, with the whole tree inside him.

Born in 1760 into the family of a younger branch of the house of Saint-Simon, Comte Henri numbered d'Alembert, one of the High Priests of the cult of reason, among his teachers and at fifteen declined to make his first Communion. He followed his father into the army. He served in the American War of Independence, was taken prisoner, and was released on the return of peace. It was not his vocation to be a soldier, he declared. 'To study the march of the human mind, to work for the perfecting of civilisation: such was the goal at which I aimed.' His most valuable service to his contemporaries was to make them think— not about politics and parties but about society, and above all about the needs of the poor. He took himself very seriously and instructed his valet to call him every morning with the words 'Remember you have great things to do.' He travelled in western Europe. On a visit to Coppet he calmly asked for the hand of Mme de Stael with the words: 'You are the greatest woman of the time and I the greatest man and our children would be greater still.' He plunged into historical and scientific studies which were to bear abundant fruit, but they took a long time to mature. Though never tempted to enter the political arena, he shared the conviction of Mirabeau and other liberal aristocrats that the *ancien régime* had outlived its usefulness, and he welcomed the opening phase of the Revolution. Chosen as the President of the electoral College at Péronne, he renounced his title and petitioned the Constituent Assembly to abolish the 'impious restrictions' of birth. Though he had committed no offence by word or deed against the new order he was cast into prison, only regaining his liberty a year later when Thermidor ended the Terror. Vivid memories of mob rule coloured his thinking for the rest of his life, and reinforced the nobleman's instinctive conviction that those who had had the best opportunities should have the chief part in serving and shaping society. His influence was increased by purchases and profitable resales of confiscated property which enabled him to entertain the political and intellectual *élite* on an extravagant scale. His marriage at the age of forty-one lasted less than one year, by which time the whole of his capital was gone. Henceforth, as before his marriage, he contented himself with mistresses. He would have been a bad partner, for he was utterly reckless when his pockets were full and shamefully dejected when they were empty. Once he attempted suicide with the loss of one eye, and for three years he lived as the guest of his former valet who had made money.

Though his brain had long been buzzing with schemes, Saint-Simon published nothing till the age of forty-three, when his *Lettres à un habitant de Genève* outlined the system which he was to elaborate in a stream of books, brochures and articles during the remaining two decades of his life. Since ideas shaped institutions, the first task was to select the finest minds of Europe to train the citizens for their responsibilities. Social order, which collapsed under the impact of the Revolution, could only be restored by the union of the intelligentsia and substantial landowners and thus deprive the ignorant of the power they had abused and would abuse again if they had a chance. In the Middle Ages the Church and the Nobility had maintained order, but the clergy had forfeited their leadership by their hostility to the new science, and scientists must take their place. Belief in providential interventions, astrology and alchemy, must give way to scientific observation, following Newton's lead. A Newton council of twelve whole-time and well-paid savants, aided by nine artists, should be chosen from the whole continent. Any subscriber to the new venture could take part in the choice. The old faith was dead or dying, and a new Church of humanity, with its temples and pilgrimages, should fill the vacuum. Here was the germ of the fantastic cult proclaimed after the death of Saint-Simon by Père Enfantin which his master would have repudiated.

Five years later a more ambitious work was published in response to a request from the Emperor to members of the Institut to summarise the achievements of science since 1789 and to offer suggestions for its further progress. The two-volume work *Introductions aux travaux scientifiques du dix-huitième siècle* was as much a confession of faith as a factual record, for it assigned to scientists the cultural leadership formerly claimed by the Church. Physicism, as he called it, would supersede theism, as theism had ousted polytheism. The transition needed time, and the traditional beliefs would continue among the ignorant till they were ripe for the new faith. The author appealed to the Emperor to take the first steps: 'A terrible general war has been raging for twenty years and threatens to devour the whole population of Europe, and has already cost several million lives. You alone can reorganise European Society. Time presses.'

After five years of further study and reflection Saint-Simon issued a short work with an ambitious title, *Mémoire sur la Science de l'homme*, modelled on Condorcet's *Progrès de l'Esprit Humain*. The author surveyed the human adventure from Egypt till his own time, when all other creeds had been superseded by the scientific spirit best described as positivism. He appealed to the Emperor to offer a prize of one million francs for the best plan for reorganisation of society, associating the Emperor of Austria and the Prince Regent of England with himself as adjudicators. If they declined, the Emperor should be the sole judge. The essays were to be sent in by the end of 1813, and the award to be issued on 1 January, 1815. Presentation copies were dispatched to influential persons with an abject appeal for help, for the death of his devoted valet had left him penniless—he never earned much by his writings. 'Sir, be my saviour, I am dying of hunger. For the last fortnight I have lived on bread and water, and I have sold my clothes to pay for printing this.' How he lived for the next three years we do not know, but in 1814, on the fall of the Emperor, he resumed contact with his Legitimist relations and received a small pension from them.

Like almost all other Frenchmen Saint-Simon welcomed the Restoration, for the country was sick of dictatorship and war. He knew little of England, but what he knew he liked. Constitutional Government, he believed, would spread over Europe. In 1814 he published the plan originally intended to compete for the prize which he had hoped the Emperor would patronise, *De la réorganisation de l'Europe*. Reconstruction required peace, and peace could only be secured by Parliamentary institutions combined with a European Parliament. While every nation would retain its independence, a European patriotism would emerge as strong as national pride. The transition would take time, but England and France acting together might make the start. The main task of the international Parliament would be to settle disputes between its units as in the Middle Ages they were referred to Rome. A hereditary king should be chosen, and should reside in some independent city. He would be assisted by businessmen and *savants*, lawyers and administrators, with elections every ten years. The author had no use for universal suffrage or universal eligibility. Only literates—relatively rare in 1814—could vote, and candidates must have a thousand pounds a year in landed property. Members of the House of Peers should be even larger landowners, and twenty of them, distinguished in science and industry, would form the executive. In an appeal to Louis XVIII he accused the nobility of striving to regain their power and dominate the King. 'Sire, your interest is to suppress the old nobility.'

The personality of Saint-Simon, no less than his writings, attracted young men of culture. The most promising, Augustin Thierry and Auguste Comte, became his secretaries and contributed to his newspapers and to some of his books. Since, however, the master was apt to change his opinions, he found it easier to win disciples than to keep them. While Thierry changed from sociology to history Comte, after years of ardent discipleship, broke away and set forth a rival philosophy in two majestic treatises.

The main constructive task of the closing decade of Saint-Simon's life was to construct a social system suitable to the new industrial age. The inventions of science in the eighteenth century had led to heavy industry becoming the chief concern of nations and the main source of their prosperity. Everyone agreed that it needed far more organisation than agriculture, but there was a sharp difference of opinion on how much control the State should exercise. Adam Smith and his school, like the leading French economist J. B. Say, argued that the national economy should not be the slave or plaything of politics. It was a science, and private enterprise knew better than state officials how a business should be run. Such was the dominant school during the years of the Restoration, and if production alone had to be considered it was difficult to challenge. But what of distribution? *Laissez-faire* economists were vigorously assailed by the historian Sismondi, and Saint-Simon followed his lead in the longest and most influential of his works.

Since political liberty, he declared, meant little to the illiterate and poverty-stricken workers and since they were incapable of helping themselves, it was the sacred duty no less than the interest of the educated Mentors of the community to create economic conditions which would gradually transform their lives. His gospel was popularised in a paper *L'Organisateur*, which ran for a year, in the system of treatises, the *Industriel* and in a brochure entitled *Catéchisme des Industriels*. All these publications, large and small, were the work of several hands, chief among them Thierry and Comte. But the master's hand was always at the helm. The programme was simple and far-reaching: government by experienced industrialists and cultural direction by savants, in a word State Socialism, not Social Democracy. Popular sovereignty, universal suffrage and absolute equality were as absurd as legitimism or theocracy or class barriers. In a reformed society the humblest citizen could rise to the top by ability, but in the absence of exceptional talent manual workers should invite their employers to rule over them henceforth. Good government was more important than self-government. Ability and education must be the sole qualifications for leadership. *La carrière ouverte aux talents*. The two obligations of government were to provide education and work for every citizen. Maximum production by private employers should be supplemented by public works such as roads and canals, bridges, ports, and the cultivation of waste and marsh lands. World trade should be fostered by construction of inter-ocean and inter-state canals, such as a Rhine–Danube and Rhine–Baltic canal. European technicians should carry their skill all over the world. The author's belief in the importance of industry and industrialists and his slogan *tout par l'industrie, tout pour l'industrie* earned financial support from the banker Lafitte and other leaders of big business who shared his opinion that economic expansion was the best hope for international peace. With a satisfactory society which worked well in every European country standing armies could be abolished.

Copies of the *Système Industriel*, consisting of brochures written in 1820, were dispatched to the King and to prominent industrialists. The tone has become more definitely socialist and the old fear that the classes should be threatened by the masses has diminished. The abolition of titles would bridge the gulf between the classes. Hereditary aristocracy had stronger roots in England, but there also it was doomed.

Saint-Simon's last message to the world in the closing year of his working life is the most attractive and the most impressive of his writings. His mature ideology is set forth in an unfinished series of dialogues between Conservative and Innovator, the latter voicing the teaching of the author. The dominant note is firmly struck in the opening exchanges:

Innovator: Back to Christ! Religion is indestructible, but it is for ever taking new shapes, since the secret of survival is transformation.
Conservative: Do you believe in God?
Innovator: I do.
Conservative: Do you believe that the Christian religion is of divine origin? If so, it cannot be bettered, yet you are always suggesting changes and are thereby contradicting yourself.
Innovator: Not at all. We must distinguish what God has said and

what the clergy has added, which is capable of improvement, as all other human knowledge.

Conservative: Which part of religion do you regard as divine and which as human?

Innovator: God said we should treat each other as brothers. That sublime precept contains all that is divine in the Christian religion and involves our organising our society for the greatest benefit of the greatest number, for the moral and material education of the largest class.

Conservative: God has left us guides. Christ charged his apostles and their successors to assume direction of human conduct. Do you regard the Church as a divine institution?

Innovator: I believe God founded the Christian Church and I have the greatest respect and admiration for the Fathers who preached peaceful co-operation of all peoples and the care of the poor.

Conservative: Do you think the Christian Church infallible?

Innovator: I regard the Fathers as infallible for their own time, but I consider the clergy of today the body which commits the most errors and their conduct is in the most direct opposition to the fundamental principles of divine morality.

Conservative: So you think the Christian religion is in a very bad way?

Innovator: On the contrary. There have never been so many good Christians, but they are almost all laymen.

Conservative: What will become of the Christian religion if its official teachers, as you believe, are heretics?

Innovator: Christianity will become the universal and sole religion. Asiatics and Africans will be converted and the European clergy will become good Christians, abandoning their various heresies. All institutions will work for the betterment of the poorest class.

Having thus delivered his message, the author proceeds to work out the consequences of its acceptance, to survey religious Europe and the New World, and to prove that what is good for the poorest class would increase the prosperity of the whole community of every nation. He was only an innovator in the sense that he pushed the application of the divine principle of morality further than anyone before him. Like other religions the New Christianity would have its dogmas and its ritual, its clergy and their superiors selected for their services to the poor. Their duty would be to preach and practise without ceasing the new religion.

The Catholic Church, declares Saint-Simon, remained very

powerful, but its strength was purely material and was only maintained by cunning. Spiritual, moral, Christian force was entirely lacking. Catholics were heretics. The Christian renaissance would abolish the Inquisition, and the Jesuit Order with its Macchiavellian doctrines. The first heresy of the Pope and the Church was the absolute subordination of the laity to the clergy. The second was the lack of capable instructors in the schools and seminaries where only theology was taught. The clergy were now being surpassed by the laity in the arts and sciences. A third heresy was the misgovernment of the Papal States and the neglect of the poor. Its record was worse and more anti-Christian than in any secular state. The failure to introduce industries led to unemployment and idleness, the root of brigandage and all vices. The fourth heresy of the Church was the support of two institutions absolutely opposed to the Christian spirit. The Inquisition stood for despotism and greed, its instruments were violence and cruelty. The Jesuits claimed authority over ecclesiastics and the laity alike. After half a century of suppression the Society was infinitely more contemptible than before in challenging the new order. 'Their missionaries are veritable anti-Christs since they preach a morality opposite to that of the Gospel while the Apostles were the champions of the poor. The Jesuits are the advocates of the rich and powerful against the poor who today find their sole defenders among the laity.'

After his flagellation of the Church of his birth the author turns to Protestantism and applauds Luther's criticism of the Papacy as a major service to civilisation. 'Without him it would have wholly subjected the human spirit to superstition by leaving morality out of sight. To him is owing the disintegration of spiritual power which was out of date.' His attempt to reorganise the Christian religion, on the other hand, merely produced another heresy, for he omitted to urge the application of Christianity to society. Moreover he had exalted the secular ruler as the source of all power, only allowing his clergy the right of humble supplication, and hereby subjecting men of peace to men of violent passions. The Reformation, the first large-scale attempt to reform the Christian Church, had failed.

Since in his opinion neither Catholicism nor Protestantism embodied the essence of Christianity Saint-Simon felt it his duty

s

to attempt its rejuvenation and purification by relieving it of all superstitions and useless beliefs and practices. The task of the new faith was to assail all combinations which sacrifice the public good to private interests, and to establish perpetual peace by allying all states against any community pursuing its private aims at the expense of the interests of mankind, and against any government so anti-Christian as to sacrifice national to private interests. The first duty of resurgent Christianity was to carry its message to the class which it would most benefit. Such apostles would be assured of a good hearing, thus securing support for their campaign against Catholicism and Protestantism. They should go to all civilised nations, employing the same methods of peaceful persuasion as the early Christians. If they met with violent resistance they should not retaliate, and they should teach their followers never to use violence against the rich or the government. There ought, however, to be no such collision, for the rich themselves would profit by raising the level of the poor.

The book concludes with an appeal to the rulers of the Holy Alliance to christianise society.

> Princes, hearken to the voice of God who speaks to you through living mouths. Cease to regard armies and nobles, heretical clergy and unjust judges, as your principal support. United under the banner of Christianity, discharge the duty it imposes on rulers to increase as quickly as possible the happiness of the poor.

Saint-Simon always wrote with his heart as well as with his head.

It was the ill-fortune of the new Messiah that the dominant group of the *Ecole Saint-Simonienne* tarnished his reputation and abused his teaching by expending their energies in fabricating a cult which a strain of mystical sensuality doomed to general contempt and speedy dissolution. The disparagement of the marriage tie by its High Priest Père Enfantin was too much for Bazard and other original members of the school, and few thoughtful Frenchmen desired a new theocracy which stridently proclaimed the rights of the flesh. A further cause of unpopularity was the repudiation of the principle of inheritance on the ground that the individual has no right to any property which is not the fruit of his own labour. There is little left of Saint-Simon, who died in 1823, except the memory of a man who earnestly and unselfishly strove to leave the world better than he found it.

18

THE OPTIMISM OF MICHELET

THE most colourful, most dynamic and most subjective of French historians was also an influential moralist and ideologist. A son of the French Revolution, he combined rapturous devotion to France with a burning sympathy with the manual worker who had never had his chance. In his early years a compositor like his father, he carried into the academic world an instinctive under-standing of the life of the poor, unattained and unattainable by the bourgeois writers and scholars from Voltaire to Thiers and de Tocqueville. Far from attempting to conceal his humble origin he regarded it as an asset in his task as interpreter of French history. Alone among nineteenth-century historians he could speak of poverty, hunger and frustration with first-hand acquaintance, and throughout his forty volumes we catch the throb of a tender and generous heart. He could hate as fiercely as he loved, and never soft-pedalled his emotions. *Liberté, Egalité, Fraternité* was no mere paper formula but the inspiration of his life, the core of a creed held with all the ardour of a missionary. No one lived more intensely, for his whole career was a crusade. Every com-munity demanded liberty, but France had discovered and pro-claimed that liberty without equality was a fraud. Never content to be a mere spectator and recorder of events, he preached the gospel of patriotism and social justice in his glittering *History of France*, his *History of the French Revolution* and a dozen other works.

Michelet owes his enduring fame to his large-scale histories, but he had made his name in the academic field with a series of works before his dazzling picture of mediaeval France took the reading world by storm. The broad sweep of his *Précis d'Histoire moderne* introduced vitality and colour into the arid world of school books, and his *Histoire Romaine* was much more than a mere summary of Niebuhr's revelations. His translation and elucidation of Vico's *Scienza Nuova* introduced to his countrymen the father of the philosophy of history and paid his debt of gratitude to the only writer whom he acknowledged as his teacher. His *Introduction à l'Histoire Universelle* he declared might have carried the sub-title *Introduction à l'Histoire de France*, for it saluted France as the pilot-vessel of humanity. Italy and France, he declared, were the joint heirs of Rome, and as such directors of the main stream of civilisation, another word for liberation. Greece had discovered the individual and Rome had given us legal rights which Christianity enlarged. France had combined liberty with equality and had not only proclaimed but implemented the Rights of Man. A visit to Germany was followed by a portrait of Luther mainly based on his correspondence and table talk, a character study, not a biography. The tone is cool, for the author was unattached to any church. Michelet applauded the Reformation, though not all its leaders, for proclaiming the rights of conscience and Luther for rejecting clerical celibacy and for composing some noble hymns.

Too little known nowadays are the four treatises which analyse the society of his time and expound his proposals for shaping it closer to the pattern of the City of God. Enriched by a wealth of personal experiences and other lands they enjoyed wide sale in France and beyond her frontiers. They retain their importance both as realistic pictures of nineteenth-century France and as powerful agents in the democratisation of her institutions and the secularisation of her thought. With Michelet at the rostrum we are never assailed by the blare of the trumpet, but there is no danger of his hearers going to sleep. Compared with the magic of his rhetorical and poetical style the narratives and treatises of most historians and publicists appear pedestrian. Even when we resent his knockabout ways we can never forget that he is a man of genius.

Le Peuple, published on the eve of the revolution of 1848, was the most significant and the most revealing of Michelet's works. When his attack on the Jesuits in his lectures at the Collège de France in 1843 made him a European celebrity he felt that the time had come to express the convictions which had long been fermenting in his mind, and they poured forth like a stream of lava. Though he earned his bread as a teacher of history and loved his work, he was even more a moralist and a reformer. Neither friend nor foe—and he had plenty of both—ever doubted his sincerity.

This book is more than a book [he announced in the dedication to Quinet]. It is myself. That is why it belongs to you. It is I and you, my friend. To know the life of the people, their labours and their sufferings, I had only to recall my memories. For I have worked with my hands. I have known the depression of the workshop, the boredom of long hours. It was a sad chapter, but what is best in me as a man and a historian I owe to these trials. I have retained above all a profound sentiment of the people and a full realisation of the treasures they contain and tender memories of the souls of gold I have known in the humblest quarters. I have shared their life and mixed with the crowd. I know their past. It is always the same people, only changed in externals.

Next to the conversation of men of genius and learning, the talk of the people is the most instructive. If you cannot converse with Béranger, Lamennais and Lamartine, go into the fields and talk to a peasant. What is there to learn from the middle-class? I have never left a salon without a chill in my heart. What has struck me most in my long studies of the people is the wealth of feeling and goodness of heart mixed with the frustration of poverty which are rare among the rich. For instance, the orphans of the victims of cholera were adopted by the poor. Devotion and self-sacrifice are my measuring-rods. Mental superiority which is partly the result of culture ranks below the faculty of sentiment.

Michelet exalts the peasant at the expense of the artisan. The land is his mistress. France belongs to him, as England belongs to the aristocracy. He made it and he loves it. If we wish to understand that love, we must remember that he made it and loves it like a human being. It is the fruit of his saving and his sweat. To get it he sometimes leaves home to work in the town for years. With it he feels free, no longer a serf or a hireling. To get more of it he borrows and stints himself in food. The town-dweller eats better every day than the peasant on Sunday. When he borrows he is charged usury rates. Sometimes he is embittered by poverty and debt. He hates the rich, and the village *curé* calls him a materialist, the only object of his worship the land. The *curé* is wrong. It is he who sees in this dirty soil the gold of liberty. 'People say the Revolution destroyed the nobility. On the contrary it created thirty-four million nobles.' His one fear is expropriation by his creditors. He and his fellows must be preserved for they are the makers and defenders of France. Yet no régime since the Revolution concerned itself with agriculture. Its younger sister, industry, has stolen the limelight. The Restoration favoured property, but only large estates and the capitalist and the industrialist are in sole command. The agriculturists furnish one-half of the revenue and the peasant is not merely the most numerous but the strongest, the soundest and on balance the best element in the national life. Having lost his old belief, and without access to modern culture, he retains the national sentiment, the great military tradition and something of the soldier's honour. Compare him, despite all his faults, with those liars the merchants. A child of the soil, he seems made in its image, greedy, determined, patient, indestructible. Do you call these faults? Without them you would have no France today. Look at our peasants as they return from the African wars and resume their labours, resume the holy task of renewing the strength of France, the marriage of man and its soil.

Life for the peasant is hard, but think what he loses if he migrates to the town. He is merely a machine himself. His food is better, but he lacks fresh air. Miserably housed, temptations surround him. He loses the possession of his soul. Visit a factory and you will see men and women standing like machines. Monotony drives to sensuality and drink. No strength needed, no skill, no thought. Nothing, nothing, nothing. The child is inferior in strength and morals to the country-cousin. Despite long hours some desire to read, but there is only one book in the home. A few become owners of a factory or merchants. Some big factories are the glory of France in the world of taste and fashion. The shopkeeper and his wife are not to be envied, for the hours are long and the uncertainties of trade are a perpetual anxiety. State and local functionaries are ill-paid and often uncertain of their tenure of office. The most important of them all is the school-master. Though he is France, his life is plagued by the hostility of the priest, himself the serf of Rome and of his Bishop.

After this depressing picture of urban life Michelet pro-nounces a blistering verdict on the bourgeoisie, the children of the Revolution, who had ruled France for half a century but were losing their grip. The cultivated classes looked down on the simple folk who were their equals in everything but education. 'I have thought to convince these classes, born yesterday, and already worn out, that they should make contact with the folk whence they spring.' Here was a task in which the author, who had known the life of the manual worker in his youth and the world of the bourgeoisie in his manhood, could play the part of a bridge-builder.

> Poor solitary dreamer that I am, what can I give to this great people? All that I have—a voice! All those who groan and suffer in silence, and all who aspire to life, are my people. Let them come along at my side. The new city must be holy ground, founded by Him who alone founds anything. And divine it will be if, instead of shutting its gates, it rallies every child of God, the lowest and the most humble, the strong and the weak, the simple and the sage, each bringing with him his wisdom and his instinct. If anyone is refused entry I will stay outside.

The happiness of a family tended to diminish as it rose in the social scale. The head of a rich household was often hard and selfish, materialist and restless. The wealthy Frenchman was the only person in the world who never rested. The author was always far too inclined to generalise, and his sweeping verdict on the French middle-class is unconvincing.

Michelet had his moments of depression when he brooded over the victims of social injustice, but there was one section of sky where shone a bright and steady light, *la Patrie*. Though he believed in the brotherhood of men he had no desire for the closer integration of the nations of Europe. They were growing increasingly conscious of their mutual interests, but let them co-exist while developing on their own lines. 'We shall always thank God for giving us our glorious country, the representative of the liberties of the world. The most attractive of nations,

France, should not indulge in utopian cosmopolitanism, and not try to copy England or any other country.' This was not blindness or ill-will, he explained, for he esteemed the great British nation as the land of wealth, where gold flows like water despite the millions of beggars—the richest people in history. France was poor, but she had exhausted herself for the world. Who else has maintained the tradition of law? Where else is Rome to be found? France has continued the Roman and Christian tradition and taught fraternity; more than England and Germany who were strangers to the great Roman-Christian-democratic tradition. They possessed portions of it, but indirectly and clumsily and without harmonising it with their own traditions.

Michelet knew little of England and English history. Crossing the Channel in 1834, he was appalled by the contrast between wealth and poverty. The Reform Bill had been passed, but the country was in the grip of the haughty aristocracy. Nothing had been done for the Fourth Estate in that country of insolence and inequality. The more he saw of England the more convinced he became of the superiority of France, for France was the Promised Land of *Le Peuple*.

In the process of social integration a vital part had been played by the schools. The need for popular education had been recognised by the Convention in the midst of bloody wars. Since those days faith in France and the Revolution had waned, and it was the task of the teachers to restore it. Nothing could be done without faith. Let them teach the children that France is a living being. Take them to see the historic buildings of Paris, to watch soldiers marching through the streets, for France was concentrated in a single city. Let all the children mix in the schools unaware of the vain distinction between rich and poor, and learn the lesson of the two redeemers, the Maid and the Revolution, the lesson of devotion and self-sacrifice.

As the Bourgeois Monarchy moved towards the revolution of 1848 Michelet interrupted his history of France to sing the praises of the French Revolution, the most glorious chapter in the national history since the Epic of the Maid. 'The Revolution', he exclaimed, 'is in us, in our souls.' It was the work of the whole people and began by loving everything, whereas the Terror was the work of a few evil individuals. The heart of France was full

of magnanimity and clemency and her soul shone forth in un-
sullied radiance. Michelet was the Victor Hugo of history, and
his *History of the French Revolution* is the epic of democracy.

Part of the same ground was covered some years later in two
books *L'Amour* and *Du prêtre, de la femme et de la famille*, which may
be regarded as the first and second volumes of a single work.
In his sympathy with suffering in body and mind Michelet had
always ranked woman above man, saluting her not merely as the
creator of life but as the guardian angel of the family. Though
generally regarded as a man of the Left, he was unashamedly
conservative in his estimate of the vocation of women. Unlike
Mill, his contemporary, who was pleading for a much wider and
richer life in *The Subjection of Women*, Michelet never ceased to
proclaim that her place was in the home and that only as wife
and mother could she fulfil her destiny. With his first wife, who
gave him three children, there was no intellectual comradeship.
The second was interested in his work, but he had little contact
and little desire for contact with the clever ladies who presided
over the salons of the capital. Yet no one has paid higher tribute
to the matchless virtues and spiritual worth of the other sex.

Every woman, he declared, was an altar just because it was a
holy task to rear a family. That her effort was often a tragic failure
was due in most cases to the husband. The perfect marriage of
his dreams rarely gladdened his eyes. Was he too severe to the
male element and did he underestimate the proportion of successful unions? He could call as witnesses contemporary novels: for
Balzac, George Sand, Flaubert, Zola and Maupassant painted
much the same dark picture of disenchantment and loveless
homes, except that in their lurid pages the responsibility for
disaster is more evenly distributed.

L'Amour opens with the declaration that love precedes the
family, for it is as old as woman; the family rests on love and
society on the family, so love is the starting-point of everything.
George Sand herself had not sounded all its depths in her novels.
Material and intellectual progress was superficial in comparison,
and Europe was confronting the industrial age with an impoverished soul. It was the task of France to change the world by
changing herself. Part of the decline was due to the increasing
use of alcohol and narcotics. Polygamy was growing, legal

marriage decreasing. Their age would be called the century of diseases of the womb. Woman was a sacred creature, the holy of holies, all pity, all tenderness, all faith. Infinitely less sensual than man, her thoughts centred on motherhood, giving pleasure and happiness to her husband more than on her own enjoyment. Nowhere is there to be found a purer, more tender or more reverent picture of a young wife. With the coming of the first child the family becomes the kingdom of God in miniature, the strong serving the weak, the smallest member of the group in full command. The celestial vision often fades with advancing years, but the elderly woman can always employ her leisure in works of mercy. With her heart full of love age is not an enemy but a friend.

The introduction to *Du prêtre, de la femme et de la famille* opens on a sombre note. Woman was being left behind by man, and the gulf was widening. How often was the hearth cold, the table silent, and the bed a block of ice! *L'Amour* had been sharply attacked, but it had been read and wept over by women. They turned to it in their spare hours. Since its purpose had been to restore woman to the hearth it could hardly please a man of the Middle Ages or a woman who preferred the cloister or the street. Adultery had almost become an institution, and in the big cities marriage was avoided unless property was concerned. Poverty drove young women to sell themselves and men preferred to change partners any day if they wished. The bachelor was afraid to marry a rich girl who was conscious of her social status and who often divided her affections between her children and her old home, leaving her husband to feel himself unwanted. Some men with modest incomes could not give their wife the smart clothes they craved, and in some cases religion was a barrier. The *ouvrière* was miserably paid and underfed and tuberculosis was rife. The educated woman who had to earn her living had no less difficulties. The governess from the country who appeared alone in the evening in a street or a restaurant was taken for a prostitute, and she was liable to be molested by the father or son in the household of her employers. The actress who received a paltry wage was advised to take a lover. No wonder that a girl, hungry and lonely, should be led astray, but a woman's soul was never so deeply corrupted as that of a man.

With decades of teaching experience behind him Michelet offers advice in education at every stage. Children, like flowers, need sunlight, books on natural history, a garden, preferably in the country. Interest them in the growth of flowers and in the way birds build their nests. Fruit and vegetables were much better for them than meat. Writing at a time of terrifying child mortality which kept the mother in a state of perpetual anxiety, he urged that everything should be done to ensure the rearing of a healthy family. The crown of education was the training of every young child to love and serve its country.

Michelet adored France to such an extent that he frowned on any mixture of European races. Profound differences, he declared, existed between French and English, even in their skeletons, and offsprings of mixed marriages were often subnormal. While the German wife was a gentle creature, French, Polish and Magyar women possessed much more personality and often dominated their husbands. The Frenchwoman, indeed, was the most many-sided in Europe and the most difficult to know, each of them differing enormously from all the others. When she gave herself for ever the bond was stronger than anywhere else. The Englishwoman, who made an excellent wife, obeyed in material things but was averse to change. The German woman, so good and gentle, wanted to belong to someone. With the pronounced personality of the Frenchwoman great care in the choice of partners was essential. And now for once the ardent patriot finds a large spot on the sun. 'The great fault of the French nation is impatience, always in a hurry about everything.' Ever too prone to far-reaching generalisations Michelet gets out of his depth in the pronouncements on the women of other countries of whom he had little knowledge. On French marriages he could speak with more authority, and here, despite his flaming patriotism, he could not find much to give him joy.

Michelet paints a touching picture of the young bride leaving the family circle and feeling at times rather lonely in her new sphere. Would she be happy? He knew of few really happy marriages. Some required a high temperature, some a medium, some zero. So one had to ask how much are they married? Everything depended on the start and it was usually the husband's fault if things went wrong. The wife should interest herself in her husband's work, play to him, and they should read books together and both should enjoy the arts. A cultivated woman enriched by a man's comradeship would become his superior. She leaned on his arm but she had wings. The book closes on the same note of something approaching adoration of woman. 'If she does not continually sanctify and ennoble the family, she has missed her vocation. Her vocation is love, her salvation making man happy. To love and have children is her sacred duty.'

Du prêtre, de la femme et de la famille may be described as a voluminous appendix to *L'Amour* and *La Femme*. It devotes hundreds of pages to the shrill complaint of priestly influence over woman as an offence against her spiritual independence and a threat to the harmony between husband and wife. The most dangerous of interlopers in Michelet's eyes were the Jesuits because they were the most powerful of the Orders, the most zealous and the most unscrupulous. He had witnessed the Catholic revival inaugurated by Chateaubriand, Lamennais and Joseph de Maistre, and the more he saw of it the less he liked it. He had been brought up without religious influences and had never felt the need of a faith, and like his parents regarded the Church as the champion of the rich, a degenerate embodiment of early Christianity. Early volumes of the *Histoire de France* had saluted St. Louis, the Maid and the *Imitation of Christ*, but in middle age his attitude to ecclesiastical influence hardened and in 1843 he and Quinet thundered against the Jesuits from their chairs in the Collège de France. The précis of Michelet's addresses, which had aroused nation-wide controversy, appeared in a little volume entitled *Les Jésuites*, which ran through six editions in eight months and was translated into many languages. Though there were only about one thousand Jesuits in France their influence was enormous and increasing; and they were growing into a national danger, for they were the police of the Pope, a worse tyranny than any political and secular autocracy. They carried treachery into the house, the wife spying on her husband, the children on their mother. Without allegiance to the local Bishop they obeyed their Superior—*perinde ac cadaver*—in order to reign themselves. With their soft wheedling voices they wormed their way into the impressionable hearts of women. They were the counter-revolution, an instrument of war, and their aim the death of liberty. Never before or after did the most widely read of French historians write a book so one-sided, so emotional and so unworthy of his fame.

Du prêtre, de la femme et de la famille was a more restrained performance. In a preface added many years later the author declared that the book, however severe, had been written without hate. He should have pronounced a still harsher verdict in view of the records of clerical sexual offences. The forty thousand confessional boxes were the strongholds of the Church and the head of the family felt lonely under his own roof as he knew that his wife and daughter told an outsider secrets of which he was unaware.

The original preface of 1845 declared that he had been violently denounced and insulted in the Catholic press which showed that they had been wounded in their most vulnerable spot, their power over women, by his taking the woman's side in family feuds. Would it not be better if the clergy were free to marry? Would not a married man understand the problems of domestic life better than a celibate? Women needed other champions than the priest, and laymen should take up their cause.

The most instructive section of the book is the survey of spiritual direction in the *Grand Siècle*. Here the publicist gives place to the scholar who supplies vivid portraits of several outstanding ecclesiastics. The story opens with François de Sales and Madame de Chantal who stand out in shining contrast to the Jesuits who were pilloried in the *Lettres Provinciales*. The Jesuits were the tempters of Kings and Popes, of the former through their lusts, of the latter by exalting their office. The quietism which Mme Guyon had learned from Molinos had its dangers, since the theology of repose weakened the sense of individual responsibility. Far worse was the sensualism of the cult of the Sacré Coeur and Marie Alacoque. The saintly Fénelon is admired as much as François de Sales and is saluted as *Le grand et bel esprit*. Bossuet, the Eagle of Meaux, an even more commanding figure, is greeted as the wisest of Directors, since he never surrendered to the fashionable quietism. After surveying the illustrious figures of the seventeenth century Michelet reiterates his detestation of 'the abdication of the soul' and of the Director's claim that he could teach the penitent what to do better than anyone else.

Passing to the nineteenth century the author notes the disap-

pearance of quietism and the survival of the system of confession
in undiminished rigour. *The Enlightenment* had bequeathed a far
less credulous France and popular education had deprived the
priests of their cultural superiority. The *curé*, often the son of a
peasant, knew nothing of society and could do little for members
of an unfamiliar superior class. On the other hand he retained
influence, the old evils persisted, the husband possessed the body
of his wife, the priest her soul. The plight of women in convents,
cut off from all contact with the life of the community, seemed to
Michelet a living death. Some inmates had been immured without
their consent and some were mentally subnormal. It was a world
of boredom and trembling obedience. Many girls received their
education exclusively from *réligieuses*. Prisons and asylums were
open to official inspection, but no secular authority was entitled
to cross the threshold of a convent. It was a dark picture and it
never occurred to the artist that many women found peace,
fulfilment and happiness in convents.

The fifth and last of Michelet's sociological works, written at
the age of seventy, appeared on the eve of the Franco-Prussian
War. *Nos Fils* is a treatise on education based firmly, as the author
explains, on thirty years of teaching experience. Many themes
discussed in his earlier books are treated at greater length, such
as the need of the study of animate and inanimate nature. Next to
natural history in the curriculum comes the literature of travel,
beginning with *Robinson Crusoe*, a book dear to the author's
heart from youth to old age. Thirdly comes history, the story of
la Patrie, 'the mother of us all'. Here as everywhere Michelet is
a preacher no less than a teacher.

His message is the goodness of human nature. Unlike the Hindu
he says Yes to life, for the world is a good place full of sunlight
and creative energies. The Middle Ages were the age of tears,
the modern centuries from the Renaissance onwards the age of
liberations. Far from needing the services of the Church, the child
requires to be saved from its false and degrading doctrine of the
Fall of Man. The Church, moreover, hated liberty, the life-blood
of humanity. 'Elargissez Dieu', Diderot had exclaimed, and
Michelet proceeds to interpret the injunction in the spirit of his
beloved Spinoza.

Enough of temples: the Milky Way is our temple. Enough of dogmas: God suffocates in these little prisons. Liberate the divine essence fermenting in our human energies and longing to pour forth in torrents and to express themselves in creative work. The soil is waiting for our aid, yearning to enrich us with its beauty. *La terre, c'est la liberté, la dignité, la moralité de l'homme.*

Michelet proclaimed the blessings of country life from the cradle to the grave. The most critical phase in education begins with school life in a big city, especially for French youth, the most precocious, impressionable and highly strung of types. The best defence against its temptations is to interest the boy in the marvels of science. Training for life must start in the home, and the mother's milk is the earliest lesson. Some German doctors declared that a child deprived of its birthright rarely laughed. In this latest treatise the author speaks of the father with more appreciation than ever before. As a rule, he declares, the French father was admirable. Both parents should be careful in their language, for a child is very observant. Himself an abstainer Michelet advises them to bring up their family without wine. The mother must strive against her instinct to bestow more of her love on a son than on a daughter.

The range of studies in universities had broadened during the nineteenth century and the classics had been supplemented by history and science. Geological and botanical excursions should be arranged and the student should never be overstrained. Two hours without a break were too long. The teacher needed an alert class as much as the class required a stimulating instructor.

A quarter of the volume is dedicated to the educational pundits of the modern centuries with Rabelais at the top of the list. Ever since his declaration of war on the mediaeval doctrine and practice of asceticism there had been a running fight between believers that human nature deserved the privilege of liberty and those who taught that all men were born sinful and need to be kept in the straight path by threat of hell and hopes of heaven. The healthy notion of the creator of Gargantua was carried on by Rousseau, Pestalozzi and Froebel. All these pioneers were inspired by a new faith, no less ardent than that of the Christian theologians, namely the faith in man. Michelet's final message to his generation was—be yourself and work with others in creative activity.

Michelet lived long enough to welcome the Third Republic in which the Church and the priest were to count for less in the life of the people than at any period in the turbulent history of France.

19

THE PESSIMISM OF TAINE

DESPITE his sufferings and sorrows Michelet journeyed through life with a song in his heart; for he adored his country and believed in the common man. Taine, on the contrary, though he never knew poverty or hunger, found little to cheer him as he peered into the boundless spaces of the universe and examined *homo sapiens* with a microscope. He would have subscribed to Gibbon's complaint that history was mainly a record of the crimes and follies of mankind. How indeed could it be otherwise? Born with teeth like the dog and the fox, man had always buried them in the flesh of other creatures, and his earliest ancestor had resembled a fierce and lustful gorilla. Scratch off the thin veneer imposed by the process of civilisation and the teaching of religions and we find a greedy and miserly animal tossed into an inhospitable world, where sustenance is difficult to find, with the instinct to acquire and retain.

That, however, is his least fault, since it can be disciplined and may become a factor of stability and conservation. Yet this is a very fragile structure, for at the least social upheaval it disappears and the primitive instinct regains control, stretching forth towards it prey. Man is by nature mad, as his body is sick. A healthy mind, like a healthy body, is a lucky accident. Reason is a weak faculty which combined numberless twisted threads to form general ideas. These, however, are cloudy and are always challenged by rival conceptions.

Thought alone raises us above the animals, but we suffer from

T   273

excess of sensibility and are liable to epidemics of credulity and superstition. Far from exalting Frenchmen as the finest of European types, Taine thought very meanly of them outside the sciences and the arts. In his monumental *Origines de la France Contemporaine*, which occupied the last two decades of his life, he found little to admire in the *ancien régime* and nothing at all in the Revolution or the Empire. And now the nineteenth century, infatuated by the slogan of universal suffrage, was galloping towards the abyss like the Gadarene swine. Could the faults of mankind be cured or mitigated by an *Être Suprème*? Certainly not, for there was no such being. No thinker of his time exerted such a profound and depressing influence on his countrymen as this high-minded scholar. He had formed his opinions long before the disasters of *L'année terrible* and the atrocities of the Commune came to confirm them. All we could do is to maintain our personal integrity, to bear our burdens bravely, to abandon our illusions, and to search disinterestedly for truth. Frederick the Great declared that he was a Stoic in the morning and an Epicurean in the evening. Taine was a Stoic all the time.

Born into a well-to-do lawyer's family, he astonished his teachers in school and in the École Normale by his precocity and his passion for work.

> He is easily first in everything [wrote Vacherot] and the most industrious and distinguished pupil I have ever known at the École Normale. His erudition is prodigious for his age, and such zeal for learning I have never witnessed. His mind is remarkable for rapidity of conception, subtlety and strength, but he judges and generalises too rapidly. He has a weakness for formulas and definitions to which he often sacrifices reality. His moral nature, however, is a stranger to any passion but truth and is above all temptation.

More than forty years later the obituaries had merely to repeat this searching analysis. We can follow his personal fortunes and the evolution of his ideas in the four volumes of his correspondence.

The revolution of 1848 was the first major political excitement in the life of a young man more interested in history and philosophy, literature and the arts than in politics or political theory, but between his twentieth and twenty-first birthday he devoted increasing attention to the plight of his country.

A week ago I came of age [he wrote from the École Normale on 1 May, 1849] but I am not voting. I have only two settled opinions in politics: the first is that the right of property is absolute and anterior to the state, like individual liberty. The second is that all political rights are reducible to one, that of consent to the existing form of government, explicitly or tacitly, for all forms derive their legitimacy from the acceptance of the nation. There are two reasons why I cannot vote. The first is that to vote I should have to know the state of France, her ideas, her ways and her future. The right government is one which is appropriate to the civilisation of the people. What suits France I know not. So I cannot vote for a republic nor for a monarchy, nor universal suffrage, nor restricted suffrage, nor for Guizot, Cavaignac, or Ledru-Rollin. The second reason is that I know too little of the merits and opinions of the candidates to choose. The two parties (royalists and republicans) disgust me. I seem to see a heap of idiots, intoxicated furies, hurling lies and filth at one another. The philosopher and artist in me rises in revolt: I should vomit with disgust if I did not laugh in contempt. I am aware that the reactionaries are the party of the present, the socialists the party of the future, but I see these two bands of fanatics wallowing in heaps of mud. In their arguments I find nothing but declamations and banalities. It is a war between those who want to let others die of hunger while keeping everything for themselves and those who wish to steal and possess. So I retire into pure science.

Politics seemed to him a dirty game now that he began to study them, and the more he saw of them during the next four decades the less he liked them. He would have agreed with Acton's aphorism that the tyranny of the many is even worse than the tyranny of the few because it is harder to dislodge.

In the autumn of the same year Taine denounced the doctrine that the rights of individuals are merely conventions, and that there are none except those established by the popular will. 'You are tyrants, for your teaching justifies the tyranny of the crowd. Liberty of speech and publication is a right. The life and property of every individual is inviolable and he has the right to retain them. The state also has the same right as the individual, namely to preserve its life and property and to defend them against enemies within and without.'

The Second Republic was bad enough but the Second Empire was worse, wrote Taine after the *coup* of 1851.

T*

So we know what is before us. For sixty years there has been a
continual oscillation from monarchy to republic, from liberty to
authority, and that will continue for some time. We are at once too
much and too little democrats to suffer either, but liberal ideas are
making their own way, and after seven or eight more revolutions
they will doubtless triumph. We are now convalescing with many
relapses, and we shall no doubt have to wait for the next century
to recover our health. So we must be patient and our children will
fare better than ourselves.

Bonaparte was no worse than the rest, he added a week later,
but law did not count, for there were only passions and instincts.
'Only science, literature, education and the slow progress of
ideas, can extricate us from this mud. I resign myself for years
to come to having no party and detesting them all. Meanwhile
I live in philosophy.'

Taine's dislike of the *coup*, though it was less virulent than
with Victor Hugo and Michelet, was sufficient to risk his academic career. Alone of the staff of the University of Nevers he
refused to sign the declaration of gratitude and devotion to the
usurper, and he paid the expected penalty of dismissal. He was
permitted to lecture at the École des Beaux Arts and published
his courses in two volumes entitled *La Philosophie de l'Art*. His
main interest in the arts was sociological rather than aesthetic,
since he always endeavoured to visualise and understand the
society which had produced the artists and their masterpieces.
The same sociological purpose dominated his first *magnum opus*,
the *History of English Literature*, which might have added as its
sub-title *The Character of the English People as illustrated in their
principal Authors*. His materialist philosophy, based on the assumption that the senses are the only source of knowledge, was explained in *Les Philosophes Classiques* and at greater length in his
major philosophical treatise *De L'Intelligence*.

'For forty years', wrote Taine at the close of his life, 'my sole
task has been psychology, pure and applied. Paul Bouget calls
me a pessimist. Poets and artists may be pessimists, but not
the man of scientific mind.' Scientists, however, like other
mortals, approach their work with prejudices or at any rate
presuppositions. Long before he reached middle life he had
formed the conviction that there was little to respect or to admire

in human beings past or present, in his own country or elsewhere.

This crushing verdict is set forth in the greatest detail and in the most uncompromising terms in his *Notes sur Paris: Vie et Opinions de Frédéric Thomas Graindorge*, edited by his executor H. Taine and published on the eve of the Franco-German War. Was it a good or a bad book? he asked on presenting a copy to his friend Sainte-Beuve. 'Was I right to write it? My friends pronounce diametrically opposite judgements. I wrote it for two reasons. I have been commended for describing the state of society in other times, so I thought I would portray the world in which I live, and my model is a man of acquaintance with Anglo-Saxon ideas.' The oracle of the literary critics diplomatically replied that it would have been better if the indictment of French society had been launched under the author's own name instead of partially concealing himself behind a Cincinnati salt pork merchant. 'I dislike this mask which is not a mask.' Assuming, as Taine's critics and biographers have done, that Graindorge is the authentic voice of the scholar and thinker whose writings filled France with his fame, we find ourselves in a society as rotten as that depicted by the Roman satirists. One of the noblest of men, living on the highest intellectual and moral plane and blessed with a happy family life, is frankly appalled by the spectacle of the materialism of the male and the utter frivolity of the female performers on the Parisian stage. Of course he is only dealing with the capital and the well-to-do bourgeoisie—there is no suggestion that the whole life of the country is being dissected and condemned. But it is depressing enough to discover so many spots on the sun in *La Ville Lumière*, and to conclude that the stern moralist sees no prospect of improvement. It is an artificial world without spiritual values, with unhappy marriages between unsuitable partners in which the contract is based on financial considerations, in which the bridegroom's heart is not seriously involved and the pitiful bride has not been consulted. The dimensions of the dowry, not mutual attraction, decide the issue.

I left Paris forty years ago [writes Graindorge introducing himself to his readers] and I returned five or six years ago. Paris is the city of balls and *soirées*, pretty women and lovely dresses. Too much is not expected either from men or women. In Paris, though not in England, a fallen woman gets a second chance. Young men prefer coarse mistresses with a loud laugh and the manners of the gutter. Husband and wife have little in common, and at table they find nothing to talk about. The young wife has too little to do, knows nothing of her husband's business and reads little, though she sometimes plays the piano. Little is heard about *La Patrie* or politics.

From beginning to end of the book there is no hint of real love, no lifting of the heart, no indication of delight in literature, the sciences and the arts. It is a world of false values and glittering trivialities. If Taine had troubled to answer charges of exaggerated pessimism he would doubtless have referred his critics to the journals of his friends the de Goncourt brothers and the novels of Flaubert and George Sand, Zola and Maupassant, and the plays of Dumas *fils*.

Taine's *Notes sur l'Angleterre* is a far more serious, comprehensive and fair-minded analysis of the character and society of a great nation. The contrast between the two peoples is always in his mind, and the estimate of France expressed in these pages is much less unflattering. If the *M. Graindorge* is the poorest of his achievements, the study of England is among the best. Interested in everything, from literature and art to ladies' dresses and food, he collects and interprets a multitude of *petits faits* which illustrate a fundamentally different society, and he finds more to praise than to blame. The main fault of the book, as of all his writings, is his habit of hasty and unconvincing generalisation.

The England of the fifties and sixties described by Taine is the England of Dickens, Thackeray and George Eliot, the country in which Disraeli's Two Nations lived side by side. It was the mid-Victorian pageant in which the aristocracy of birth, education and wealth remained in command, in which there was no smiling Welfare State to help the Fourth Estate in its misery or out of its misery. The England he studied, note-book in hand, on his successive visits, was a community of sharply differentiated classes, where the superiority of the upper strata was overtly or tacitly recognised by everyone, while France was the child of the Revolution. Without an aristocracy, declared Taine, a civilisation was incomplete, and the British nobility retained their vitality through frequent marriage into the bourgeoisie.

At the heart of the social system lay the conception of the gentleman, for which there was no word in French because there was no such thing, just as there was no equivalent for the word lady. With his incurable distrust of democracy Taine found a good deal to admire in a stratified society where political and social leadership was in the hands of an *élite* with a fine tradition of public service, discharging their official and unofficial duties with far greater competence and zeal than the state which grossly neglected the welfare and education of the manual worker. The glaring contrast between rich and poor was the abiding impression left on the visitor's mind, as he learned to know and enjoy the carefree and cultured atmosphere of the great country houses, with their enormous staffs of respectful domestics, their stables and their spacious domains.

Back in London Taine is appalled by the prostitution in the Haymarket, the squalor of the slums and the all-pervading ravages of drink, at once the sole delight and the chief enemy of the 'submerged tenth'. Nowhere in Paris, Lyons or Marseilles, he asserts, is such utter degradation to be seen. There are ugly faces everywhere, but nowhere quite so hideous as in London. Liverpool and Manchester are described as monsters, and the smoky towns of Lancashire were equally a disgrace. Some chapters read as if they were lifted from General Booth's *Darkest England* a generation later. Apart from this abyss of urban vice and misery, England struck him as possessing a higher standard in family life. The *fine fleur* of English society was to be found in the Athenaeum, of which he was elected an honorary member and where he talked with Thackeray, and in the common-rooms of Oxford, where he enjoyed the society of Max-Müller, Jowett and other academic celebrities.

England pleased the visitor as the country of the middle way, of political moderation, the home of toleration. The constitution was a skilful compromise between aristocracy and democracy. There was no more characteristic embodiment of the cool English temperament than the Anglican Church, anchored in mid-stream between Rome and Geneva. High Church and Low Church made no appeal to the Positivist. The Broad Churchmen, such as Dean Stanley and Jowett, who were more interested in the moral teaching of the Saviour than in dogmatic theology, seemed to sound just the right note in an age when science was beginning to sap inherited beliefs.

The chapter entitled *L'Esprit Anglais* compares the English brain to a Murray Guide, full of facts but with few ideas, whereas the Frenchman loved ideas for their own sake. The Englishman knew twice or four times as much but derived less advantage from his knowledge, rarely leaving the beaten track or making his readers think. The Frenchman enjoyed intelligent conversation ranging over many fields. The prevailing philosophy of Mill and Herbert Spencer avoided lofty flights. Life was less colourful and less exciting, John Bull's pulse was steadier and his food less tasty. *Punch* carefully avoided scandal. London on Sunday resembled a cemetery, and the only choice lay between church and a public-house. No words could describe the horrors of a winter fog. The educated Englishwoman was usually better-looking and healthier owing to outdoor life and exercise; but she was less coquette and less piquant, and she lacked some of the graces which rendered Frenchwomen more attractive to men. Frenchmen were gayer and got more happiness out of life, yet the English were a friendlier nation.

After completing his studies of French and English society Taine planned a companion volume on Germany where he had visited friends in the spring of 1870, but the outbreak of war convinced him that the remaining years must be devoted to the study and service of his country. Like most open-eyed observers of the Second Empire he concluded that it was only the latest in a series of revolutions and that it would not be the last. The ruler's health was failing and Ollivier's *L'Empire Libéral* was obviously a mere parenthesis. 'This is the dissolution of France,' he wrote in March 1870. 'The people are tired of their leaders. The sense of our impotence and unreason is desolating. I feel I am living in a madhouse and I have lost the capacity of indignation. There are about fifty thousand *déclassés* in Paris at thirty *sous* a day. Never was social disintegration so manifest. Blood has flowed and more is to come. We are on the verge of civil war and massacre.'

The defeat of France was generally expected except by the noisy mob which surged through the streets of the capital shouting *à Berlin*. But could the disaster be attributed merely to military inefficiency and unpreparedness? 'Our duty will be to confess our faults publicly,' wrote Taine to Sorel in December. Military defeat, though bad enough, was a familiar experience, but the bestialities of the Commune were unique. 'Europe has pitied us,' he wrote, 'now it has the right to despise us. Paris is mad and vile. It is hard to think badly of one's country. To me it is like a close relative, almost a father or mother. I judged her incapable, now I find her grotesque, odious, low, absolutely incorrigible, destined to be a criminals' prison and a madhouse. The army is worn out. We are among the perils of primitive anarchy. Thiers cannot trust the troops, Bonaparte is largely behind the revolt. I am in a condition of dry-eyed despair and dumb rage.'

What could be done to cure the spiritual sickness of France? While the anticlericals who dominated the Third Republic believed that a better type of citizen would be evolved by the extension of *L'école laïque*, Taine felt that reforms were required at the top of the academic ladder, and he encouraged his friend Émile Boutmy to establish an *École libre des Sciences Politiques*. Its purpose was to provide intensive training in political science and economics, history and sociology, for young men seeking a career in public life or a chair in the universities. A distinguished staff was formed, including Sorel, Rambaud, Anatole and Paul Leroy —Beaulieu, Boutmy, the Director himself, and eager young students flocked to its classrooms. Its success was one of the few satisfactions of his later life.

How had France fallen into the lamentable condition in which Taine found her? His answer was given in an analysis of her political régimes, social systems and ideologies from the eighteenth century onwards. Six volumes of *Les Origines de la France Contemporaine* filled the last twenty years of his life. Since *homo sapiens* had so much of the ape and the tiger he required exceptional wisdom to train and to discipline him, but France had had no luck with her successive tutors. For Michelet the Revolution meant regeneration, for Taine degeneration. The former, believing in the people, demanded more democracy; the latter longed to curb its growing power though with little hope of closing the floodgates which had opened in 1789. 'You know how I love the Revolution,' he wrote in bitter irony in 1874. 'Seen at close quarters it is the insurrection of mules and horses against man under the lead of monkeys with the larynxes of parrots.'

The Preface to the volume on the *ancien régime*, published in 1875, sharply challenged the whole theory of democracy. Millions of ignorances did not add up to sound knowledge. The people knew what sort of government they wanted but not what they needed. Full credit is given to the Monarchy, the Noblesse, and the clergy for building up the nation, but their best days were over. The chief sufferer was the peasant who was crushed by taxation, but the grievances of the *Tiers État* were sentimental rather than practical. Already, before the final crash, France was in dissolution because the privileged classes had forgotten their responsibilities. There was no firm hand at the helm. The only available leadership was that of the *Philosophes*, of whom the author speaks with horror, not for the usual clerical or royalist reasons, but because they filled the brains of their readers with utopian ideas, some utterly false, others unrealisable. France was like a man of rather weak constitution who drank greedily of a new liquor and fell to the ground foaming at the mouth.

On reaching the Revolution, Taine casts all restraint to the winds. When the Duc de la Rochefoucauld-Liancourt brought the news of the destruction of the Bastille, Louis XVI remarked: 'It is a revolt!' 'Sire,' retorted the Duke, 'it is a revolution.' As the courtier corrected the Monarch, so Taine corrects the Duke. It was much more than a revolution, it was a dissolution. With the fall of the central government the security of life and property disappeared. The customary distinction between the principles of 1789 and the Terror of 1793 is contemptuously dismissed, and the golden dawn, the thought of which almost brought tears of joy to the eyes of Michelet, never existed. Moderate men were never in control. Bloodshed and rapine began at once throughout France when the human tiger bounded forward from his lair. The Revolution in its essence, he declared, was a transfer of property. In the second and third of the volumes devoted to the Revolution the author's voice rises to a scream and we listen to a pessimist in a passion. His picture of the Jacobins, for whom the sovereignty of the people meant the mob of Paris, is the French equivalent of Burke's *Reflections on the French Revolution* and *Thoughts on a Regicide Peace*. Though a friend and admirer of

Saint-Beuve, he had no use for his maxim *La vérité est dans les nuances*. He had collected a mass of documentary materials from the archives but never learned how to deal with them, selecting only what confirmed his interpretation. Man was evil and during the Revolution he was at his worst.

The temperature of the volume on Napoleon is less feverish, but the verdict is scarcely less severe. It was natural that Taine should detest the heir of the Revolution, but his readers were surprised by the unrelieved darkness of the picture. 'I am going to write about Napoleon as I did about the Revolution,' he announced in 1876, 'as a pure naturalist, without any political intention.' There was not much of a Darwin or Pasteur about the author who reminds us rather of John Knox denouncing sinners from the pulpit. In the most celebrated superman and autocrat of modern times he finds no spark of humanity. He lived in complete moral isolation, we are told, and the only signs of feeling were exhibited at the deaths of his Marshals, and they were quickly forgotten. He regarded human beings as tools, not fellow-citizens. He was like a hunter intent on his prey. Principles and patriotism, affection and gratitude had no meaning for him and he believed they had no meaning for others. On hearing of what sounded like a disinterested act of kindness he inquired 'What does he want?' He was mean, petty, vulgar, utterly lacking in self-control and self-respect, with the worst faults of the parvenu. As Wellington remarked, he was not even a gentleman, and he cheated at cards. He told Josephine of his amours, and we cannot be sure that he did not seduce his sisters. Under other circumstances he would have been a convict and the princesses prostitutes. Beneath the sumptuous robes we detect the naked animal. He was an Italian of the Renaissance, a *condottiere*, a contemporary of the Malatestas and the Borgias. He caused the death of two or three millions, and deprived France of fifteen Departments acquired by the Revolution. The portrait of the Emperor is as unconvincing as the portrait of the Jacobins, for the author's emotions blinded his vision. No one could be surprised that Princess Mathilde banished him from her salon where he had been an honoured guest. The tone of the sixth and last volume, designed as a prologue to the history of the Restoration which he did not live to write, was infinitely calmer, for there was little in the reign of Louis XVIII to excite him or anyone else. The whole work was at once a sermon and a political testament.

The Third Republic reminded Taine of a ship without ballast or keel. The rise of Gambetta, whom he regarded as a mere demagogue, increased his alarm, and MacMahon's attempt to hold him in check seemed like a belated cavalry charge after the victory of the enemy. 'In my opinion the social and political battle was lost long ago, and universal suffrage is sufficient to ruin France. As we are in the hands of animals we must try to tame them and above all feed them. In power we shall be inferior to Italy and perhaps on the level of Spain—better we cannot be. The Marshal's tentative proposals can only exasperate them and hasten their triumph.' Taine belonged to no party, but his special hatred was reserved for the rule of the crowd.

> The well-fed, well-to-do and well-educated classes of good family have no influence in France [he complained]. The shopkeeper, the partisan, the peasant, have only to inquire for whom such people vote and then they vote the other way. Gambetta will raise his voice to a shout and let loose his rabble. He will come back more fanatical than before, the President will have to go, and in four months Gambetta will succeed him. Instead of a slow descent to a vulgar democracy it will come with a run.

As man becomes more cultivated he becomes more sensitive, a misfortune outweighing all the benefits of civilisation. The republicans, he declared, would become more and more radical, the conservatives more and more clerical. The democrats would win and would wish to suppress the upper class as clerical, useless, degenerate. Whatever happened in politics would be for the worse. 'I expect a *coup d'état*, a Bonapartist restoration. I see no hope in any direction.'

Four years later the prospect seemed equally dark. 'Under the name of the sovereignty of the people we have had insurrections and *coups d'état* and probably we shall have more. We have excessive centralisation; state interference in private life everywhere, and universal suffrage produce a system at once apoplectic and anaemic.' Shortly before his death he felt that much of his life-work had been in vain. 'Probably I was wrong twenty years ago in undertaking this series of works which have saddened my old age. From the practical point of view I feel they are of no use. A powerful and rapid current is carrying us away, so what is the good?' Since hope was extinct it was time for the curtain to fall.

20

GEORGES SOREL AND
REVOLUTIONARY SYNDICALISM

No French sociologist of the twentieth century has attracted so much attention, and no one outside the communist fold has issued such an audacious challenge to the system and record of the Third Republic, as Georges Sorel. While Taine looked for leadership to the educated middle class, Sorel, who belonged to the same social stratum, declared war on the bourgeoisie which in his eyes had demonstrated its incapacity to rule, and whose congenital selfishness could only be overcome by force. Though he called himself a socialist he scorned the Parliamentary socialists led by Jaurès who believed in constitutional methods and aspired to graft their principles on the bourgeois stock to which he belonged. Such men seemed like traitors to Sorel, engaged in a sham fight, with socialist formulas on their lips but more interested in securing the amenities of office and a good living for themselves. Parliamentary government in France was a game of intrigue, democracy a sorry farce. Society was sick and required a purge in the shape of a general strike in order to overthrow not merely the political supremacy of the bourgeoisie but the state itself in a conflict as decisive as the battle of Austerlitz. Power would then be assumed by the proletariat grouped in *Syndicats* of producers, who, ever mindful of their national responsibilities, would step up production and thereby increase general prosperity.

Sorel declined to indicate even the more important measures they would introduce, but he believed that there was nothing to fear from a syndicalist revolution and that bloodshed was improbable. The Terror of 1792–4 had been the work not of the proletariat but of lawyers and other middle-class fanatics. These revolutionary notions were ventilated in numberless articles before being fully explained in *Réflexions sur la Violence* published in 1903. No one could accuse the author of concern for his personal fortunes. He had no wish for power or a role in political life, and no student of his writings can doubt his sincere desire for a better life for the common man. His friend Croce pronounced him and Marx the only original socialist thinkers. Sorel acknowledged his debt to Marx but never called himself a Marxist. He remained a lonely figure to the end. Thinking almost as meanly of human nature as Taine, he never expected any form of society to be very satisfactory.

Georges Sorel, a cousin of the historian Albert Sorel, was born in 1847 into a middle-class Catholic family at Cherbourg. After distinguishing himself in mathematics at the École Polytechnique in Paris he entered the Ministry of Roads and Bridges and rose to be Chief Engineer whose duties frequently called him to the provinces and the colonies. Retiring from the Civil Service at the age of thirty-nine on inheriting private means he devoted his remaining years to study and authorship. He had always read omnivorously in philosophy and sociology, history, political science and economics. In middle life he attended the lectures of his friend Bergson whose emphasis on the *élan vital* he found greatly to his taste. He enjoyed conversation and testing his ideas on his wide circle of friends. His system was only ready for presentation to the world when he was nearing sixty, and when at last it emerged it exploded with the force of a bomb.

His *Reflections on Violence* is a trumpet-call to arms. The existing political and social system, dominated by the bourgeoisie, is portrayed as beyond redemption, needing to be destroyed by direct action since no gentler methods would suffice. History is a record of ceaseless conflict, and such imperfect civilisation as we possess has been achieved in a running fight with the blind and arbitrary forces of nature. Democracy in its present form must disappear since it weakens the moral fibre and unfits us for the struggle which demands faith no less than muscle. The task of creating a better society was urgent, so no compromise, no conciliation, no parleyings could be tolerated. When the politicians talked of social reform and put a few measures on the statute book they were merely postponing the hour of liberation. For such a task heroic virtues were required, and heroism was only generated by the same apostolic zeal which inspired the early Christians and the front-line warriors of the French Revolution. The conviction that a better order was in sight should be enough to inspire the proletariat to epic deeds, and the irresistible weapon of a general strike was in their hands. The utmost care must be taken to avoid a premature *coup*, and the ground needed careful preparation by a revolutionary *élite*. Properly organised proletarian violence would surely triumph over bourgeois apathy, and direct action need not involve bloodshed. Production was the key to national well-being. Free producers, no longer servants but their own masters, would justify their revolution by increasing output to the maximum.

The lengthy Introduction sounds the uncompromising note which echoes through every chapter. The class war was a very old story, and the time had arrived for the last to be first. Jaurès was a highbrow, and the significance of the intelligentsia was grossly exaggerated. They knew nothing of the feeling of the manual worker who must henceforth look after himself.

> My reflections [declared Sorel] are inspired by passionate love of the truth, and I have spent years unlearning the formulas of my youth. I write for the few and I cannot found a school, but I have made people think. I have tried to show that a new society might spring from the struggle of the proletariat.

The Syndicalists desired to destroy the state in order to prevent some other minority government. They were also anti-militarist since the army was the chosen instrument of the executive. The Parliamentary Socialists attacked individual politicians but not power nor the arm of power, convinced that they would need it if they took office. Do not touch pitch, cried Sorel, or you will be defiled. By entering bourgeois institutions and taking part in political debates revolutionaries soften into mere radical reformers. Historians would regard the entry of the anarchists into the *Syndicats* as one of the greatest events of the time. They had taught the workers that they need not be ashamed of acts of violence and had arrested a threatened deviation towards middle-class ideology.

After this elaborate exordium the author proceeds to expound the new gospel in a series of incandescent chapters. Writing at the time when Bernstein was recommending revisionism to his German colleagues in the socialist party, Sorel complains that the French Parliamentary team, though not quite so frank, was just as bad since they had abandoned all idea of insurrection. Jaurès detested the thought of violence, and his casuistry recalled the subtleties of seventeenth-century Jesuits. The upper bourgeoisie were ignorant, impotent, and as stupid as the eighteenth-century *Noblesse*, and Jaurès lulled them to sleep with humanitarian platitudes. If their stultification continued, exclaimed the author in bitter scorn, our official socialists might reasonably hope to reach the goal of their dreams and sleep in sumptuous mansions. What did the future of the country matter if the new régime provided a good time for a few professors who imagine they have invented socialism? Before the working-class could accept this dictatorship of incapacity it would have to become as stupid as the middle-class and lose all its revolutionary dynamism. Socialists should not try to prepare the middle-class for the transition to a better social system. Their sole duty was to explain to the proletariat the magnitude of their revolutionary task: to build up institutions on the foundation of their *Syndicats*. Any *rapprochement* between classes was undesirable. Militant capitalism bred a corresponding militancy among the workers, who would promptly suppress the Parliamentary Socialists who posed as leaders of the working classes and guardians of social order.

Democracy meant corruption. Look at Tammany Hall! Some French towns were bad enough. The great art of the financiers and politicians was to bleed the taxpayer without driving him to revolt. Parliamentary Socialists despised morality as much as the stockbroking bourgeoisie. The proletariat had none of the servile instincts of democracy. President Faure was a ridiculous creature and a snob. Socialism represented the highest moral ideal ever conceived by man, but syndicalism alone was true socialism. Syndicalists could save civilisation by the total elimination of the bourgeoisie of which Renan had despaired. Religion having been discarded, there was nothing to fill the gap. In the total ruin of institutions and morals there remained a force new, powerful and intact. The proletariat would survive if the worker possessed the energy to bar the road to bourgeois corrupters and repelled their advances in the bluntest terms. Socialism owed to the principle of violence the high ethical values which would bring salvation to the modern world. At last the world would belong to the workers and not to the politicians, socialist or capitalist, and a new civilisation would dawn.

How could an elderly man of such intellectual calibre believe that it was the duty of the manual workers to overthrow the bourgeoisie by force? And why did he expect them to govern more unselfishly? He had never been an optimist about *homo sapiens* like Michelet, so how could he imagine them to be immune to the common failings? It was a classic example of wishful thinking.

Sorel's exasperation with the working of democracy under the Third Republic was widely shared, and in 1910 Emile Faguet, the oracle of literary criticism, launched a violent attack in *Le Culte de l'Incompétence*. While business and the professions were managed by people who understood their job, he complained, the political guidance of the nation was left to amateurs. The principle of democracy was the cult of incompetence. The voter instinctively chose the candidate who shared his opinions, prejudices and passions, and was often as unfit for the grave duties of a legislator as himself. Selection and promotion by merit was unpopular since it required inequality, whereas the religion of democracies was equality. Moreover the Deputies were tied by instructions from their constituents, and Ministers were bossed by the Chamber. The same system of selection by opinion instead of by fitness largely prevailed throughout the sphere of administration, even extending to appointments to the judiciary. Democracy tended to socialism, which envisaged an increase in the number of officials chosen for their opinions. Democracy in fact meant doing everything badly, a case of the blind leading the blind.

Sorel founded no school; France was more interested in the struggle with the Church, the prospects in Morocco, the Russian alliance and the German fleet, than in a social revolution. Moderate socialists such as Jaurès were returned to Parliament at free elections in undiminished numbers while revolutionary syndicalists remained an insignificant minority. The old doctrinaire found more to encourage him abroad, particularly in Italy. In 1915 the foundation of Mussolini's Fascist Revolutionary Party aroused his interest. 'Our Mussolini is not an ordinary socialist,' he remarked to a friend. 'Perhaps you will see him one day at the head of a battalion saluting the Italian banner with a sword. He is a *condottiere* of the fifteenth century. The world does not know him yet, but he is the only man of energy capable of redressing the feebleness of government.' Mussolini returned the compliment in his article on 'Fascism' in the *Italian Encyclopaedia* in 1933: 'In the great stream of Fascism are to be found the ideas which began with Sorel, Péguy and Lagardelle.' Caring nothing for political liberty, or the rule of law or the rights of minorities, Sorel welcomed the Russian revolution in 1917 but deplored the bloodshed, and Lenin dismissed him as a mischief-maker with absurd ideas. Since he died on the eve of the march on Rome we can only guess what would have been his reaction. That he would have applauded the overthrow of Parliamentary democracy is certain, but his ideal was the dictatorship of a particular class, not of a superman. His campaign had failed and he knew it. When he died in 1923 he could detect no ray of light in the French political sky. The Third Republic emerged from Armageddon in precisely the same form as in 1914, not indeed greatly respected by the nation but with no rival system in sight.

DATE DUE

OCT 22 '65			
OCT 9 1970			
GAYLORD			PRINTED IN U.S.A.